Composition and the Rhetoric of Science

Composition and the Rhetoric of Science

Engaging the Dominant Discourse

Michael J. Zerbe

Southern Illinois University Press
Carbondale

10 09 08 07   4 3 2 1

Library of Congress Cataloging-in-Publication Data
Zerbe, Michael J., date.
    Composition and the rhetoric of science : engaging the
dominant discourse / Michael J. Zerbe.
        p. cm.
    Includes bibliographical references and index.
    ISBN-13: 978-0-8093-2740-9 (pbk. : alk. paper)
    ISBN-10: 0-8093-2740-6 (pbk. : alk. paper)
    1. English language—Rhetoric—Study and teaching.
2. Interdisciplinary approach in education. 3. Report
writing—Study and teaching. 4. Science—Study and
teaching. I. Title.

PE1404.Z475 2007
808.042—dc22   2006033693

Para Carmen

The greatest enterprise of the mind has always been and always will be the attempted linkage of the sciences and the humanities.

—Edward O. Wilson,
Consilience: The Unity of Knowledge

One must attempt to understand how the world is represented if one is to attempt to change it.

—David J. Hess (paraphrasing Marx on Feuerbach), *Science Studies*

Contents

Preface

"Scientific discourse is a 'power rhetoric.' Rhetoric must attend to discourses that matter." So stated Jack Selzer when he introduced a session on scientific discourse at the 2005 Conference on College Composition and Communication in San Francisco. Yet this session was one of fewer than a half dozen sessions on scientific or medical discourse presented at the conference—a conference that typically contains more than five hundred sessions. And the year 2005 was no different than any other. Scientific discourse is not a major concern in the field of rhetoric and composition, despite this discourse's evident dominance in Western societies. No other discourse has as much power to both define culture at large and shape individual identity as scientific rhetoric does. Unfortunately, though, with only 1 percent of sessions at its most important conference devoted to scientific discourse, rhetoric and composition is not attending to this "power rhetoric."

This book seeks to change that. In doing so, it attempts to move rhetoric and composition in an entirely new direction—to sustained inquiry into and interrogation of dominant discourses in our society. To take the first step in this new direction, I undertake two primary missions in the book: first, to persuade compositionists, writing across the curriculum specialists, and technical communicators to consider scientific discourse an integral part of their research and teaching, and second, to convince rhetoricians of science, who already do conduct research on scientific discourse, to think about pedagogy and literacy. I want to make the study *and* teaching of scientific discourse—the most powerful rhetoric of Western culture—a central disciplinary issue in rhetoric and composition.

This book is directed at the field of rhetoric and composition (including writing across the curriculum and professional writing) as a whole, although taking such a holistic approach has become increasingly difficult as the discipline has matured and specialized. I contend, though, that careful attention to dominant rhetorics, no matter what form they take, should always be a front-and-center concern for the entire field. Rhetoricians, compositionists, and their students need to understand how scientific discourse operates and how to produce it so that they may become fully informed, literate participants in civic life. Much civic discourse—especially the type used to make decisions—is scientific discourse. We need to be more than simply stakeholders with respect to scientific rhetoric.

This book also seeks to transcend the theory–practice boundary. It is both a theoretical and a pedagogical text; the two are not easily separated. Ideas that I discuss in the book come from both reading theory and teaching students. It is my hope that an equilibrium can be established in which theory is informed by what happens with scientific discourse in rhetoric and composition courses and, conversely, pedagogy is influenced by rigorous theory.

The time is right to become much more active with respect to the rhetoric of science. Prestigious conferences in rhetoric and composition (e.g., the Conference on College Composition and Communication and the Penn State Conference on Rhetoric and Composition) have, in recent years, started to include presentations on scientific discourse, albeit in small numbers. Additionally, the American Association for Rhetoric of Science and Technology, at their 2003 meeting, called for study of pedagogical issues, which have not traditionally been a concern of this group. This book answers that call.

Acknowledgments

A multiplicity of voices inhabits this book. Friends, colleagues, and mentors who have read and commented on drafts of parts of this work are Michelle Comstock, Bill Hart-Davidson, Tom Moriarty, Tim Peeples, Ed Nagelhout, Graham Smart, Bud Weiser, Janice Lauer, Patricia Harkin, Johndan Johnson-Eilola, Janet Zepernick, and Dominic DelliCarpini. Neither their contributions to this book nor my appreciation for them can be underestimated. I have enjoyed enormously fulfilling conversations about rhetoric, composition, and/or science with Bill Voige, Dan O'Sullivan, Paul Anderson, Jean Lutz, Bill Hardesty, Paul Puccio, Shirley Rose, Jeff Jablonski, Carlos Salinas, Jon Bush, Baotong Gu, Jim Porter, Cindy Ryan, Elizabeth Pass, Alice Philbin, Mark Hawthorne, Roger Munger, Brenda Orbell, Jack Selzer, Amanda Young, Barbara Heifferon, Harrison Carpenter, and Charles Bazerman. Chris Strickling was kind enough to provide a syllabus for her fascinating composition course at the University of Texas that focused on weight loss. I received valuable advice from Bruce McComiskey, and I am grateful for it. Students at York College of Pennsylvania, James Madison University, and Purdue University have listened and responded to my ideas about rhetoric and science with patience and enthusiasm. I have learned a great deal from them.

I am grateful to York College of Pennsylvania and to Purdue University for research grants that allowed me to pursue this project. Additionally, I am indebted to many helpful people from libraries at York College of Pennsylvania, Penn State University (University Park campus, Harrisburg campus, and College of Medicine), Messiah College, James Madison University, Idaho State University, and Purdue University. Administrative support from Deb Staley, Sandra Diener, Judy Powell, Lisa Hartman, Benita Smith, Jill Quirk, and Julie Knoeller has been invaluable. I thank AAAS for permission to reproduce the illustrations in chapter 7.

At Southern Illinois University Press, I thank Karl Kageff for his steadfast support and helpful suggestions. I am also grateful to Bridget Brown, Barb Martin, and Kathleen Kageff at the Press for their assistance. Louie Simon performed an absolutely fabulous editing job. The detailed suggestions of Alan Gross and Tim Peeples, who reviewed this manuscript for SIU Press, helped transform this project into a much more coherent and forceful text.

Carmen, Alejandro, and my family have been with me every step of the way. I could not be more fortunate.

Composition and the Rhetoric of Science

Introduction

The publication of *The Bell Curve* by Richard Herrnstein and Charles Murray in 1994 ignited a firestorm of controversy and, as one might expect, generated a tidal wave of reviews. Essentially, the book's authors, after extensive study of decades worth of IQ data, concluded that intelligence is determined more by heredity than by environment; by extension, the authors then suggested that Americans of African descent were genetically less intelligent than Americans of European or Asian descent. The response to Herrnstein and Murray's work was immediate and heated.[1] Dismayed by what many perceived of as the latest instantiation of eugenics, not to mention a poorly executed study, a number of reviewers, especially those with science or social science backgrounds, castigated the work. For example, economists Goldberger and Manski maintain that Herrnstein and Murray, in Part 1 of their book, "offer only scattered anecdotes, hypothetical vignettes, and selective citations" (774), and the reviewers then conclude that "*The Bell Curve* is driven by advocacy for [Herrnstein and Murray's] vision, not by serious empirical analysis" (775). Kamin, a psychologist, utterly dismisses Herrnstein and Murray, saying "The book has nothing to do with science" (99). Finally, sociologist Patterson takes no prisoners: "The authors develop their argument in a scattershot way in which all positions and available data are indiscriminately thrown at the reader, including positions that flatly contradict their own" (191).

Many reviewers with roots in the humanities critiqued *The Bell Curve* as well. However, a certain tentativeness pervaded a disturbing number of these critiques (Gould, "Curveball" 15). For example, in *The New Republic*, which devoted an entire issue to the *Bell Curve* controversy, senior editor Mickey Kaus equivocates, saying, "As a lay reader of *The Bell Curve*, I'm unable to judge fairly." Leon Wieseltier, the *New Republic's* literary editor, vacillates: "Murray . . . is hiding the hardness of his politics behind the hardness of his science. And his science, for all I know, is soft. . . . Or so I imagine. I am not a scientist. I know nothing about psychometrics."

Finally, *New York Times* reviewer Peter Passell hedges: "But this reviewer is not a biologist, and will leave the argument to experts" (all quoted in Gould, "Curveball" 15).

What is going on here? Why were reviewers—especially those who write for publications as influential as the *New York Times* or the *New Republic*—walking on eggshells when it came to critiquing *The Bell Curve*? Why drastically weaken critiques that were almost invariably right on target? One answer to these important questions is that many of the reviewers who wrote critiques of the book don't know how to approach scientific discourse. The bewildering terminology, the hopelessly complex and mind-numbing statistics, the seemingly authoritarian, objective, and neutral tone—the whole package is just simply too overwhelming for many nonscientists. As noted Harvard paleontologist and popular science writer Stephen Jay Gould pointed out in his take on the controversy: "*The Bell Curve* is even more disingenuous in its argument than in its obfuscation about race. The book is a rhetorical masterpiece of scientism, and it benefits from the particular kind of fear that numbers impose on nonprofessional commentators. It runs to eight hundred and forty-five pages, including more than a hundred pages of appendixes filled with figures. So the text looks complicated, and reviewers shy away with a knee-jerk claim that, while they suspect fallacies of argument, they really cannot judge" ("Curveball" 15).

Indeed. Surely the unwillingness or inability of these reviewers—and all those who consider themselves rhetoricians[2]—to critique scientific discourse consistently and reliably hinders the ability of the vast majority of our population who do not have an academic or professional background in science to participate actively in our science- and technology-dependent democracy. Scientific rhetoric is among the most powerful of discourses. It *is* the way the world is represented (as Hess states in the epigraph above). Like any other powerful cultural institution, science must be watched carefully—and checked when necessary—in an effort to prevent abuses. As Rorty points out, "Much of the rhetoric of contemporary intellectual life *takes for granted* that the goal of scientific inquiry into man is to understand 'underlying structures,' or 'culturally invariant factors,' or 'biologically determined patterns'" (22, emphasis added). Shouldn't a postmodern rhetoric and composition call this goal and many other assumptions about science into question? Among the many responsibilities of rhetoric and composition should be a constant dedication to keep a close eye on powerful discourses. An unwillingness or inability to engage scientific discourse meaningfully bodes ill for our society.

Another example may help to illustrate this point. Just over one hundred years ago, as Gould points out in another essay, intelligence was calculated not by IQ but by careful measurement of skull size. This "science" was called craniometry. Under its auspices, renowned French surgeon Paul Broca unequivocally (at least for him and his supporters) determined in 1873 that women were less intelligent than men after discovering that women's brain sizes in terms of volume were, on average, smaller than men's. In performing his research, Broca followed the scientific method to the letter. First, he carefully built on work that had already been performed: Rousseau, for example, had reasoned that women's minds were weaker because their bodies were weaker and that men must retire to men-only clubs for earnest intellectual stimulation (Wertheim 146–47). Similarly, de Malebranche had pointed to women's softer "cerebral fiber" to reach this conclusion (Tuana 68).

Armed with this information, Broca proceeded apace. He took meticulous care of the bodies—most of which had undergone autopsies at Paris hospitals—from which he was extracting brains. He painstakingly measured each and every brain to gain accurate data. He used a large sample size so that his conclusions were statistically valid (Gould, "Women's Brains" 152–53). Who could argue with such precise methodologies and obvious results?

As any good scientist should, Broca considered the difference in size between men and women as a factor in the determination of brain size. Broca dismissed this issue, though, saying "we must not forget that women are, on the average, a little less intelligent than men, a difference which we should not exaggerate but which is, nonetheless, real. We are therefore permitted to suppose that the relatively small size of the female brain depends in part upon her physical inferiority and in part upon her intellectual inferiority" (quoted in Gould, "Women's Brains" 154). Of course, as Gould points out, Broca's experiments were supposed to test this theory, not assume its validity *a priori* ("Women's Brains" 154). The *fin-de-siècle* scientific community and Western culture at large did not, however, see this lapse of logic as a problem. Now, over one hundred years later, almost any reasonably educated person can read Broca's work and, despite its precision, quickly deduce that it is bogus. We should not, however, need to wait more than one hundred years for the population at large to decide that some of the science out there is—well—*bad*. Too much potential for harm exists, both to human beings and to the planet on which we live.

Scientific rhetoric—and here I mean discourse in which science is actually *performed*, not discourse such as essays and news reports that is simply *about* science—is potent. It carries a great deal of weight. Every day, using discourses of scientific research for support, policymakers reach conclusions about who may or may not (or who should or should not) perform certain actions. Decisions affecting millions if not billions of people—decisions about health (e.g., whether mammograms are effective for women in their forties), education (e.g., whether this child should be tested for Attention Deficit Disorder), travel (e.g., whether travel to Asia should be discouraged because of the risk of contracting avian flu), and the environment (e.g., what effects will building a subdivision have on a nearby stream)—are made on the basis of someone's interpretation of scientific discourse. Also, as the above examples concerning race and gender indicate, scientific discourse constructs identity. Indeed, with the advent of a new era in which the entire human genome has been deciphered, scientific discourse will not just construct identity, it will *define* or even *create* it. What scientific discourse says about fundamental issues of identity results in material effects that are more profound than those caused by virtually any other type of discourse because scientific discourse reifies prevailing biases in society, causing their acceptance among a vast number of people. As Hess indicates, "general cultural values can come to be seen as natural after they have been encoded in scientific representations" (115).

The power of scientific discourse reaches into almost every corner of human experience. Aronowitz writes, "claims of authority in our contemporary world rest increasingly on the possession of legitimate knowledge, of which scientific discourses are supreme" (ix). Echoing this sentiment, Lewontin states that science is "the chief legitimating force in modern society" (8). Moreover, Aronowitz adds, "modern scientific rationality is the privileged discourse, and all others are relegated to the margins. As result, institutions of the state as well as the economy—education systems, government bureaus, the law and criminal justice systems—emulate scientific procedures within the constraints imposed by their own traditions and exigencies" (8). The constraints that Aronowitz mentions, however, are not often recognized. Indeed, because science, no matter what institution has appropriated it, is generally perceived publicly as a positive and trustworthy institution, its conclusions are viewed as Truth and as Progress by a significant portion of the population. According to the National Science Foundation, for example, "overwhelming majorities" (i.e., between 85 and 89 percent) of survey respondents agreed that "Science and technology are making our lives healthier, easier and more comfortable," "Most scientists want to work on things that will make life better for the average person," and "Because of science and technology, there will be more opportunities for the next generation" (*National Science Foundation*, "Science and Engineering Indicators—2002" 7–12).

Over the past two decades, interest in scientific discourse by rhetoricians has increased greatly. This interest is both welcome and extremely necessary, and the body of work produced by rhetoricians of science has illuminated the operations of scientific discourse in many striking ways. However, most rhetoricians of science do not consider how to make this work available to and accessible by a larger community; in other words, they do not consider scientific *literacy* to be a priority. In composition studies, on the other hand, pedagogy and literacy issues are always at the forefront of disciplinary discussions, but scientific discourse is not a rhetoric of concern in the vast majority of first-year or even advanced composition courses. Given that an oft-stated goal of composition studies is to prepare students for the kinds of reading and writing that they will need to perform as literate, informed students and citizens, it is dismaying that scientific discourse is largely ignored by compositionists.

Rhetoric and composition studies cannot claim to be fulfilling its mission of providing its students with the intellectual vigor and depth required for successfully navigating twenty-first-century America without more attention to scientific discourse. It is a vexing paradox that scientific rhetorics are so powerful and yet form such a small part of our discipline. Rhetoric and composition instructors, as experts in language, owe it to their students, to the public at large, and to themselves to identify and interrogate the discourses that influence society most keenly. Rhetoric and composition studies should be a place in which students learn, among other things, about the history, underlying assumptions, and rhetorical conventions of our society's dominant discourses. Students enrolled in rhetoric and composition courses should gain a sophisticated appreciation for understanding and using these discourses. Absent this understanding, the vast majority of our students face a lifetime of stakeholder status relative to scientific rhetoric that deprives them of any meaningful chance of participating in making decisions that are based on this dominant discourse.

Many people rely on the mass media to keep them abreast of scientific and medical developments and to publicize dishonesty or shortcomings in science. Unfortunately, however, the mass media cannot be counted upon to portray science accurately or to provide necessary critical scrutiny. Interestingly and perhaps paradoxically, scientific discourse remains one of the most powerful discourses in Western society even as the many scientists—the everyday writers and readers of this discourse—have become more cognizant of its limitations. Many journalists, though, do not include this recognition in news reports that are directed to the general public. For example, a prominent feature of contemporary scientific discourse is the "Further Study" hedge. Almost ubiquitous today, this hedge appears most often near the end of a scientific research study, when authors carefully seek to limit the generalizability of their results. For instance, in a randomized trial of a low-carbohydrate, high-fat, high-protein diet (the so-called Atkins diet) that appeared in a 2003 issue of the *New England Journal of Medicine*, the authors write, "our findings should not be generalized to overweight subjects or to obese subjects with serious obesity-related diseases, such as diabetes and hypercholesterolemia. Additional studies are needed in these populations to evaluate the safety and efficacy of low-carbohydrate, high-protein, high-fat diets" (Foster et al. 2089). This hedge, however, did not appear in the CNN website account of the trial ("Vindication for the Atkins diet?"). The failure of the mass media to inform the general public about the limitations of scientific studies appears to be common (MacDonald). Additionally, scientific knowledge in general is often recontextualized from a forensic to an epideictic rhetoric when it moves from scientific journals to the popular press (Fahnestock, "Accommodating Science" 279, *see* also Nelkin's *Selling Science*).

Even when media reports are accurate and balanced, our students do not necessarily understand them. A 2003 study found that university students who were asked to read popular media reports describing scientific research "displayed a certainty bias in their responses to questions regarding truth status, confused cause and correlation, and had difficulty distinguishing explanations of phenomena from the phenomena themselves." The amount of science education that the students had received seemed to have little impact on the results. Worst of all, many of the students seemed to think that their understanding of the science presented in the media reports was both accurate and adequate; it was neither (Norris, Phillips, and Korpan 139).[3]

It is my belief that rhetoric and composition studies offers the institutional, intellectual, and cultural capacity necessary to develop a widespread, sophisticated, and sorely needed scientific literacy. Institutionally speaking, composition studies maintains a prominent position in most American college and university curricula, and the field reaches most students who pursue postsecondary education. Intellectually speaking, rhetoric and composition instructors regularly help students to interrogate, produce, and manipulate complex, powerful discourses that they will use often in college and in life. Culturally speaking, rhetoric and composi-

tion studies classrooms regularly provide a setting in which open dialogue and grappling with complex issues is welcomed. Because scientific
rhetoric influences students so profoundly—even and perhaps especially
those who do not major in a science—it is incumbent upon rhetoric and
composition studies to provide an opportunity to students to develop or
hone the requisite intellectual skills to engage this discourse in a fully
informed way.

Rhetoric and composition studies needs to contribute to the development of a sophisticated scientific literacy to further challenge modernist
claims to progress, objectivity, truth, and universality in science. The consideration of these claims has become more and more important as science's
influence has increased exponentially over the last three centuries. These
claims, held by scientists and nonscientists alike, are too often used to support the production of scientific knowledge without any attention to ethics
or effects on the culture at large. Indeed, despite its many truly world-
transforming, salutary, and labor-saving achievements, science has not
been without its failures and disappointments, some of them spectacular.
For example, earlier this century, a vaccine for polio was developed only
a few years after the first use of the atomic bomb. Although automobiles
and jet aircraft whisk us quickly and (sometimes) comfortably from place
to distant place, oil spills and carbon monoxide pollute the environment
in which we live. Chemicals of all sorts make our world a better place
to live—providing us with everyday, indispensable items such as plastics
and medications—but the escape of deadly gases from a Union Carbide
chemical plant killed thousands of people in Bhopal, India. We have renew-
able spacecraft, but included in the cost of using them are the lives of the
Challenger and *Columbia* crews. Airbags in automobiles save many lives,
but, tragically, we discovered that, in their earliest versions, they could kill
children and small-boned adults. Drugs once regarded as miracles, such as
penicillin, are found now to be ineffective because of bacterial evolution,
adaptation, and resistance. As with all other human vocations, science has
acknowledged and adjudicated episodes of misconduct, dishonesty, and
fraud. And finally, people all over the world struggle with questions about
the use of science and technology by nation states and violence-minded
groups for political and military gain.

The failures and disappointments of science, though, have not made
much of an impact on the culture at large, perhaps because of its many
triumphs, its enormously successful institutionalization, and its aggres-
sive maintenance of its image as objective and universal. Western culture
expects—even demands—that, despite its potential problems, science

must make air travel safer, determine how to build faster computers, find cures for diseases, and improve the acoustical quality of stereo speakers. Science (and engineering) often delivers. Thus, science is generally perceived positively as a way of thinking and as a methodological process by which measurable human progress can be made rapidly and unproblematically. Accompanying this positive view of science, however, is often a superficial understanding of science. Because science is so often successful, our culture at large has not determined that sufficient grounds exist to understand and critique it, as we do with other cultural institutions. This shortcoming is unfortunate. A grounding in the rhetorical conventions of scientific discourse—incorporating both production and analysis—can help rhetoric and composition students learn to recognize the underlying assumptions and agendas inherent in scientific arguments. Such recognition would potentially enable these students to make more informed choices as citizens of a highly scientific and technological society.

In this book I want to explore the relationships and possibilities between rhetoric and composition studies and scientific discourse. To begin with, in chapter 1, using both theoretical and empirical means, I demonstrate that scientific discourse, and here I refer to the peer-reviewed scientific research article, is indeed the dominant rhetoric of twenty-first-century Western culture. Then, in chapter 2, I examine the state of scientific discourse as an area of study in rhetoric and composition studies. In chapters 3 and 4, I use cultural studies and literacy studies, respectively, as theoretical gateways for incorporating scientific discourse into rhetoric and composition studies more effectively than it has been to this point. In chapter 5, I expand my definition of scientific discourse to include popularizations and demonstrate how these works have the potential to do a lot of the cultural contextualization that needs to be performed so that a more robust scientific literacy can be established. Chapters 6, 7, and 8, then, introduce specific pedagogical scenarios for the study and production of scientific discourse. Each scenario is built around a peer-reviewed scientific research article and incorporates cultural studies and literacy practices discussed in chapters 3 and 4. More specifically, in chapter 6, I show how comparing Western scientific discourse with non-Western scientific discourse reveals cultural assumptions about science that may be called into question. In chapter 7, I demonstrate how the study of a classic (i.e., well-known) scientific text can help demystify scientific rhetoric for students and illustrate its powerful influence. Finally, in chapter 8, I show that scientific discourse about students is used to define them and that it is possible to teach students how to play a role in this characterization.

By thinking about scientific discourse as a cultural studies issue and a literacy issue, rhetoric and composition can implement an effective pedagogical framework that capitalizes on cultural studies and ideological literacy so that students can gain confidence and fluency reading and writing this rhetoric. Such a framework might look like this: first, students would read one or more carefully selected primary scientific texts. Selecting texts that discuss topics that many students find interesting and that are, with reasonable effort, accessible to students would be most beneficial, and I have tried to meet these criteria in the pedagogical scenarios presented in chapters 6, 7, and 8.[4] As is typical of writing courses, further reading, most likely in the form of science popularizations, class discussion, and group work could be used to help clarify concepts, define important issues, suggest additional sources to consult, link the science to politics, the economy, and religion as well as to local and/or personal concerns, and develop arguments and evidence for writing. These additional reading and discussion activities would provide the cultural studies framework (foregrounded in chapter 3) needed to understand the cultural origins and implications of the knowledge produced by the scientific texts that the students read—implications that are often difficult to extract from the texts themselves.

After reading primary and popular literature and other sources, students would be asked to join the ongoing scientific debates by either proposing or conducting scientific research and writing about these endeavors. Most of the research would likely be proposed, but some more social science-oriented research may actually lend itself to being conducted. These proposals or reports would follow the IMRAD (Introduction, Methods, Results, and Discussion) organizational plan—for proposals, students would discuss hypothetical results and conclusions—and students would be encouraged to discuss what they see as the strengths and weaknesses of this genre, a discussion that can be much more substantive when students actually practice writing it.[5] In the discussion section of their proposals or reports, it will be important for students to think hard about the limitations of their research. Possible issues to consider are study design validity and reliability, correlation versus cause and effect, ability to generalize, unproven assumptions, and uncontrolled or not fully controlled variables. The idea is to get students beyond the ubiquitous "possible human error" and "further study is needed" hedges that are typical in (and that tend to terminate) these sections in lab reports.

Writing and reading about scientific discourse promotes ideological scientific literacy—the most sophisticated of the three forms of scientific literacy presented in chapter 4—in a number of ways. First, it asks students to examine *texts*—the most important and common product of science—that present explicit claims not only about the topic being studied, but implicit claims about the role and methodology of science as well. As they gain experience reading scientific texts, students will begin to recognize these claims, even though many of the more explicit ones will be cloaked in the impartial, authoritative language characteristic of Western science. Second, students will begin to recognize how science gained and maintains its privileged status in Western culture. The texts students read, for example, will list grants from the United States federal National Science Foundation or National Institutes of Health, or from large, powerful, and well-known energy, transportation, consumer product, or pharmaceutical corporations that were used to support the research. The list of authors will often be over a dozen names long and include individuals who hold prestigious positions at the world's best-known universities and who are featured in mass media accounts of their research. Third, the additional reading and discussion activities discussed above will illuminate the connections between the sciences and economics, politics, and history. Fourth, students will become much more critically proficient in their analysis of experiments as they learn to ask questions about scope, isolation of variables and the impact of variables on each other, sample size, statistical significance, and other important issues associated with this methodology. Fifth, learning about the kinds of research conducted by scientists will lead students to ask questions about the ethical implications of such work: who will benefit from the research, who will not; what are the costs of the research, how else could the money be spent; and if people are involved in the research, how are they are informed of the research methodology, potential risks, and results (e.g., with the oversight role of an Institutional Review Board), what to do if people are not adequately informed. Sixth, students will begin to appreciate the ways in which the knowledge produced by the experiments they read and write about impact them directly and personally: how does, for example, the science change their daily routine and those of their families and friends, or how might the students imagine such changes in the future? Seventh, students will learn to invent and develop arguments, as they deem necessary, that advance alternative interpretations of the results of scientific studies, question the validity or replicability of research or the generalizability of its results, or appraise the necessity or implications of the research they analyze.

While this book appears to adhere to a fairly traditional theory–practice split, it is my real hope that the ideas presented here initiate an equilibrium: the use and modification of the pedagogical scenarios presented in the last three chapters of the book will, of course, lead to new questions and problems that will need to be theorized, which will in turn lead to new pedagogical approaches, and so on. I have just barely started to use some of the strategies that I discuss in my own courses, and they have already generated a host of questions and exciting possibilities.

This book should not be misconstrued as an argument that a composition course—especially a first-year course—should focus *exclusively* on scientific rhetoric. It most certainly should not. Similarly, this work does not maintain that scientific discourse should be the only dominant discourse studied, although it certainly could be in a special topics or graduate-level course. Discourses of religion, economics, quality control (see, for example, Dickson and Barton), and, most recently, security from terrorist attack are also legitimate candidates for dominant rhetorics that deserve close study. This book should, however, be understood as an argument that rhetoric and composition studies should pay a lot more attention to our society's most powerful discourses. I believe wholeheartedly that it is possible to artfully discover and incorporate into our courses scientific rhetoric and other dominant rhetorics in ways that students—no matter what their major or area of interest—would find interesting and relevant.

In addition, this book does not contend that rhetoricians and compositionists should perform more empirical research at the expense of theoretical research. Along with many in the field, I find both theoretical and empirical work to be valuable and enlightening. My argument for the study of scientific discourse in composition and rhetoric classrooms does, however, recognize that the egalitarianism enjoyed by theoretical and empirical research in rhetoric and composition studies does not extend to the society at large, where scientific discourse (or discourse that at least purports to be scientific in nature) reigns supreme.

This work draws on the rhetoric of science, history of rhetoric, cultural and science studies, composition theory, writing across the curriculum research, research that investigates public understanding of science, and literacy studies. In a sense, its mission perhaps follows most closely the important work of M. A. K. Halliday and J. R. Martin and several other Australian linguists, education specialists, English scholars, and communication theorists who have carefully studied the professional discourses of science, science popularization, and science education.[6] The Australian School has been concerned about both "professional" science literacy and "school" science literacy; these terms are Halliday and Martin's from *Writing Science: Literacy as Discursive Power*. They note a critical distinction: professional literacy is concerned with "construing nature," while school literacy is concerned with "construing knowledge" (v). The authors examine each of these rhetorics as part of a larger discourse and literacy picture; most research in the United States focuses on just one of these areas at a time.

The present work, however, differs from this Australian tradition in two ways. First, I call for scientific literacy—not just the study of scientific discourse by a small community of theorists, be they linguists, education specialists, sociologists, or rhetoricians of science—to be a much more important concern of rhetoric and composition studies than it is at present. The status of scientific discourse as the dominant rhetoric in Western society obligates the discipline of rhetoric and composition to prioritize it and think about how to teach it to our students rather than study it in isolation without any pedagogical aim. Second, I call for the use (both reading and writing) of *primary* texts—scientific research articles or proposals—by all students in conjunction with science popularizations to achieve such a literacy. Halliday and Martin's distinction between professional and school scientific literacies abundantly clarifies why students should be moving more and more to primary scientific texts: the way scientists attempt to make sense of the world is by their use of language. To not be exposed to that language is to not understand how science works. By the time students are in college, they are reading primary texts in rhetoric, philosophy, literature, history, and politics. There is no good reason why they shouldn't be reading primary scientific texts as well. If carefully chosen, primary scientific texts can be, with reasonable effort and contextualization with the aid of popularizations and media accounts, comprehensible to students.

Martin illustrates why exposure to primary, peer-reviewed scientific discourse is important. He characterizes science textbooks as "the main source of models of written scientific language for most students" ("Chapter 9" 167). However, the discourse of most science textbooks—again, language *about* science—bears little resemblance to that of scientific research articles—again, language that *performs* science. The use of textbooks is essentially analogous to using only secondary reports on Cicero rather than reading Cicero himself. As Martin notes, "What seems to have gone wrong in the development of science textbooks over the years is that an attempt has been made to make science more accessible by downplaying science literacy. . . . To rehabilitate literacy in science teachers and students will have to work towards a much clearer grasp of the function of language as technology in building up a scientific picture of the world. Technical language has evolved in order to classify, decompose, and explain. The major scientific genres—report, explanation and experiment—have evolved to structure texts which document a scientist's worldview. The functionality of these genres and the technicality they contain cannot be avoided; it has to be dealt with" (202). To put it in analogous terms, reading Cicero himself is undoubtedly more complex than reading a textbook about Cicero; nevertheless, we rightly insist that our students read *De Oratore* and perhaps use textbooks and other materials as aids. We should apply this thinking to science as well. Primary scientific discourse can be quite complex, but with some work and contextualization much of it is ultimately accessible. Students need to see scientific discourse in action, right at the point at which it attempts to accomplish its epistemological and ontological goals.

In a broader sense, beyond the examination of the relationships between scientific discourse and rhetoric and composition studies, this book argues for the reconnection of composition studies and rhetoric, especially rhetoric in terms of the study of public or civic discourse, of which scientific rhetoric is a neglected part. As I discuss in chapter 2, scientific discourse does get some attention from rhetoricians of science and others in the field. But the important work of rhetoricians of science—such as that of Charles Bazerman, Jeanne Fahnestock, Alan Gross, Marie Secor, Celeste Condit, Greg Myers, Leah Ceccarelli, Dwight Atkinson, Carolyn Miller, Davida Charney, James Zappen, Jack Selzer, and John Battalio, to name a few—is not typically read by compositionists, and, conversely, this work rarely if ever considers issues of pedagogy, about which compositionists would think seriously, in its analysis of scientific discourse.[7] This lack of synergy is troubling. Compositionists should be interested in teaching students about one of Western society's most powerful discourses, and rhetoricians of science should be interested in thinking about how their important work can be used in a classroom setting specifically and to achieve scientific literacy more generally. This work cannot occur if compositionists and rhetoricians of science do not read the same journals, attend the same conferences, and genuinely reach out to each other.

By studying scientific discourse, rhetoric and composition students and instructors will become part of exciting work that is occurring in many disciplines. Over the past two decades many different types of humanities scholars and social scientists have begun to question more actively and critically how and why science operates as such a powerful cultural institution. Leading the way have been researchers in women's studies (e.g., Keller, Haraway, and Harding), cultural studies (e.g., Herndl and Aronowitz), literary theory (e.g., Rosner), linguistics (e.g., Myers), and sociology (e.g., Knorr-Cetina), who have demonstrated that scientists cannot escape cultural prejudices. These critics conclude that science is a social construct that is significantly influenced by politics, economics, history, and other forces. In recent years, scientists have been joining the discussion as well. In a stunning move, the British journal *Nature*, perhaps the world's preeminent science journal, editorialized in 1997 that social constructionists of science should not be ignored since "fashionable ideas on the design of experiments to the negotiations that take place through the peer review process" can affect what becomes recognized and accepted as scientific truth ("Science Wars" 373).[8] The popular press has picked up on the idea as well (see, e.g., "The Science Wars" in the April 21, 1997, issue of *Newsweek*). Reading and writing scientific discourse will enable instructors and students in writing courses to become a part of this increasingly vital and sophisticated debate on the place and practice of science in society. As Charney observes in the introduction to the 2004 special issue of *Written Communication* on the rhetoric of popular science, "Perhaps it is time to start thinking about popularizing the rhetoric of science" ("Introduction" 5). Whether she refers to scientific discourse itself, research conducted by rhetoricians of science, or—most likely—both, Charney recognizes that our culture needs to have a much deeper and widespread understanding of the scientific enterprise.

In the end, in rhetoric and composition studies, we need to think about "keeping" science in two ways that must balance each other, that demonstrate both the promise and the limitations of science. First, we must "keep" science in perspective as a fundamentally human activity, full of uncertainty, political intrigue, and emotion. This perspective has not been articulated by science or by the mass media. As Gregory and Miller note, drawing on Collins and Pinch, "If the scientific community, in cahoots with the media, thought it was doing the public a favor by not troubling them with the complexities of scientific research as it is really carried out, it was mistaken. The shock of being disabused of the simple picture of science is a vital one. 'The point is that for citizens who want to take part in the democratic process of technological society, all the science they need to know about is controversial': so it is the mess, the disagreements, and the uncertainties of science that matter most in the public sphere" (*Science in Public* 61). These "complexities" are many and multifarious in nature, ranging from design to methodology to the interpretation and application of results. Second, we must "keep" science lest we lose it in the name of increased irrationalism or mysticism and autocracy. Holton, a physicist, historian, and Nazi refugee, argues that "History has shown repeatedly that a disaffection with science . . . can turn into a rage that links up with far more sinister movements" (quoted in Gregory and Miller, *Science in Public* 58). The future health and stability of democracy[9] quite literally depends on our informed critique of and enthusiastic participation in science. Rhetoric and composition has a great deal to contribute to this mission.

Part 1

Contexts and Gateways

1 The Dominance of Scientific Discourse: Theoretical Contexts

Generally, scientific discourse can be understood to be the language used (a) to ascertain, describe, and explain the workings of our bodies and our surroundings and (b) to validate the methods used to accomplish these objectives (Kinneavy 78). Scientific discourse is a culturally contingent rhetoric, one that is dependent on cultural norms and historical periods (Zappen, "Historical Perspectives" 15). A wide range of discourse can be described as "scientific," and, over time, many different forms of scientific discourse have appeared. As scientists have developed more sophisticated techniques to conduct their investigations, recognized biases and conflicts of interests, and noticed flaws of logic and mismatches between evidence and hypotheses, they have criticized earlier forms of scientific discourse as naive and sadly misinformed. Kinneavy recognizes this progression in his discussion of scientific discourse: "Though we are justly proud of modern science's attainments, . . . they have been made possible only through the efforts of some whom we must now disclaim in our attempts to progress. At the same time, it might be properly humbling to reflect that if history pursues its same track, future science may in like manner look upon our own contemporary exploits as childish, amateurish, folklorish, and mythical. In consequence . . . a view must be taken of scientific discourse broad enough to include, at least in a generic way, the attempts of previous eras to represent the universe. Therefore, some myths, legends, folklore, religious cosmologies, and past metaphysics can be valid corpora of scientific discourse" (77–78). Kinneavy borrows the term "ethnoscience" (78) to refer to this phenomenon. Although by the late Renaissance scientific discourse had taken a form that would be recognizable to readers of contemporary scientific prose, the myths, legends, and other genres that Kinneavy mentions all can be understood in a broad sense to be forms of scientific discourse.

For the purposes of the first four chapters of this book, however, scientific discourse is characterized much more narrowly, as discourse that describes empirical research using the familiar IMRAD (*I*ntrodcution, *M*ethods, *R*esults *a*nd *D*iscussion) organizational scheme. For the most part, this discourse is disseminated in peer-reviewed, scientific research journals that are read chiefly by scientists who work in the specialty area on which the journal focuses.[1] This discourse is used throughout the physical sciences, life sciences, and social sciences in both experimental (e.g., a pharmacologist's testing of a new diabetes drug) and descriptive (e.g., a botanist's account of the types of plants found on a remote mountaintop in Papua New Guinea) frameworks and in both qualitative and quantitative work. Ideally, the authors describe their research with a degree of thoroughness that allows their research to be replicated and thus confirmed or contested.

The narrowly defined scientific discourse described above has, since its inception in western Europe just three hundred years ago, become one of the powerful discourses in Western society. It is the discourse that is most often associated with knowledge production, descriptions of reality, Truth, impartiality, progress, and universality. It is certainly not the only form of professional scientific discourse: grant proposals, reviews, and editorials are also regular features of scientific journals and have a large role to play in the enterprise of science. But day to day, it is the scientific journal's original research article that currently performs the work of making sense of our physical surroundings, our behavior, and our society at large.

Early on, scientific discourse held the promise of being a democratically produced, widely accessible, and easily and openly debated rhetoric. As it inevitably became institutionalized and politicized, though, this promise has faded. Halliday and Martin put it this way: "It is not too fanciful to say that the language of science has reshaped our whole world view. But it has done so in ways which (as is typical of many historical processes) begin by freeing and enabling but end up by constraining and distorting. This might not matter so much if the language of science had remained the special prerogative of a priestly caste (such a thing can happen, when a form of a language becomes wholly ceremonial, and hence gets marginalized). In our recent history, however, what has been happening is just the opposite of this" (10–11). With the use of a dauntingly complex vocabulary and of various methods of scientific discourse forum control,[2] such as peer review and denial of publication or other form of visibility (both of which generally occur in private), and correction and ridicule (both of which generally occur in public) (Sullivan 128), gatekeepers in science keep a tight reign on the nature of and access to scientific discourse. Scientists must comply or risk their career. As a result, the liberating potential of scientific discourse has been tempered.

This constraint, however, has done little to damage scientific discourse's sterling cultural reputation. Indeed, this rhetoric has only grown in power. Because of the epistemological and ontological authority accorded to this rhetoric, it is not uncommon for scientific discourse to be appropriated in an effort to frame arguments more convincingly—not as arguments at all but as established Truth. Examination of this practice begins to reveal the degree to which scientific discourse is valorized in Western society. As Halliday and Martin continue, "A form of language that began as the semiotic underpinning for what was, in the worldwide context, a rather esoteric structure of knowledge has gradually been taking over as the dominant mode for interpreting human existence. Every text, from the discourses of technocracy and bureaucracy to the television magazine and the blurb on the back of the cereal packet, is in some way affected by the modes of meaning that evolved as the scaffolding of scientific knowledge" (11). One of the most obvious and compelling recent examples of this appropriation can be found in the creation science movement (which has now been largely supplanted by the intelligent design paradigm). In the 1980s and 1990s, practitioners of creation science sought to prove by scientific means that the formation of the earth and of human beings occurred as described in Genesis, the first book of the Bible, and to disprove what they saw as heretical explanations such as the Big Bang Theory and Darwinian evolution. Typically, creation scientists used established methodologies in their disciplines to gather data. For example, one creation physicist reported that "A preliminary analysis . . . of 'creation light' (now microwaves) data from the Wilkinson Microwave Anisotropy Probe (WMAP) . . . shows a remarkable orientation around a definite axis through the cosmos. The axis points roughly toward the constellation Virgo, very close to the plane of the earth's equator. . . . The existence of an axis (whether from rotation, a magnetic field, or some other cause) is strong evidence against the big bang theory. That is because the big bang presupposes a boundless cosmos with no special places (such as a center of mass) and no special directions (such as an axis through a center of mass)" (Humphreys). A mainstream physicist would most likely be more than surprised to see microwaves characterized as "creation light," and may take issue with the notion that the existence of an axis casts doubt on the Big Bang Theory.[3] But what is important to recognize is that many people who would otherwise be at least somewhat skeptical of evangelical Christianity may decide to take creation science seriously because it is presented *as a science*. It is conducted in university science departments. It uses scientific methods. And, most importantly, it uses scientific discourse unabashedly. It is an example of the many areas of inquiry that appropriate features of scientific rhetoric in an effort to strengthen arguments. Indeed, as Longo maintains, language is often recast "into scientific discourse that can partake of the cultural power residing in scientific knowledge" (55).

What is perhaps even more interesting is that the converse appropriation is not seen: scientists, especially evolutionary biologists, geologists, and physicists in this case, do not turn to Biblical scripture to bolster support for evolution, although they did early in the institutionalization of science to gain favor from the church, a much more powerful entity at the time. Despite the fact that religious discourse is another potent rhetoric in American society and that most evangelical Christians view the Bible, not scientific discourse, as the ultimate discursive authority, it is revealing that creation scientists found it necessary to appropriate scientific discourse to further their cause: even a discourse as authoritative as religious rhetoric appropriates scientific rhetoric to convince people of its truthfulness.

Rhetorics associated with the economy also hold significant sway in Western society and directly impact material conditions. Markets react almost instantaneously with the publication of reports on unemployment, productivity, quarterly earnings, and real estate sales. Like the discourse of creation science, though, economic rhetoric is made to appear scientific. Although not based on experimental research, this rhetoric is presented numerically, and the quantitativeness of the discourse lends it a scientific aura that it would not otherwise have. For example, one anxiously awaited economic report is the monthly Consumer Confidence Index. This report is turned inside out, upside down, and backward to glean every possible shred of meaning from its text. Wall Street analysts not only read between the lines, but through and beside them as well to determine what impact, if any, the report will have on the performance of a particular company and stock. However, the Consumer Confidence Index is simply a self-reported survey distributed to five thousand people: each respondent is asked to rate as positive, neutral, or negative his or her own economic situation, the economic state of the country, and future prospects. Survey results are then quantified—perhaps we should say "scientized"—to be presented to the public as the Consumer Confidence Index (*Conference-board*).

Finally, since the events of 9/11, the rhetoric of security has quickly established itself as another hegemonic discourse. In the United States, a change in alert status from yellow to orange results in an enormous number of material effects: people may alter travel plans, report activity to authorities that may have gone unremarked before the change, or worry that what they check out of the library will be reported to law enforcement. It remains to be seen whether the rhetoric of security will appropriate features of scientific discourse. It most likely will. Growing frustration with delays, cancellations, and other inconveniences will lead to calls that the imposition of security measures be substantiated. Scientific methodologies would then be devised to determine the necessity of the measures.

The obvious and virtually automatic attempts practitioners of religious and economic rhetorics—and perhaps security rhetoric in the future—to ride the coattails of scientific discourse clearly demonstrates the authority with which scientific rhetoric is held. People in many fields appropriate features of scientific discourse in an effort to take advantage of its rhetorical capital. The purpose of this chapter is to examine the dominance of science and scientific discourse—a dominance manifested by the above examples of its appropriation—in some theoretical contexts that are widely accepted and respected in rhetoric and composition. These contexts—postmodernism and Marxism—need to be explored because rhetoricians and compositionists, while making wide use of these theories over the past two decades, have not sufficiently considered what they say or imply about scientific discourse.

In this chapter and elsewhere in this book, *science* and *scientific discourse* are used interchangeably, given that scientists are "compulsive and almost manic writers . . . who spend the greatest part of their day coding, marking, altering, correcting, reading, and writing" (Latour and Woolgar 48–49) and that all cultural apparatuses—science is characterized as a cultural institution throughout this study—operate discursively. Leitch has characterized this connection: "Through various discursive and technical means, institutions constitute and disseminate systems of rules, conventions, and practices that condition the creation, circulation, and use of resources, information, knowledge, and belief. Institutions include, therefore, both material forms and mechanisms of production, distribution and consumption and ideological norms and protocols shaping the reception, comprehension, and application of discourse" (quoted in Longo 55). Foucault also connects disciplines directly to discourse, claiming that disciplines are actually one way in which discourses are controlled. "A discipline is defined," says Foucault, as "a domain of objects, a set of methods, a corpus of *propositions* considered to be true, a play of rules and *definitions*, of techniques and instruments." In addition, Foucault maintains that "in a discipline . . . what is supposed at the outset is not a meaning which has to be rediscovered, nor an identity which has to be repeated, but the requisites for the construction of new *statements*" ("Order of Discourse" 59, emphasis added). Discourse, says Foucault, "normalizes" the content and method of a discipline ("Means of Correct Training" 195). In short, he contends, "A 'power of writing' was constituted as an essential part in the mechanisms of discipline" ("Means of Correct Training" 201). Thus, because the discourse of any cultural institution is a manifestation of the institution itself, discussion of the dominance of scientific discourse can be discussed as a matter of scientific rhetoric specifically or as a matter of science generally.

Postmodernism and the Dominance of Scientific Discourse

Although postmodernism has met with some success in calling attention to modernist limitations of science, rhetoricians and compositionists have generally not paid heed to these discussions, focusing instead on discourses associated with race, class, gender, technology, and labor. The attention to these discourses is, of course, enormously warranted. But given the extent to which science strongly influences all of these discourses—as with the construction of racial and gender identity, for example—it is surprising that scientific discourse has never gained traction as a prominent issue of concern in rhetoric and composition (see chapter 2 for a more detailed discussion of this issue). This oversight is all the more startling given that several prominent postmodern theorists—Lyotard, Žižek, and Foucault among them—identify scientific discourse as the most influential contemporary rhetoric or science in general as the most powerful institution in contemporary culture.

Lyotard, in his report to the Conseil des Universités in Québec on the state of knowledge as stated in *The Postmodern Condition*, bases his distinction of modernism from postmodernism almost entirely on science: "To the extent that science does not restrict itself to stating useful regularities and seeks the truth, it is obliged to legitimate the rules of its own game. It then produces a discourse of legitimization with respect to its own status, a discourse called philosophy. I will use the term *modern* to designate any science that legitimates itself with reference to a meta-discourse of this kind making an explicit appeal to some grand narrative" (71–72). The act of contextualizing the distinction between modernism and postmodernism as a matter of science indicates just how seriously Lyotard views this institution. Lyotard recognizes that the grand narrative to which modernist science aspires is a thoroughly entrenched one: it is a heroic and masculine story of forward progress that entails the impartial and complete description of universal natural laws, an endeavor that will inevitably lead to the betterment of humankind. Lyotard contends that postmodernism can be understood as an "incredulity toward metanarratives" (72); in a postmodern critique of science from Lyotard's point of view, then, key notions of the grand narrative of science are called into question. For example, the notion that science has always resulted in positive progress can be interrogated. This critique has been made by researchers such as Usher and Edwards, who argue that "the notion of inevitable progress has been thrown into doubt, rendered 'incredible' by the continuation of want, disease, famine, destruction, and the recognition of the ecological costs of 'development'" (9–10).

Lyotard distinguishes narrative knowledge from scientific knowledge, noting the cultural superiority of the latter. Although scientific knowledge indeed takes narrative form, especially as a series of denotative statements, it refers to objects that "must be available for repeated access, in other words, they must be accessible in explicit conditions of observation; and it must be possible to decide whether or not a given statement pertains to the language judged relevant by the experts" (74). The ability to verify or refute scientific statements independently thus renders it distinct from other forms of narrative knowledge, which are typically viewed by scientists as not being subject to rigorous argumentation or proof, as scientific discourse is. Nonscientific discourse is dismissed, then, as "belonging to a different mentality: savage, primitive, underdeveloped, backward, alienated, composed of opinions, customs, authority, prejudice, ignorance, ideology. Narratives are fables, myths, legends . . ." (83). Lyotard's separation of a purely scientific discourse from other forms of discourse contrasts sharply with Kinneavy's focus (see my comments in the introduction) on the *similarities* of various types of discourses used in an effort to explain biological and physical phenomena. Lyotard does not think that the separation is right, however. He maintains that the unequal relationship between scientific discourse and other forms of narrative is responsible for "the entire history of cultural imperialism from the dawn of Western civilization" (83). Such is the astonishing power that Lyotard accords to scientific discourse.

For Žižek, like Lyotard, scientific knowledge is a form of narrative knowledge, and, as with all forms of narrative knowledge, it has material effects. Scientific discourse is an especially powerful narrative, though, because it describes effects that are not immediately verifiable to the five senses. Discussing the radiation poisoning that resulted from the Chernobyl disaster, Žižek points out that "The [scientific] experts themselves admitted that any determination of the 'threshold of danger' was arbitrary. . . . We do not see or feel radioactive rays; they are entirely chimerical objects, effects of the incidence of the discourse of science upon our life world" (36). This notion—that scientific narratives attempt to describe phenomena that cannot be detected by nonscientists but that nonetheless have significant effects on human beings—is a factor that leads to the dominance of scientific discourse. Most people do not have everyday access to ultraviolet spectrometers, the Hubble telescope, or even raw data from sampling and surveys or quantitative descriptive techniques used by social scientists; thus, it is difficult if not impossible for a "lay" person to verify results and conclusions from scientific discourse independently. Scientific discourse is, in effect, the only manifestation of the radioactive rays that Žižek discusses. Specifically, with respect to radioactivity, while a person can certainly see and feel the terrible *consequences* of radioactive rays, she cannot see or feel the radioactive rays themselves. The only description of these rays available to her is scientific discourse; if she does not have access to it or a good understanding of it, she cannot confirm or challenge this description as she would with a nonscientific narrative, such as a witness' account of a traffic accident.

Of all postmodern theorists widely read in rhetoric and composition, the one who is most concerned with scientific discourse is Foucault. First, through his work on knowledge production, Foucault recognizes the rise and dominance of scientific discourse and uses it to illustrate some of his most important points. Foucault develops his concept of *episteme* (i.e., "the set of total relations that unite, at a given period, the discursive practices that give rise to epistemological figures, science, and possibly formalized systems" [quoted in Hess 116]) by examining the epistemological shifts in science over time: from scientific thought based on "resemblances" during the Renaissance to "representation" during the classical era to "time, function, and dynamicism" during the modern era (Hess 116–17). More specifically, for example, Foucault maintains that the new scientific knowledge of the seventeenth century resulted from the spatialization of knowledge. Referring to the work of Linnaeus, an eighteenth-century Swedish botanist and physician famous for developing the plant and animal classification systems still in use in the biological sciences today, Foucault points out that "If the natural history and the classifications of Linnea were possible, it is for a certain number of reasons: on the one hand, there was literally a spatialization of the very object of their [seventeenth-century scientists'] analyses, since they gave themselves the rule of studying and classifying a plant only on the basis of that which was visible. They didn't even want to use a microscope. All the traditional elements of knowledge, such as the medical functions of the plant, fell away. The object was spatialized" ("Space, Knowledge, and Power" 254). More broadly, what Foucault is saying is that the study of physical objects in science is based on the fragmentation of those objects into their component parts; eventually, using the microscope and other tools (despite the initial reluctance of the botanists alluded to in the above quotation), each level of an object's components is divided in turn in an effort to discover its most basic, fundamental structure. In addition to fragmentation, spatialization refers to an isolation of the object of study. In traditional botany, the plant is studied only for itself; *uses* of the plant are not considered. It is in a "space" all its own.

Foucault could have chosen to explore knowledge production in more general terms or to explore it in several different disciplinary contexts. He doesn't. Foucault specifically focuses on science to explicate the shifts in knowledge production over the past several centuries because he knows that the production of scientific knowledge is the type of production that has influenced humankind most profoundly during this time period.

A second area in which Foucault uses science to epitomize his ideas is disciplinarity, as alluded to earlier in this chapter. One of Foucault's most important projects as a philosopher was to study how human sciences such as linguistics and economics became disciplines in general and *sciences* in particular. Foucault undertakes this work because, in contemporary society, he contends, "'Truth' is centered on the form of scientific discourse and the institutions which produce it" ("Truth and Power" 73). Foucault focuses on psychiatry in his discussions of disciplinarity as the primary manifestation of power in contemporary society. This branch of medicine is a classic example for Foucault of a discipline that "fixes" knowledge, establishes firm hierarchies, and suppresses spontaneously arising multiplicities ("Panopticism" 209).[4] His explication of how a scientific, discipline-specific discourse and institutions such as asylums were established in psychiatry demonstrates how a science can quite literally change Western civilization. In addition, Foucault is interested in how a more aesthetically inclined field like architecture wavers, as a discipline, between "exact" and "inexact" sciences ("Space, Knowledge, and Power" 255–56). Finally, Foucault points to atomic scientist Robert Oppenheimer as a manifestation of the shift from an earlier "universal" intellectual to a contemporary "specific" intellectual. In this latter capacity, intellectuals such as Oppenheimer concentrate on specific problems in small, well-defined cultural spaces rather than on the problems that confront humanity as a whole. In all cases, contends Foucault, "biology and physics were to a privileged degree the zones of formation of . . . the specific intellectual" ("Truth and Power" 71). However, Foucault concedes, contemporary specific intellectuals have actually reconnected with the public at large in a number of ways: one of these is the way in which localized, specific scientific knowledge, in this case the knowledge of how to initiate a nuclear chain reaction, affects all humanity in a drastic way ("Truth and Power" 68–69). The point is, though, that Foucault's entire discussion of disciplinarity and its associated changes in the nature of the intellectual is contextualized within the sciences, despite the fact that other types of disciplines gained recognizable form during the time periods that he studies. Thus disciplinarity, as a manifestation of Foucault's notion of power, is tied inextricably to the rise of science.

A third argument in Foucault's central focus on science is his notion that attempts to control discourse occur in all societies. A number of procedures are used to achieve this control. One of these is the "opposition between reason and madness" ("Order of Discourse" 53)—a form of control based fundamentally on the use of scientific procedures in the field of psychiatry to establish distinct boundaries between sane and insane and, in turn, to dismiss the discourse of individuals relegated to the latter category. Another, more important, procedure used to control discourse is the "will to truth" ("Order of Discourse" 54–56). To illustrate this principle, which involves the question of whether a proposition succeeds or fails in becoming part of the "truth" of the day, Foucault recounts the Austrian botanist Mendel's efforts to convince his peers of the existence of hereditary traits—the foundation of genetics. Mendel's ideas were summarily dismissed by the scientific community of the mid-nineteenth century because, contends Foucault, even though "Mendel spoke the truth . . . he was not 'within the true' of the biological discourse of his time" ("Order of Discourse" 61). Mendel constituted the genetic trait as an entirely new kind of biological object, and he used methods and a theoretical foundation that were simply too far beyond the boundaries of the nineteenth-century biology discourse community ("Order of Discourse" 61). As with knowledge production and with disciplinarity, Foucault could have chosen a failed proposition from any field to demonstrate his notion of the will to truth. Again, though, he uses a scientific example, perhaps implying that truth is more strongly associated with scientific propositions than with propositions from any other source.

The work of Lyotard, Žižek, and Foucault demonstrates the high level of interest and concern with which postmodernism has approached science. Postmodernism has, in fact, influenced science profoundly. It is redefining questions, procedures, and interpretations within science as part of the constant exchange between science and the culture of which it is an inextricable part. To this end, complex, multi-dimensional webs are taking the place of linear cause-and-effect chains, long-established categories are being upended, and disorder is valorized. As Hess notes,

> In the sciences, outlines of postmodern theorizing are seen in a number of fields. In biology, the evolutionary theory of the nineteenth century has undergone another shift from the equilibrium models of the modernist period to new theories based on computer simulations and nonlinear dynamics. Likewise, molecular biology destabilizes conventional species categories by focusing on genes, their recombination, and their transmission. In physics, there is less sense that an ultimate foundation particle will be found, and chaos/complexity theory has provided a new framework for the analysis of areas previously seen as merely random. In general, the shift in emphasis toward open systems and patterns of self-organization marks a "postmodern" style in scientific theorizing. (133–34)

Despite attention from theorists of the postmodern whom many rhetoricians and compositionists esteem and changes in science that have occurred as a result of this attention, though, scientific discourse remains largely absent from rhetoric and composition.

Science as an Ideological State Apparatus

Marxism also provides a valuable theoretical lens that can be used to view the dominance of scientific discourse (Hess 116). Because of the enormous magnitude to which science is supported and practiced by large corporations and the state, science can be understood as an Althusserian ideological state apparatus (ISA) that operates discursively. Althusser defines such entities as "a certain number of realities which present themselves to the immediate observer in the form of distinct and specialized institutions" (143) that not only reproduce the skills and labor needed for their continued existence but also reproduce "the submission to the ruling ideology for the workers . . . and the ability to manipulate the ruling ideology correctly for the agents of exploitation and repression, so that they, too, will provide for the domination of the ruling class 'in words'" (132–33, emphasis added).

Althusser does not include science in his list of such apparatuses, which includes religion, education, the family, the legal system, the political system, trade unions, mass media, and the "cultural ISA (Literature, the Arts, sports, etc.)" (143). In fact, Althusser would most likely strongly object to the inclusion of science as an ISA. Despite his theoretical stance as an anti-positivist (see, e.g., Aronowitz 176 and 184), Althusser separated science from other institutions because part of his task was to portray Marxism as scientific and thus independent of cultural influence. According to this view, says Aronowitz, "Science is somehow separate from the class struggle, even though class and class struggle may be the object of knowledge of scientific investigation provided they are viewed from the mechanism of structural analysis. . . . Althusser holds to the eternity of the distinction between ordinary ideological discourse and scientific discourse" (173, 175–76).

Nonetheless, once one accepts the notion that science is a cultural institution, science meets Althusser's criteria for ISAs. First, the disciplines and institutions that refer to themselves as scientific, like other ISAs, take great pains to distinguish themselves from other fields or institutions that are fraught with political and economic concerns. Also, similar to the other ISAs, science functions primarily by ideology and not primarily by violence, as would a repressive state apparatus such as a secret police force (145).[5] Finally, like other ISAs, science produces a product—discourse—and, simultaneously, reproduces the means and conditions of its production (128) with a well-defined hierarchy of training in undergraduate, graduate, and postdoctoral programs (for labor/skills) and with well-established sources of income from government and private industry (for capital).

With the use of a musical metaphor, Althusser argues that "This concert [of ideological state apparatuses] is dominated by a single score" (154); for Althusser, that single score is education, which Althusser declares to be the most powerful ideological state apparatus, replacing the church. Some contemporary theorists echo this contention: Usher and Edwards, for example, state that "modern forms of governance and social discipline are secured through education; in an important sense, they work through educating. In modernity, education replaces premodern coercion and subjugation" (84). For Althusser, the educational establishment is the dominant ISA for several reasons: it has charge of children for a highly significant portion of time, and it presents itself and appears as ideologically neutral to society at large (156–57). However, the institution of science, which is the means by which many education theorists create and validate knowledge in their field, develop new curricula, and determine a child's potential for learning, is, in fact, more powerful on a fundamental level than education. This movement toward and dependence on science by education has been recognized. For example, Longo discusses the "*academic* and economic systems which tend to reproduce our culture's *dominant scientific model*" (59, emphasis added). Althusser points out that the school is "as 'natural,' indispensable-useful and even beneficial for our contemporaries as the Church was 'natural,' indispensable and generous for our ancestors a few centuries ago" (157). But what caused this historic shift from church to school? One of the most important provocations was science.

It is in his discussion of how ideology interpellates individuals as subjects that Althusser, finally, tangentially but specifically acknowledges the power of scientific discourse: "It is essential to realize that both he who is writing these lines and the reader who reads them are themselves subjects, and therefore ideological subjects. . . . That the author, insofar as he writes the lines of a discourse which claims to be scientific, is completely absent as a 'subject' from 'his' scientific discourse (for all scientific discourse is by definition a subject-less discourse, there is no 'Subject of science' except in an ideology of science) is a different question which I shall leave on one side for the moment" (171). Despite the fact that Althusser does indeed leave the question of identity in scientific discourse unexplored, he seems to recognize the dominance of this rhetoric. In addition, somewhat ironically, Althusser himself relies on scientific rhetoric here and elsewhere to bolster his ethos even as he claims that this type of discourse is subject-less. At one point, discussing the reproduction of labor power, he says, "To put this more *scientifically*, I shall say that the reproduction of labor power requires not only a reproduction of its skills, but . . . a reproduction of its submission to the rules of the established order" (132, emphasis added). In addition, he likens the Marxist theory of the State to "great *scientific* discoveries [that] cannot but help through the phase of what I shall call *descriptive 'theory.'* This is the first phase of every theory, at least in the domain which concerns us (that of the *science* of social formations)" (138, "scientific" and "science" emphases added). In essence, then, Althusser felt he needed to ground his arguments in what would be viewed as truth-revealing and truth-producing rhetoric. For this purpose, he chose the rhetoric of science.

Althusser returns to the power of science when he decides, ultimately, that scientific knowledge is the type of knowledge that is used to deny ideological allegiance: "what thus seems to take place outside of ideology

. . . in reality takes place in ideology. What really takes place in ideology seems therefore to take place outside it: one of the effects of ideology is the practical *denegation* of the ideological character of ideology by ideology: ideology never says 'I am ideological.' It is necessary to be outside ideology, i.e. in scientific knowledge, to be able to say: I am in ideology (a quite exceptional case) or (the general case): I was in ideology. . . . Ideology *has no outside* (for itself), but at the same time . . . *it is nothing but outside* (for science and reality)" (175). Thus, a person uses the "subject-less" scientific discourse in an attempt to renounce any kind of ideological leaning and perhaps to accuse others of ideological bias. However, this discourse is, like all language, inherently ideological in nature despite protestations to the contrary—a conclusion that Althusser readily admits even as he uses the rhetoric of science to appear ideologically neutral.

Conclusion

No rhetoric becomes dominant by chance alone. Specific historical, political, economic, and social conditions have contributed directly to the increased influence of scientific discourse. Longo observes that "Those of us living in the United States in the late twentieth century take for granted the dominant place of science in our culture. We often assume that science gives us objective truths. We do not readily see scientific dominance as an outcome of contests for knowledge legitimation that came to a head in our culture some three hundred years ago—and are still waged today" (65).

During the eighteenth century, despite the thoughtful critiques of Vico and Pascal and the scathing satires of Swift and Addison, the discourse that came to be associated with the alleged epistemological and ontological certainty of science won the day. By this time, the *Philosophical Transactions of the Royal Society*, the first scientific journal published in the English language, was regularly including texts that would be easily recognized as IMRAD scientific discourse today. According to scientists and their defenders, the new scientific method was the best course of action available to investigate and solve problems of any sort. The alleged absence of rhetoric in scientific discourse, and the epistemological assumptions, ethos, and generic practices initiated by Renaissance scientists and their benefactors (e.g., members of the Royal Society, which was chartered by King Charles II in 1660 to advance the cause of science) have become standardized over the last three hundred years.

Many contemporary, authoritative style manuals associated with scientific disciplines manifest the Renaissance assumptions made about scientific discourse. According to these manuals, scientific writing aspires to be

- Acontextual: According to the *American Medical Association Style Guide*, "All the emergency room physician cares about is that 'The patient has been shot in the hand'—not that 'A policeman had shot the patient in the hand'" (1.14).
- Impersonal: The *Council of Biology Editors Style Manual* advises scientists that "A scientific article should hold the attention of its readers by the importance of its content, not by the presentation calculated to impress the reader with the author's intellect and scientific status" (35).
- Factual: The *American Chemistry Society Style Guide* informs scientists that "phrases like 'we believe,' 'we feel,' 'we concluded,' and 'we can see' are unnecessary, as are personal opinions" (Dodd 3).
- Precise: "Scientific writing serves a completely different purpose from literary writing, and it must therefore be much more precise," adds the *American Chemistry Society Style Guide* (Dodd 3).

In addition, the trend to develop a new, highly complex vocabulary for the language of science, started by Linneaus and his French contemporary Lavoisier, has continued unabated. As a result, many people who are unfamiliar with the terminology have difficulty comprehending scientific discourse—and in fact most people don't even bother trying. Indeed, Kinneavy had a difficult time selecting a piece of scientific discourse for his book: "After several months of a frustrating and vain quest for a piece of strict scientific prose that would at once be intelligible to the general student for whom this book is intended and that would sacrifice nothing to scientific integrity, I am inclined to agree with J. Robert Oppenheimer, who maintains that the language of science is now 'almost impossible to translate' into conventional lay language" (74). It is *not* impossible for a nonscientist to understand scientific discourse—or any other complex discourse, given reasonable effort by those who read scientific discourse and a genuine attempt at clarity by those who write scientific discourse. But we have allowed scientific discourse, as a discipline and a culture, to locate itself outside and above culture at large.

C. P. Snow's two cultures thesis, which radically separates the humanities and sciences, is cited so often that it is virtually household knowledge (Snow 4–5). Counters Swan, much more recently: "we need a populace literate in both language and science, one that is technically competent and able to cross disciplinary boundaries in discoveries of ideas that affect us all. The time is past when we could afford to maintain two separate cultures" (72). Swan is right. Today, because of the work of theorists such as Lyotard, Žižek, Foucault, Althusser, and others, we find ourselves in a situation that is historically similar in several fundamental ways to that of the seventeenth-century western Europeans. We realize that one grand narrative, religion, has been replaced with another, science, and we are skeptical of modernist assumptions about science. We have reservations about science's ability to answer important questions and solve important problems. Science soon will be able to explain to us how to engineer genes and clone animals and humans, but enormous ethical questions must be addressed. And, despite a declaration of war on the disease over thirty years ago by President Nixon and billions of dollars of research support, cancer still plagues us, as does AIDS. Postmodernism and Marxism, as well as feminism and other forms of theory, have put science's promises into critical perspective, yet even now scientific discourse dominates the rhetorical landscape. Rhetoricians and compositionists need to take a much more active part in the important discussions that scientific discourse engenders.

2 The State of Scientific Discourse in Rhetoric and Composition

As they progressed from primary school to more advanced study, students of rhetoric in ancient Greece and Rome de-emphasized other types of texts—most notably works of literature—and began to spend a great deal of time analyzing and composing texts about law. Indeed, it is no coincidence that one of Greece's most famous rhetoricians, Isocrates, was a court logographer, and that two of Rome's most famous rhetoricians, Cicero and Quintilian, were well-known lawyers. The connection between rhetoric and law was strong, and this connection was reflected in the education of the rhetor. Quintilian frames his rhetorical education in terms of law, saying, for example, "What is there in those exercises of which I have just spoken [i.e., declamation] that does not involve matters which are the special concern of rhetoric and further are typical of actual legal cases? Have we not to narrate facts in the law-courts?. . . . Are not eulogy and denunciation frequently introduced in the course of the contests of the courts? Are not commonplaces frequently inserted in the very heart of lawsuits . . . ? These are weapons which we should always have stored in our armoury ready for immediate use as occasion may demand" (II.i.10). The twelfth and final exercise—the capstone experience—in Hermogenes' *progymnasmata* is "Laws" (Murphy 61) and Quintilian, speaking of this exercise, states that "The praise or denunciation of laws requires greater powers; indeed, they should be almost equal to the most serious tasks of rhetoric" (II.iv.33). These "most serious tasks" are those pertaining to declamation, which is itself often contextualized as a legal practice. The two primary types of declamation were *suasoria*, which required a student to urge a person (such as a judge) or group (such as a jury) to act in a certain way, and *controversia*, which required a student to prosecute or defend "a person in a given legal case" (Murphy 62).[1]

Why such focus on law and legal discourse? Teachers of rhetoric in ancient Greece and Rome recognized legal discourse as the rhetoric that made their cultural world go round.[2] The rhetoric of law was the dominant discourse of the day, and rhetoric teachers took seriously their responsibility to ensure that their charges were well-prepared to handle the myriad complexities and situations associated with it.[3] Similarly, in later centuries, rhetoric was closely associated with the discourse of the church: witness *ars prædicandi* as one of the three medieval arts and, starting with St. Augustine, the large number of rhetoricians who were also clergy. Students in medieval and Renaissance schools were required to study Biblical scripture, a curricular fact that is unsurprising given that so much of the educational establishment was controlled by the church. Just as legal discourse was the dominant discourse for the ancients, then, so was the rhetoric of Christianity for the Middle Ages and Renaissance. Teachers of rhetoric recognized the importance of these dominant discourses—their association with the civil affairs of the day and their ability to define and shape identity—and taught their students accordingly.

Today, however, virtually no rhetorician is a scientist, or vice versa.[4] There is little connection between rhetoric and one of the most dominant discourses of the era. It is curious and disturbing that rhetoric and composition, the contemporary institutional forum in which writing teachers have the most access to students and the most opportunity to help them develop as critical readers and writers, largely fails to address scientific discourse—the discourse that drives our contemporary cultural world. This chapter seeks to demonstrate that scientific rhetoric is not a primary concern of rhetoric and composition studies and to articulate reasons why this situation exists. Included later in the chapter are analyses of how scientific discourse is presented (or not presented) in the subfields of composition, ecocomposition, writing across the curriculum, rhetoric of science, medical rhetoric, and technical communication and an explanation of why these efforts do not meet the threshold of establishing the rhetoric of science as a primary concern in the field.

Disinterest and Intimidation

Scientific discourse is essentially ignored in composition theory and practice. Journal articles and conference presentations in the field rarely mention science, and scientific discourse is not studied or produced in composition classrooms. In a typical composition course, especially one with a WAC focus, students may at most read an essay or two *about* science; in most composition courses, though, science or related topics are not discussed at all. On the rhetoric side of the discipline, scientific discourse receives more attention. Articles appear occasionally on scientific discourse in rhetoric and in technical communication journals; these studies typically fall under the purview of the rhetoric of science. From 1999 through 2005, a total of about thirty articles have been published in *Rhetoric Society Quarterly, Rhetoric Review, Rhetorica, Written Communication, Technical Communication Quarterly,* the *Journal of Technical Writing and Communication,* and *CCC.* In *CCC,* considered by many to be the flagship journal of rhetoric and composition as a whole, only one article on the rhetoric of science was published during this six-year span. The bulk of the rhetoric of science articles appeared in special issues of other journals: a Summer 2000 special issue of *Technical Communication Quarterly* on medical rhetoric, a January 2004 special issue of *Written Communication* on the rhetoric of popular science, and a Summer 2005 issue of *Technical Communication Quarterly* on the rhetoric of science. (All three of these special issues followed a 1996 special issue of *Rhetoric Society Quarterly* on the rhetoric of science.) Over this period, though, the number of articles published by these influential journals combined exceeds five hundred. Rhetoric of science articles represent only 6 percent of this total.

In addition to journal articles, a few books on scientific rhetoric have been written, and the American Association of the Rhetoric of Science and Technology holds a small annual pre-conference the day before the National Communication Association conference begins. Medical rhetoricians conduct a special interest group at the annual Conference on College Composition and Communication. Overall, however, the community of rhetoricians of science (including medicine) is tiny in comparison to composition, literacy, writing and technology, rhetorical history and theory, and professional writing as a whole, and its efforts receive scant attention. Moreover, most of the work in the rhetoric of science takes the form of rhetorical criticism.[5] This body of work, while fascinating from an analytical point of view, fails to consider issues of pedagogy and literacy—in short, the impact of scientific discourse on identity and culture. Because the work is not visible beyond a small academic community, its impact is severely limited.

Why is scientific discourse not a major concern of rhetoric and composition as a whole? This question can be answered initially in at least two ways: rhetoricians and compositionists are, in general, either uninterested in scientific discourse or intimidated by scientific discourse. In terms of being uninterested, rhetoricians and compositionists may simply find most scientific discourse to be . . . well . . . boring. Who in rhetoric and composition studies, for example, can get really worked up about the following?

> Like in the condensed phase, without an external input of energy, at room temperature only exothermic or approximately thermoneutral reactions can take place with measurable rate constants as long as entropic effects do not play a major role. Because the interaction between an ion and a dipole (permanent or charge-induced) always is attractive, there are no thermochemical constraints with respect to the formation of ion-molecule complexes in the first step. The fact that rate constants measured for formation of such complexes in the highly diluted gas phase are often quite small is readily explained by the absence of a heat bath, which could consume the excess energy released during complex formation and thus prevent its dissociation in the back-reaction. In contrast, efficient reactions are observed in many cases if the collision complex can be stabilized by elimination of a fragment carrying away the excess energy. (Koszinowski et al. 5000)

And this passage does not even contain any numbers, equations, or formulas! Indeed, the vast majority of scientific discourse presents research—like this example—on what Kuhn refers to as "normal, puzzle-solving science" (35), done by scientist–technicians, as opposed to the more celebrated paradigm-busting type. This research, especially basic (not applied) science in the biological and physical sciences, such as this text from the *Journal of Physical Chemistry A*, does not have any apparent or immediate application to issues of language, power, and pedagogy that rhetoricians and compositionists find important. It represents that infinitesimal step forward—adding just a little bit more to the corpus of scientific knowledge. Even in more applied sciences and in medicine, this research often represents such a small piece of the puzzle (whatever it may be) that it hardly warrants special attention.

Another reason that rhetoricians and compositionists may find scientific discourse uninteresting is because it adheres slavishly to one of the most thoroughly entrenched organizational schemes in the history of language: IMRAD structure. Students begin to practice the genre as early as fifth or sixth grade, when they begin to write their first lab reports; by the time they are in high school, they have internalized the IMRAD drill. Rhetoricians and compositionists likely view such a fixed scheme with the same distaste they reserve for formulaic literary genres and the dreaded five-paragraph theme. Similarly, scientific discourse is not known to reflect contemporary standards of good prose style. It is, in fact, the type of writing many of us try to teach our students to avoid. Ubiquitous passive voice; long, convoluted sentences; endless noun strings; hidden agents; few action verbs—all of these features are hallmarks of what many rhetoricians and compositionists see as simply bad writing. It is bad in terms of rhetorical ethics in addition to terms of quality. With the use of passive voice, responsibility is hidden. Comprehension is delayed, if not obscured altogether. Grace and elegance are wanting. Rhetoricians and compositionists react with dismay.

In addition, rhetoricians and compositionists may be unconcerned with scientific discourse because its ties to classical rhetoric, upon whose foundation much of rhetoric and composition studies is founded, may not be as strong as these connections are for other types of discourse, such as forensic and deliberative. For example, Bazerman, who himself has done a great deal of work on scientific rhetoric, states that "For issues of rhetoric of science and writing in the disciplines, I find classical rhetoric of some, but limited use" (H-Rhetor). Instead, Bazerman goes on to say, sociology, psychology, and literacy studies provide more theoretical muscle to explore discourse in these areas.[6] One reason why scientific discourse seems to be distant from classical rhetoric may be that contemporary scientific discourse has its roots in a significant misreading of the Ciceronian plain style (Halloran and Whitburn 64–67); the connection of scientific discourse to classical rhetoric is thus tenuous because this misinterpretation has become institutionalized and codified.

Classical rhetoric is designed for specific situations for which an audience and situation are projected; a student of classical rhetoric learned to plan a text for that occasion. The publication of a scientific research article is a much different type of situation than that envisioned by classical rhetoricians: an absent, dispersed audience upon which *pathos* appeals cannot be overtly utilized. Also, classical rhetoric does not address intertextuality well; this issue is of critical importance in scientific discourse. Finally, for a discourse to be analyzed productively with classical rhetoric principles, says Bazerman, the discourse needs to be public: "In matters of pubic deliberation and decision, classical rhetoric is much more consistently useful and revealing. Matters of public deliberation, political persuasion, and legal choice-making are precisely the kinds of occasions classical rhetoric was designed for" (H-Rhetor). Thus scientific discourse may also not warrant interest from rhetoric and composition because of the perception that it is absent from the public spaces with which we normally associate civic discourse: government institutions, major newspapers and news magazines, television and radio news programs, talk shows, and the like.

Another reason rhetoricians and compositionists largely ignore scientific rhetoric is perhaps because so little research or discussion in rhetoric and composition uses this type of discourse. Perhaps more than any other discipline or set of disciplines except the fine arts, English studies has resisted the scientism that pervades once much more theoretical fields such as political science, economics, psychology, and sociology. In English studies, although qualitative empirical studies in the forms of ethnographies and case studies are now commonplace, quantitative scientific discourse is restricted primarily to some areas of linguistics and English education research that is often performed in education departments rather than in English departments.[7] As a result of this paucity of scientific method-based research in English studies, graduate students in rhetoric and composition have at best limited exposure to scientific discourse. Even if some attention is given to quantitative research methods and elementary statistics in a graduate research methods course, as is often the case, the vast majority of graduate students (and their dissertation directors) pursue research projects that are either theoretical or empirically qualitative in nature.[8] In addition, many rhetoricians and compositionists move into the field from other areas of English studies, especially literature. Graduate students coming out of literature programs are even less likely to have worked with scientific discourse than students coming from other disciplines.

Rhetoricians and compositionists may ignore scientific discourse because they have also had other pressing concerns. Chief among these has been gaining a foothold and institutional authority within academia. Struggling for recognition, fair working conditions, and equitable treatment with regard to promotion and tenure, rhetoricians and compositionists have had to perform the vital tasks associated with building a new discipline. Working in a field only forty years old, rhetoricians and compositionists have perhaps not had ample time or opportunity to examine the discourses prevalent in society at large; they have, understandably, been dealing with dominant discourses (such as literature) closer to home. In addition, many graduate programs in rhetoric and composition were founded at land grant universities, where science and technology prevail. Some may have thought it politically unwise to pursue research agendas that involved critique of scientific discourse at this type of institution.

Just as important as disciplinary arguments about the lack of interest in scientific discourse from the perspectives of rhetoric and composition instructors are discussions that consider our students' points of view. Let's face it: the prevailing assumption is that most students who take composition and rhetoric courses are even less interested in scientific discourse than their instructors are. And rhetoric and composition instructors tend to value rhetorics that students find exciting because students produce more sophisticated, interesting texts when they use these rhetorics; thus, because it does not meet this criterion, scientific discourse is not considered for inclusion in rhetoric and composition curricula. Many rhetoricians and compositionists claim that the use of discourses that students will find familiar, relevant, and interesting, both for reading and writing, captivates students and increases the likelihood that they will produce informed, enthusiastically written papers. Thus, for example, I and many other rhetoric and composition instructors will, in a first-year writing course, ask students to write a review of a film or CD that has made an impact on them. We attempt to teach the students how to "dig in" to a film, to recognize what's happening (or not happening) in terms of casting, acting, plot, cinematography, and production, or for a CD, to carefully analyze lyrics, vocal and instrumental talent, instrumentation, innovation, and arrangement of tracks. We strive to explain clearly to our students that it is not enough to simply describe the film or CD; they must evaluate it as well. In other words, they must argue effectively that the film or CD is good, mediocre, or terrible, and many of them do so successfully. Indeed, many students enjoy writing about a film or CD that they feel in a sense belongs to their generation. Most do not, however, enjoy writing about science, with which most of our students feel little connection.

In addition to being uninterested in scientific rhetoric, rhetoricians and compositionists and their students may be intimidated by it. This intimidation results from, among other things, jargon and the use of numbers and statistical analyses. The jargon problem is a difficult one. Despite Bishop Thomas Sprat's plea in the late seventeenth-century *History of the Royal Society* for budding scientists to prefer the "language of Artizans, Countrymen, and Merchants" (113), lexical invention and change in scientific disciplines, subdisciplines, and super-narrow specialties occur with dizzying speed, and each discourse community in the sciences (there are thousands) has its own vocabulary. Even a seemingly well-defined field such as cancer research has a large number of disparate discourse communities who find it difficult to communicate with each other. For about three years, I worked as an editor for the *Journal of the National Cancer Institute*, a prestigious twice-monthly cancer research journal that prides itself on its multidisciplinary focus. A typical issue may have a pharmaceutical article on a Phase I clinical trial of a new cancer drug regimen followed by a basic science article on genetic origins of breast cancer followed by an epidemiological article on the incidence of leukemia in a certain geographical area. Because the editorial staff of the *Journal of the National Cancer Institute* strives to make each issue's content accessible to readers from across the entire spectrum of cancer research, a large part of the editing work that goes into each article is adding explanation, spelling out abbreviations, and making field-specific assumptions visible to a wider audience. It is not an easy task. In my experience, it was not uncommon for an author to object to my modifications on the grounds that the text I often added was elementary knowledge in the author's field that did not deserve mention and that in fact embarrassed the author if articulated. The author's peers, the argument went, would be insulted because they would be forced to read this elementary material and waste valuable time. The author did not always agree with my rebuttal, which invoked the *Journal of the National Cancer Institute's* multidisciplinary mission; she or he often pointed out that they thought it unlikely that specialists from other fields would in fact read the article. The point is that if even fellow scientists are put off by scientific discourse outside of their narrow specialty area, how can rhetoricians and compositionists be expected to make sense of it?

Similarly, scientific rhetoric's reliance on numbers and statistics sends many a compositionist, rhetorician, or student racing in search of more palatable, textually based reading material. For most in the field, the use of statistics renders a text more unintelligible by at least an order of magnitude, what with the reader trying to make sense of all kinds of variables, correlations, interactions, and statistical significance. This recoil occurs because most rhetoricians and compositionists have not made an effort to understand the function of statistics and how they contribute to the argument posited by the author(s) of a scientific research report. Because we have not shown statistics to be the rhetorical constructs they are, we and our students suffer.

Whether disinterest or intimidation or a combination of each, the disconnect between rhetoric and composition and scientific discourse is unfortunate and troubling. True, with respect to its style and organization, scientific discourse does not move many of us in the same way that well-written essay prose or literary discourse does.[9] However, discourses of power, since the demise of oral cultures, have never been literary in form. Dominant discourses may have literary or poetic elements—the Psalms and Proverbs and the Song of Solomon of the Christian tradition come to mind—but these elements lack the material clout that other perhaps less poetic parts of the Bible carry, such as the Ten Commandments or the Gospels. Legal discourse has never had a literary element; indeed, in 2003, a judge in Pennsylvania who wrote some of his decisions in verse was censured by a higher state court for trivializing the serious work of interpreting law. With scientific discourse, though, even Kuhn's normal, puzzle-solving science needs to be taken seriously. It is this discourse that our society assigns the responsibility of performing the day-to-day work of making sense of ourselves and our surroundings, both epistemologically and ontologically. This authority should be reason enough to make scientific discourse a central component of rhetorical study for all students, despite its alleged lack of literary merit

Although the disinterest argument about scientific discourse's lack of ties to classical rhetoric may have merit, several theorists have attempted to establish a link. Gopen, for example, argues that the typical IMRAD arrangement parallels that of a Ciceronian oratory. Alford suggests that Thucydides' account of a plague in 430 B.C. Athens uses conventions of scientific writing that are now an established part of the scientific research article genre (133). Fahnestock has analyzed the use of *incrementum* and *gradatio* in Darwin's writings, and Miller and Selzer have investigated generic, institutional or organizational, and disciplinary "topics" in engineering reports. Miller has also written an essay on "*Kairos* in the Rhetoric of Science." Additionally, a body of work investigates the use of the classical tropes of analogy and metaphor in scientific discourse (see, for example, Graves, "Marbles," and, more recently, Little, "Analogy in Science," or Ceccarelli), and Fahnestock's *Rhetorical Figures in Science* examines the use of other schemes in scientific discourse such as the *antimetabole, ploche, agnominatio,* and *polyptoton*. Finally, Zappen maintains that since the mid-1970s, most work in the filed of the rhetoric of science has emphasized the similarities between classical rhetoric and scientific discourse rather than the differences ("Historical Studies" 288).

Additionally, scientific discourse can be said to be strongly tied to classical rhetoric given what some theorists in the field see as a recent shift to a neo-Sophistic rhetoric. To the extent that the current state of rhetorical theory demonstrates some similarities to that of past Sophistic eras, as scholars such as McComiskey argue (12), the scope of rhetoric as an academic discipline has expanded in a way that Sophists (past or present) would contend includes the discourse of science. For example, from a rhetoric of science perspective, Alan Gross argues that claims made by science are "solely the products of persuasion" (3) and are thus wholly suffused with rhetoric. Gross declares that "brute facts" of nature exist, but these facts by themselves are meaningless. Statements must be used to explain and interpret facts; in turn, persuasion must be used to convince others of the truth of these statements. Gross's rhetoric is, in many ways, Aristotelian; he claims Aristotle's *Rhetoric* as his master theoretical text.

43

However, Gross acknowledges that the rhetoric of science is decidedly un-Aristotelian in one key respect: by extending the scope of rhetoric to include science, Gross rejects Aristotle's partitioning of knowledge into categories of probable and certain and thus gives rhetoric a Sophistic strain that Aristotle would not have tolerated. Scientific discovery is, according to Gross, equivalent to rhetorical invention—a Sophistic move and a stark contrast to Bacon's famous bifurcation of the two forms of invention in *The Advancement of Learning*. And, declares Gross, the rhetoric of science should be "updated" (18) from a strictly Aristotelian perspective by taking into account the ideas of modern rhetoricians. He sees analogy and taxonomic language as well as the more traditional concerns of invention, arrangement, and style as important aspects of the rhetoric of science.

From a Sophistic theory perspective, Gross's efforts, as well as those of other rhetoricians of science, suggest that the neo-Sophistic movement described by theorists such as McComiskey is underway. Indeed, as McComiskey notes, drawing on an aphorism from Adorno, "Adorno suggests that 'steady drops hollow the stone' . . . and although sophistic 'drops' may have been suppressed for many years, they are once again flowing, hollowing the stones of realism and foundationalism that stifle the most vital functions of rhetoric—its social functions" (117). No new Sophistic is complete without an engagement of the discourse of "realism and foundationalism"—the rhetoric of science. Scientific discourse can be characterized as one of the realist, foundationalist stones—ponderous, unbreakable—that is seemingly immune from the messy complexities of rhetoric. Scientific discourse's supposed immunity is, of course, a sure sign instead of its rhetorical sophistication. This assertion has been posited by Latour, who, when he introduces his readers to the term "rhetoric" in *Science in Action*, states, "Rhetoric is a fascinating albeit despised discipline, but it becomes still more important when debates are so exacerbated that they become scientific and technical. . . . Scientific or technical texts . . . are not written differently by different breeds of writers. When you reach them, this does not mean that you quit rhetoric for the quieter realm of pure reason. It means that rhetoric has become heated enough or still so active that many more resources have to be brought in to keep the debates going" (30–31). Many neo-Sophists were and are attuned to the rhetorical nature of all language. In a Sophistic age, no discourse, and especially dominant and allegedly non-rhetorical discourses, can be left unexamined. An association of scientific rhetoric with a currently perceived neo-Sophistic environment clarifies its ties to classical rhetoric.

Then there is the disinterest argument of the lack of *public-ness* of scientific discourse.[10] Why isn't scientific discourse public? For the most part, it is certainly available and accessible, and there's a lot of it. But, except for health[11] and the environment (including—and perhaps especially—the weather), scientific issues are not part of the public sphere. *Scientific American* is the most well-known science popularization magazine, but its circulation is miniscule compared to magazines such as *People* or *Rolling Stone*. Scientific issues are not often discussed by the water cooler or at Friday afternoon happy hour. The reasons for scientific discourse's lack of visibility in the public sphere are complex, but they most likely have something to do with the rise of the Romantic individual—the isolated scientific genius is a figure similar to the isolated literary or artistic genius—and with the fragmentation and compartmentalization of knowledge in the modern university. In addition, and more importantly from the perspective of this book, scientific discourse is not public *because rhetoricians and compositionists have not made it public*. Modernist assumptions about the impartiality and universality of scientific discourse have remained largely unchallenged by rhetoricians and compositionists, especially with respect to teaching.

With respect to the disinterest argument that scientific discourse itself does not play a significant role in the research agenda of rhetoric and composition, it must be again stated that this absence should be seen as a boon and not a drawback. Rhetoric and composition prides itself on being a home for both theoretical and empirical means of investigation—a "multimodal discipline," as Lauer calls it (44). Nevertheless, all graduate programs in rhetoric and composition (as well as the other humanities-oriented disciplines) should retain a special and constant interest in scientific discourse and, for that matter, any dominant discourse. An active focus should be maintained on how such discourses operate (i.e., the material effects of such discourses), how they attained dominance (i.e., how they were made dominant), how to identify discourses that are suppressed as a result of the dominant discourse and the mechanisms of such suppression, and how dominant discourse should be studied in rhetoric and composition classrooms. Now that rhetoric and composition has solidified its place within the academy, the discipline may feel secure enough to engage public and/or dominant discourses more readily. While the discipline-building activities and institutional self-reflection have been vital to the coalescence of rhetoric and composition as a legitimate academic enterprise, the time has come to look increasingly outward, beyond disciplinarily comfortable discourses.

Certainly the argument to make use of discourses that students express an attraction to and will enjoy deserves merit as a pedagogical approach. While it is entirely understandable and justifiable, though, this approach fails to fully acknowledge that students may value rhetorics that they do *not* already have considerable experience in analyzing and using. Perhaps, at least in part because of the consumer orientation that pervades so much of higher education, we overdo the emphasis on working with rhetorics that our students find interesting or familiar at the expense of working with rhetorics that our students will have to engage as active citizens of a society in which important decisions are made on the basis of scientific research. Rare is the first-year writing student, for example, who cannot conduct a fairly well-informed analysis of an advertisement produced for mass media. Today's students have been exposed to these advertisements since they were toddlers old enough to focus on a television screen or computer monitor. Rhetoric and composition instructors should bring their expertise to bear in a concerted effort to introduce students to society's dominant discourses, demonstrate how they work, and show students how to use and analyze them effectively.

Also, the assumption itself that most students (not to mention instructors) do not find scientific discourse to be interesting deserves renewed attention. Given the enormous popularity of television programs such as *CSI*, which portrays heroic scientists working diligently in the laboratory and in the field to solve all manner of crimes, we can see earlier stereotypes of incredibly intelligent but socially awkward, isolated scientists breaking down. *CSI* and other programs like it are associated with a flood of student interest in forensic chemistry, a trend that I noticed when I taught an all-chemistry majors section of a technical communication course for three years. Also, there are indications that the popularity of science-related books is increasing; Hawking's *A Brief History of Time* has been widely read, and Sagan received a $2 million advance for *Contact*, a science fiction novel upon which a subsequent successful film was based. At the time, the advance was the largest ever received by an author for a work of fiction (Lewenstein quoted in NSF, "Info Brief" 7–6).

With respect to the intimidation argument, students and instructors in rhetoric and composition classrooms must realize that science can be read, understood, and even improved upon by nonscientists. Studies in anthropology and sociology "demonstrate that lay groups develop fairly sophisticated understandings of science when it is in their interest to do so" (Hess 142). And beyond merely understanding, local knowledge possessed by nonscientists can often provide scientists with a much more complete picture of the phenomenon under investigation. Hess, citing Wynne, discusses nonscientists' understanding of radiation pollution in northern England's Lake District during the Chernobyl disaster in 1986: "The Chernobyl incident was accompanied by high levels of rainfall in this region, and sheep farmers subsequently learned that their flocks were contaminated. However the government intervention came via a series of mixed messages, and scientists did not take local knowledge into consideration as they developed their analyses. As a result, some of the scientists' recommendations were ludicrous in light of lay knowledge about grazing patterns, local ecology, and local soil types. Furthermore, long-standing suspicions about contamination from the nearby Sellafield Nuclear Plant reemerged as farmers began to suspect that the Chernobyl incident was being used to cover up a local radioactive contamination problem. (142) In this case, scientists failed both 'technically and politically'" (Hess 142). The farmers quickly and easily recognized that, despite their credentials, the scientists' recommendations were seriously flawed; the farmers developed "a relatively sophisticated skepticism of expert knowledge" (Hess 142). These flaws, in turn, fueled suspicions that the scientists were protecting the nearby nuclear plant, thereby discrediting the scientists entirely.

Undoubtedly the vocabulary of the sciences is complex and likely represents one of the primary reasons for intimidation. However, scientific vocabulary is no more difficult than the intricate lexicon of rhetorical theory or any other advanced intellectual operation. There are ways to address this complex vocabulary in any discipline. For example, in some instances, complex discourse can be comprehended more quickly if one reads related texts that are published in the same rhetorical space. In some scientific research journals, especially those in the medical sciences, the article that the editorial board feels will generate the most publicity in that particular issue is accompanied in the same issue by one or two editorials written by a prominent physician or scientist in the field of which the authors of the featured article are a part.[12] The editorial writers often ask broad, compelling questions about the featured article: they are, then, engaging in textual criticism of scientific research. Once nonscientist readers who read the featured article and accompanying editorial realize that they are witnessing cutting-edge *debates* in science, they may well begin to be less intimidated by the authoritative tone and recognize the *logos*, *ethos*, and *pathos* appeals contained in scientific discourse and thus be more motivated to look up definitions of unfamiliar terms.

For example, in the May 14, 2003, issue of *JAMA* (formerly the *Journal of the American Medical Association*), researchers report that high blood pressure occurs 60 percent more frequently in western European adults than in their North American counterparts (Wolf-Maier et al. 2363). In a separate editorial in the same issue, Staessen et al., on the basis of their reading of the article, note that "the study by Wolf-Maier et al . . . breaks new ground by raising the hypothesis that the average level of BP [blood pressure] and its age-related increase might differ across populations" (2421). However, Staessen et al. add,

> Undetected selection in the enrollment of study participants, divergent lifestyle factors (including salt intake, smoking, or alcohol consumption), secular trends in BP among surveys published over a time span exceeding 1 decade, and climatic influences on BP are among the confounders unaccounted for in the assessment by Wolf-Maier et al. Furthermore, in all of the population studies reviewed by Wolf-Maier et al., BP was measured by auscultation of the Korotkoff sounds, except for 1 survey in England, in which an oscillometric device with doubtful precision was used. This technique of BP measurement is prone to error and is difficult to standardize even among skilled observers. . . . Thus, disparities in both the technique and in the conditions of BP measurement may have inflated the apparent between-country differences in the study by Wolf-Maier et al. (2421)

This research article and editorial appeared in one of the most prestigious medical journals in the United States. Most rhetoricians and compositionists will not recognize terms such as "auscultation," "Korotkoff," and "oscillometric" readily—but they will recognize the editorial writers' overall goal. It is to engage in the same kind of scholarly debate and exchange that occurs in all vibrant discourse communities, and rhetoricians and compositionists are adept at discovering the rhetorical practices that occur in these forums.

Additionally, rhetoricians and compositionists—and their students— need not be statistics virtuosos to engage scientific discourse intelligently. Indeed, many of the most influential scientific texts use few if any numbers (for example, see Watson and Crick's "A Structure for Deoxyribose Nucleic Acid"). And the numbers themselves are not what are most important to nonscientists: instead, broader questions on the study design's validity and reliability, its execution, and interpretation of the study's results need to be asked. In terms of statistics, though, a recognition of the correspondence between statistical "moves" and corresponding textual "moves" may help to alleviate a lack of familiarity. Statistics are essentially equivalent to Toulminian warrants in text: a claim is made, evidence is provided to support the claim, and statistics are employed in an attempt to demonstrate why the evidence can be argued to support the claim—the same function a Toulminian warrant serves.

Below is an excerpt from a social science research article that relies heavily on statistics. This passage is taken from an educational psychology study on how well second- and fourth-grade Chinese students learn to pronounce unfamiliar Chinese compound characters on the basis of partial information about the pronunciation that is visible in the characters themselves. In the first sentence of the Results section, the authors report the following: "The major finding of the study was that type of character strongly influenced the learning of pronunciations, Wilks's λ = .123, $F(3, 235)$ = 556.88, p < .01, $\acute{\eta}_p^2$ = .877. The high value of partial eta squared ($\acute{\eta}_p^2$) confirms a very large effect size; nearly 88% of between-characters sample variance is explained by type of character. Planned comparisons indicate that, as expected, performance was better on regular, $t(207)$ = 36.09, p < .01, and tone-different, $t(207)$ = 19.76, p < .01, characters than characters with unknown phonetics" (Anderson et al. 54). Although no editorial that would help to understand these data accompanies the article, thirty minutes with a statistics dictionary, Google, and a small book entitled *Statistics Without Tears* provides enough context to ask meaningful questions about the study. Indeed, the only symbol I knew when I initially read this work was p, which, when it is less than .05, is an indicator of statistical significance (i.e., given a random sample, there is less than a 5 percent chance that the results occur by chance).[13] In this, case, the authors claim that there is less than a 1 percent chance that the results occurred by chance; thus, the results are indeed statistically significant. Wilks' λ, according to my brief foray into statistics, is a test to determine if differences exist between multiple groups (presumably groups of students in this study) and across multiple dependent variables (e.g., type of character). The F symbol refers to a ratio of variance within groups to variance between groups; it is used to attempt to prove that the variance does not occur by chance and instead is a result of an effect being studied (Rowntree 148), in this case, being able to pronounce the word. Partial eta squared, $\acute{\eta}_p^2$, measures the correlation between an effect and a dependent variable; in this study, the authors claim that the type of character (the dependent variable, of which there were four types) that students were introduced to strongly influenced how well they were able to pronounce the word (i.e., the effect). The t symbol refers to a test of statistical significance.

Ultimately, statistics is a language. Like all other languages, it has rhetorical conventions and rules that can be learned and then, as necessary, interrogated. In fact, statistics have become much more visible with the popular SPSS program, which many universities own. In addition to the traditional foreign languages, graduate students in some rhetoric and composition programs can fulfill a language requirement by studying a computer programming language; however, no program that I know of allows a graduate student to take statistics to fulfill a language requirement. Perhaps this step should be considered.

The Treatment of Scientific Discourse in Rhetoric and Composition

Because of disinterest and possible intimidation and perhaps other as yet unarticulated reasons, then, scientific discourse does not occupy the place of privilege in rhetoric and composition communities that one might expect of a dominant discourse in a Sophistic-leaning age. However, some efforts have been made. The remainder of this chapter explores in more detail the place of scientific discourse in rhetoric and composition. This discussion must be framed with the realization that the work that I mention represents a fraction of the work that occurs in rhetoric and composition as a whole. The purpose of this discussion is, then, to introduce and promote work on scientific discourse to the wider rhetoric and composition community and to discuss its strengths and weaknesses. The discussion begins with composition and moves to writing across the curriculum, rhetoric of science, medical rhetoric, and technical communication. Overall, the discussion demonstrates that even when science becomes an area of interest, which is, again, rare, rhetoric and composition does not engage scientific discourse head-on: either scientific discourse itself is ignored in favor of texts that are simply *about* science (as is generally the case with composition and technical communication), or scientific discourse is analyzed but issues of pedagogy, literacy, and culture are disregarded (as is largely the case with the rhetoric of science). Thus, in terms of our students' understanding, issues of scientific discourse's dominance and power are overlooked. In other words, rhetoric and composition dances *around* scientific discourse for the most part, and even when it does take this discourse for a spin, as in the case with the rhetoric of science, the dance occurs in private.

Composition Readers

Three readers that deal exclusively with science[14] and that are aimed at the composition market have been published since 1990. The first science reader to appear was HarperCollins's *Science and Society*, published in 1992. It contains a total of twenty-seven essays that describe science, differentiate it from "pseudoscience," contemplate the relationship between humanity and nature, discuss science and ethics, analyze the costs and benefits of medical technology, and predict the future of science and technology. Macmillan's *The Culture of Science: Essays and Issues for Writers*, edited by Hatton and Plouffe, appeared in 1993. Much larger than *Science and Society*, it is divided into three sections entitled "Science and the Broader Culture," "The Enterprise of Science," and "Some Issues for the Nineties." The last section contains chapters on issues such as science and the abortion debate, science and the environment, science and gender, and science and education. Finally, St. Martin's *Science and Technology Today: Readings for Writers*, edited by MacKenzie and published in 1995, is the most recent and perhaps the most useful of the three readers to composition instructors interested in the ways in which writing shapes reality. It contains an entire section called "Writing to Construct Science and Technology" that, in part, attempts to teach students that scientific writing is negotiated, persuasive, biased, and open to interpretation.

These readers are notable because they represent the first attempt within the field of composition to study science as an institution. From a cultural studies standpoint, they seek to demystify a dominant cultural institution that is often taken for granted. All three readers contain selections that attempt to define science, explain its processes, and assess its impact on identity and on culture. In addition, the authors of the three readers include essays that seek to explain the relationship between science and nature and other selections that illustrate ethical dilemmas in science. Finally, each of the readers contains some pedagogical apparatus at the end of every selection: both *Science and Society* and *The Culture of Science* include "Suggestions for Discussion and Writing," while *Science and Technology Today* offers "Discussion Questions," a "Journal Entry," "Writing Projects," and a "Collaborative Project." These prompts can potentially lead students to gain confidence in writing about scientific issues.

The readers may help students to become more critically literate in science issues. As defined later in this book (chapter 4), critical literacy moves beyond simply reading and writing; the critical literate can think analytically by questioning sources, recognizing assumptions and intentions, breaking down arguments, and synthesizing different points of view. Students may be able to accomplish these tasks as a result of enrolling in a course that uses one of these readers. More awareness can be gained, though, if a course that makes use of one of these readers addresses issues of context specificity, shifting subject positions, and the immediate impact of science on students' lives and the ability of writing to foster change—features associated with cultural studies that are discussed in more detail in chapter 3.

However, while the contextual knowledge about science that is gained from these readers is useful, they will not ultimately help students navigate the rhetorical complexities of scientific research articles and sophisticated science popularizations. Awareness is not enough. Indeed, the pedagogical approach espoused by these readers strongly resembles methodologies promoted in critical multiculturalism pedagogies (such as those advocated by, for example, Giroux and McLaren) that focus on understanding dominant cultural institutions and diverse historical narratives. Although noble in its intent, this approach assumes, incorrectly, that awareness leads to agency and ability. As McComiskey points out, "While Giroux, McLaren, and many other critical multiculturalists have done much to develop pedagogies in which students critique dominant hegemonic culture and its globalizing representations, they have done little to help students develop specific rhetorical techniques that can chip away at the institutions that most affect their lives. They send students into battle with knowledge of the enemy but no ammunition. In other words, through critical multicultural pedagogies, students learn to critique structures of domination, but they learn no tactics of their own, no means to counter hegemonic structures" (116). The sidestepping of learning to read and write primary scientific discourse in these readers is similar to the drawbacks McComiskey describes, and this shortcoming limits the readers' ability to teach students to engage scientific discourse meaningfully. A much more pragmatic concern also arises: none of these three readers has appeared in a second edition, a possible and unfortunate indication of lackluster sales.

Composition Courses

Besides readers, at least one composition course that focuses on science has been offered, at Princeton University. In 1995, Swan, who has a Ph.D. in biochemistry and teaching experience in both composition and scientific communication, published a description of a course she taught that combined composition and environmental chemistry. As she explains in "Reflections Across the Divide: Written Discourse as a Structural Mirror in Teaching Science to Nonscience Students," the course was aimed at first- and second-year nonscience and science students (despite the title of the essay, some of the students were science majors [69]) who enrolled to satisfy either Princeton's writing requirement or laboratory science requirement (56). Swan's innovations in the course as far as science education is concerned reflect her experience as a compositionist: they included con-textualizing knowledge by presenting a familiar environmental studies context (e.g., water pollution) first before explaining underlying chemi-cal principles (usually, science educators present the general principles first) so that students' interest would be piqued and maintained. She also encouraged student participation by questioning and polling students frequently so that they were engaged in the construction of the class as a knowledge-making community, a contrast to the more common science education pedagogy of presenting material via lecture (63). Indeed, Swan emphasizes that empowerment was a major goal of the course (67). To advance this goal, students were asked to complete writing assignments and group projects on environmental issues that were presented as part of a symposium to which the university community and general public were invited so that a real audience existed—one that was encouraged to discuss and evaluate the students' work. Swan states that "the projects . . . took the science out of the classroom and into students' lives" (68). In addition, students were asked to complete in- and out-of-class writing assignments that emphasized both writing and science as processes instead of "a set of correct answers" (68). These assignments stressed the role of interpretation, authority, and persuasion in science (70).

The type of course that Swan taught—as with the readers mentioned above—allows students to gain an appreciation and better understand-ing of science. Swan's course moves beyond the readers in demonstrating that the specific environmental issues that are addressed in the course il-lustrate how knowledge is always part of a broader context. In addition, the course engages students by asking them to study environmental issues and highlights the change potential of writing by establishing a forum in which the students addressed a knowledgeable and perhaps powerful audience. Swan's course drives home the point that science is argument and that science is public. It is unclear, though, whether students gained any experience in reading or writing IMRAD-based scientific discourse. Nevertheless, Swan's integrated course is the best work to date with respect to calling attention to the importance of discourse in science and to making science understandable and accessible to students through writing.

Ecocomposition

Ecocomposition focuses on the environment as its area of inquiry rather than on more traditional first-year composition topics such as academia and other cultural institutions, multiculturalism, self-reflection, and civic rhetoric. The number of ecocomposition texts and courses has proliferated over the last two decades, and the authors of these texts and the instructors of these courses should be applauded for bringing the critically important issue of the environment to the composition classroom. Certainly increased awareness of the environment has resulted. But is it enough? Do our students, even those who complete a first-year writing course that focuses exclusively on ecocomposition, have the necessary understanding and tools to engage environmental issues actively, accurately, and convincingly? The environment, even when it is being protected, is managed, as in the case of thinning forests to prevent catastrophic forest fires. The vehicle of this management is scientific discourse, especially that of forestry, oceanography, wildlife and marine biology, botany, and atmospheric science. Ecocomposition courses should incorporate this discourse in both choice of textbooks and subject matter.

Writing Across the Curriculum

Efforts to increase the amount of writing students do in all classes, not just those in English departments, have met with some success over the past several decades at least in part due to the WAC movement, and it is WAC that has done the most to involve texts about science in writing courses. Arguing that writing can both help students to learn subject matter and to become familiar with the rhetorical conventions of different fields (McLeod 3–4), WAC practitioners have designed and conducted faculty workshops (see, e.g., Magnotto and Stout 33–45 for a description), authored grant proposals (Walvoord 25), and studied the writing of scientists, lawyers, psychologists, corporate executives, and professionals in other fields (see, e.g., Bazerman's "What Written Knowledge Does: Three Examples of Academic Discourse" for an example of analyses of writing from molecular biology, sociology, and literature) in an effort to increase the amount of writing that students do while attending college. In its most successful manifestations, WAC can be a compelling model of interdisciplinarity: the movement has allowed and even encouraged the establishment of mutually beneficial relationships among faculty and administrators and a collective appreciation of the work done in these disciplines.

The interaction between WAC and science has been profitable in many respects. Students have used writing to learn various scientific concepts, and they have also gained some familiarity with the genres and other rhetorical conventions common in science. These two activities correspond to McLeod's dual functions for WAC: the cognitive function, or "write to learn," and the rhetorical function, or "learn to write" (3–4).[15] These functions are not easily separated. As LeCourt points out in a discussion of her own WAC practices, "The two [functions], of course, are always related in my discussion. I emphasize how learning to write according to the disciplinary norms of a certain profession is inextricably linked to encouraging the type of thinking valued in that tradition" (389). For science students, this knowledge is especially helpful for enculturation purposes; for others, science-related WAC provides some more general insight into the potential of writing to come to a more complex understanding of an issue and some appreciation for the kinds of discursive activities that occur in science.

The articulation of the rhetorical function of WAC has its roots in the close study of discourses used in the college coursework of different disciplines. (For science, notable examples of this type of analysis are Herrington's work on writing in chemical engineering courses.) Russell notes that as early as the mid-1970s, the most prestigious national organization for science in the United States, the National Science Foundation, sponsored research on the improvement of students' laboratory observations through writing (16). While some scientists and science educators endorsed WAC, however, others regarded WAC as a threat: in a 1985 *Journal of Chemical Education* editorial, Labianca and Reeves provide what they call a "heretical" perspective, arguing that, in the teaching of science, "writing across the curriculum causes problems in terms of time, training, and techniques" (400).[16] Despite the alarm bells sounded by these authors, mutual interest has remained between WAC practitioners in English and rhetoric departments and science teachers. Randy Moore, a biologist, is one of many scientists who advocates pedagogical practices that are consistent with WAC goals: biology instructors should, says Moore, "help students get their ideas on paper and show the students that writing is a powerful tool for discovering information as well as for organizing and communicating it" and ask students to "consider how to write for different audiences" such as peers, grant-sponsoring organizations, and the general public (614–16).

Although the amount of writing about science in composition courses and the amount of writing in science courses has most likely increased as a result of the WAC movement, the writing that students do that is related to science generally does not help them to gain an understanding of primary, peer-reviewed scientific discourse and its power. As Peritz points out, "As an ideological formation, writing to learn tends to reinforce the politically liberal belief that more learning is key to the achievement of socio-cultural equity, not merely because it means more access to better employment opportunities but most of all because it furthers democratic communication, consensus, and community" (438). The cognitive and rhetorical functions of WAC, then, are more directed at teaching students to become professionalized within disciplines instead of at an understanding of the discipline's positive and negative roles in society and the impact of the discourse on identity. LeCourt lists a number of statements from WAC literature that reveal a tendency for WAC practitioners to construct students as uncritical disciplinary novices:

> Professionals within a discipline share a knowledge of the conventions of written discourse used by that discipline. Such knowledge needs to be shared with students, too. English faculty can, with the help of others, encourage this sharing by introducing students to the written work of professionals in various disciplines, by showing them how to read that work for conventions as well as context, and then *by asking students to try their hands at apprentice versions of such writing* (Peterson 61).

> This dialogue [between faculty in the humanities and other disciplines] must work toward balancing humanistic methods of encouraging more active and collaborative learning [write-to-learn activities] in WAC courses with *reinforcing the ways of knowing and the writing conventions of different discourse communities* (Jones and Comprone 61).

> In writing-intensive courses focused on disciplinary writing, students achieve an understanding of the "relationship between writing (the writing in the assigned texts and the writing prepared by students) and what it means to become *members of that discipline's intellectual community*" (Slevin 13).

> Although this approach ["writing in the disciplines"] does not exclude writing-to-learn assignments, it emphasizes more formal assignments, teaching *writing as a form of social behavior in the academic community* (McLeod 5).

> From studies of writing intensive classes . . . [w]e have a much better understanding of how WI [writing intensive] instructors' classrooms really function as "interpretive communities." . . . More important, perhaps, we have a much fuller sense of what [course] goals mean to the *members of that classroom's and that discipline's "culture"* (Farris and Smith 83–84) [394–95, all emphases, citations, and clarifications are LeCourt's]

Taken together, these statements demonstrate that WAC is often more focused on a form of enculturation that reinforces existing power relationships, epistemologies, and ideologies (LeCourt 395). The potential for recognition of how disciplines can limit discursive activity and of resistance and change is thus not realized.

This normalizing trend is reflected in the treatment of science in many WAC textbooks. Some WAC theorists, such as Krieger, Saint-Amand, and Emery in *Dialogue and Discovery: Writing and Reading Across Disciplines*, rightfully encourage students to "Be skeptical of absolute statements. Be skeptical of anyone who maintains that science has proved anything. Be skeptical of anyone who dismisses scientific research because some studies have been wrong in their conclusions or misguided in their methods" (492). However, none of the texts that I have encountered encourages students to understand "disciplines as socially negotiated territories and conventions as representations which emanate from a discipline's center of inquiry" (Kirscht et al. 373). Indeed, Norgaard argues that "WAC texts (especially anthologies) still labor under a tyranny of content surprisingly similar to the focus on topical coverage common in the disciplines themselves" (WAC-L).

Although not restricting themselves to science, several WAC theorists have called for the consideration of the cultural contexts of disciplines that WAC involves. For example, LaSalle University's WAC literature states that "Students should be aware of the different purposes and audiences for writing in their major. This awareness can lead them to understand the social, political, and ethical dimensions of their field of study" (Soven 81). This awareness not only has the potential to help students; it can help WAC faculty understand culturally influenced disciplinary practices as well. For example, Kaufer and Young discovered, much to their chagrin, that their efforts to increase the amount of student writing in their laboratory notebooks in a biology class met with resistance. The authors did not understand the role of the laboratory notebook in science, specifically, that it can be used for patent applications and product litigation (80). Too much information in a laboratory notebook can, then, actually result in harmful consequences.

The most explicit and theoretically informed attempt to link WAC to cultural studies has come from LeCourt. In her 1996 article "WAC as Critical Pedagogy: The Third Stage," she draws on cultural studies as well as critical pedagogy to propose a critical model of WAC that problematizes conceptions of disciplines as closed, relatively unified systems and that asks students to be (recognized as) active participants in the construction of disciplines, especially in terms of questioning dominant paradigms (397). LeCourt argues for her model by comparing WAC with cultural studies-influenced first-year composition: "It seems that the field's approaches to WAC are subject to the same description and critique of how academic discourse seeks to inscribe students as subjects that has been forged against composition instruction in English departments. . . . While much of the work in first-year writing presumes that writing instruction should study how cultural discourses position those who seek to be a part of them and offer strategies of resistance to such discursive positions, WAC focuses upon accommodating students to that discourse" (390). As a result of current WAC practices, students are, says LeCourt, enculturated into already normalized disciplinary discourse communities; thus, dominant ideologies are reproduced and differences are suppressed (390). And, although the recent research on writing in the disciplines has highlighted how knowledge production occurs in different fields, the goal when it comes to students, says LeCourt, is still enculturation: "While making the process by which knowledge is made more explicit has critical potential, the goal of such an approach is almost always put in terms of teaching or initiating the student into a certain way of thinking valued by the discipline" (LeCourt 393).

A critical third stage of WAC, according to LeCourt, should "re-constitute" community. Drawing on the work of Myers, Trimbur, and Faigley, LeCourt argues that discourse communities should be understood as places in which, first, conflict takes place continuously and, second, wider social discourses that take place primarily outside of the community exert considerable influence. To avoid forcing such a conceptualization on her students, LeCourt encourages them to study discourse and arrive at their own conclusions. She states, "What seems both a pragmatic and a viable way to facilitate students' critical consciousness about disciplinary procedures would be to have students conduct such investigations themselves" (398). As a result of such an analysis, students might be able to articulate an example of what counts as knowledge in a particular discourse community and another example of what does not—and be able to explain why.

A critical third stage of WAC should also provide space for and encourage the discussion of student writers' "multiple discursive positions as a way of allowing for student difference and alternative literacies" (399). This space would allow students more of a chance to resist dominant practices in the discourse community by recognizing that their own experiences are valuable in shaping the discipline. LeCourt points to the work of Spanier, whose feminist theory-informed students were better able to situate their knowledge from biology courses into a broader cultural context (401).

Compared with a traditional WAC approach, a more critically informed WAC program applied to science, then, would ask students to understand scientific disciplines as culturally interactive and influenced systems rather than discrete entities impervious to societal pressures. In addition, this approach would recognize and explain how science reproduces itself through education and other forms of enculturation and would ask students to consider whom this reproduction benefits (and how it does so) and whom it does not. Students would learn that, in science, argument is an entirely normal activity that must occur for new knowledge to be created. At the same time, students would also realize that certain viewpoints—and the people who hold them—are always occluded, even though it is conceivable that these opinions may be valuable. A more critical WAC would invite students to recognize that their actions—especially their writing—have the capability to profoundly influence science's arguments and scope and shape its relationship with culture.

Rhetoric of Science

As mentioned in the introduction, interest in scientific discourse by rhetoricians has increased significantly in the last two decades. However, the academic community of the rhetoric of science is still quite small relative to the overall enterprise of rhetoric and composition. Theorists who work in this community are the rhetoricians (and a few compositionists) who are most comfortable with scientific discourse. In their work, most rhetoricians of science have focused on discourse analysis—specifically, the analysis of scientific texts—with the intention of discovering rhetorical techniques used by the authors of these texts and demonstrating their inherent rhetorical nature. The work focuses on historical as well as contemporary instantiations of scientific discourse and texts associated with Kuhn's normal, puzzle-solving science, performed by scientists who are not widely known, as well as classics such as Carson's *Silent Spring* and Watson and Crick's "The Structure of Deoxyribose Nucleic Acid" that manifest Kuhn's paradigm-shift science, performed by scientists whose names are virtually household words. Many rhetoricians of science read and discuss scientific discourse with admirable fluency.

No genre of scientific writing has attracted as much attention in terms of discourse analysis as that of the peer-reviewed, IMRAD-based scientific research article, the workhorse of scientific rhetoric. Rhetoricians have broken down the scientific research article into its component parts and carefully studied each of them to ascertain their rhetorical infrastructure. For example, research article introductions have been studied by Swales and Najjar, while results sections have been analyzed by Thompson. Swales and Najjar demonstrate that research article introductions change over time and from discipline to discipline. In her case study of results sections from biochemistry journals, Thompson uses a Toulminian approach to demonstrate different types of rhetorical moves made by scientists. Structured abstracts and their potential application to the texts of scientific research articles have been studied by Hartley, while Burroughs-Boenisch has investigated reading strategies for IMRAD articles. In chapter 6 of *The Rhetoric of Science*, Gross contends that the arrangement of the typical experimental scientific research article relies on Baconian induction, while theoretical scientific papers are deductive (85–96). The intertextuality of research articles has been illuminated by Berkenkotter and Huckin in "You Are What You Cite: Novelty and Intertextuality in a Biologist's Experimental Article." Bernhardt has shown that, despite efforts to the contrary, the writers and readers of scientific articles are often brought to the textual "surface" through a variety of rhetorical moves.

While scientific research articles have undergone the most study, presumably because they are the most common means of communicating science, other genres of scientific discourse have not gone unnoticed by rhetoricians of science. Myers ("Social Construction") has placed scientific grant proposals under the rhetorical microscope, concluding that the biologists whom he studied modified their *ethos* and their relationship to the literature of their field in revisions of their work. Studying the formation of public policy related to science, Waddell has highlighted the use of *pathos* appeals by scientists to nonscientists in the 1976–77 moratorium on recombinant DNA research in Cambridge, Massachusetts. Notes and raw data kept by scientists in the laboratory have been scrutinized: Alan Gross has analyzed Darwin's famous Red Notebook, which Darwin used to record his observations during his round-the-world journey aboard the *Beagle*, while Holmes has demonstrated how writing up laboratory data allowed Lavoisier to come eventually to a correct understanding of human respiration. Book-length scholarly essays in psychology, linguistics, and sociobiology have been labeled a "hybrid genre" and studied by Varghese and Abraham (201).

Other theorists have studied scientific writing more generally, though they still concentrate on textual analysis. Lessl focuses on *ethos* in scientific writing, calling the presence that scientists establish "the priestly voice." Halloran and Bradford demonstrate the use of metaphor in scientific and technical writing; Ceccarelli focuses specifically on the use of mixed metaphors in genomic science ('Neither Confusing"). In an essay published in *American Scientist*, Gopen and Swan argue that interpretation of scientific texts be considered a part of science and suggest several "writing principles" that can help readers and writers of scientific discourse recognize "interpretive clues readers derive from structures" (558). Coletta argues that scientific and technical writing is not neutral in "The Ideologically Biased Use of Language in Scientific and Technical Writing." Linguistic work on specific types of wording has been done by Myers ("Out of the Laboratory"), Vande Kopple ("Noun Phrases" and continued work on spectroscopic articles from *Physical Review*), and others.

It is also in the area of discourse analysis of scientific texts that book-length studies of the rhetoric of science have been published. The writings of Newton, Copernicus, Boyle, Darwin, Einstein, and Watson and Crick are taken up by Gross in *The Rhetoric of Science*. Ceccarelli analyzes the scientifically interdisciplinary works of Dobzhansky, Schrödinger, and Wilson in *Shaping Science with Rhetoric. Understanding Scientific Prose*, edited by Selzer, is a fascinating collection of essays that focus on a single scientific text, "The Spandrels of San Marcos and the Panglossian Paradigm: A Critique of the Panglossian Paradigm," by Stephen Jay Gould and Richard C. Lewontin. The piece was originally published in the *Proceedings of the Royal Society of London* in 1979. Each contributor to Selzer's book reads the text through a different theoretical lens: deconstruction, Marxism, feminism, narratology, psychoanalysis, sociolinguistic analysis, and others. What Selzer demonstrates with this collection is how differently the text can be interpreted from one theoretical context to the next. His work provides a number of valuable analytical tools and strategies to rhetoricians of science.

In his book *A Rhetoric of Science: Inventing Scientific Discourse*, Prelli continues the textual analysis of IMRAD-based scientific discourse. However, unlike Gross, Prelli focuses almost exclusively on the creation and evaluation of scientific knowledge. Drawing on the work of Popper, Polyani, Kuhn, Toulmin, Feyerabend, and other scholars, Prelli states that science depends on interpretation as well as on formal logic and that rhetoric operates in both of these spheres. Scientific discourse is a "special" type of language that has its own rhetorical principles: in specific, Prelli asserts that "scientific discourse aims at producing cooperative attitudes and actions from a particular kind of situated audience" (258). Scientists' rhetorical choices depend in large part on values and propositions that are considered legitimate in science. The process of agreeing on the issues that face science is, according to Prelli, analogous to the *stasis* questions used in legal discourse: in other words, scientists look for or create dissonance in situations that call for scientific communication. Once the issues have been decided upon, an established set of *topoi* is used to develop scientific claims; it includes problem-solution, evaluative, and exemplary topics. Examples of problem-solving *topoi* are replication and precision, examples of evaluative *topoi* are accuracy and consistency, and examples of exemplary *topoi*, which are typically associated with *ethos*, are universality and skepticism. Prelli also discusses the use of analogy in the invention of scientific texts.

As the above paragraphs demonstrate, the rhetoric of science as a field has spent significant effort on the discursive analysis of scientific texts and on the methods that should be used to study them. Some theorists, however, drawing especially on work in the sociology of science such as Latour and Woolgar's *Laboratory Life: The Social Construction of Scientific Facts* and several books and articles by Knorr-Cetina, have considered the environment in which these texts are produced, namely, the laboratory. An example of this type of work is that of Kinsella, who maintains that his analysis "focuses on the laboratory as rhetor, rather than upon the rhetoric of individual scientists" (65). Kinsella's study is a two-year ethnography of the writing of nuclear fusion scientists at the Princeton University Plasma Physics Laboratory. In another longitudinal study, Haas focuses on the rhetorical development of an undergraduate biology major and demonstrates that her increasing rhetorical prowess (with respect to scientific writing) over four years allowed her to become part of the laboratory. Nagelhout performs a similar study with graduate students in biology at Purdue University.

Some authors have gone one step further and examined not just the laboratory context but broader cultural contexts in which scientific texts are produced as well. Bazerman's study of the history and development of the component parts of the scientific research article in *Shaping Written Knowledge: The Genre and Activity of the Experimental Article in Science* approaches genre as a socio-psychological construction and demonstrates how the scientific research article genre changed as science shifted historically from empiricism (observation) to rationalism (experimentation); his concern with prevailing cultural epistemology continues in his analysis of twentieth-century physics. Halloran argues that *ethos* as expressed in scientific discourse (in this case, that of molecular biology) is a critical feature of scientific discourse communities ("Birth of Molecular Biology" 71), and Herndl, Fennell, and Miller consider institutional context in "Understanding Failures in Organizational Discourse: The Accident at Three Mile Island and the Shuttle *Challenger* Disaster." Finally, Moss has done historical work that focuses on the "interplay" between rhetoric and science in seventeenth-century Italy and, in a book-length work, on the cultural context surrounding the Copernican controversy. In this latter work, Moss demonstrates in vivid detail how Galileo violated conventions and expectations of his most important audience, the church.

Rhetorical studies of disasters such as Herndl, Fennell, and Miller's work on the *Challenger* explosion and the near meltdown at Three Mile Island; of pseudoscience such as Dombrowski's study of the Russian botanist Lysenko; of scientific and medical fraud such as Zerbe, Young, and Nagelhout's work on the falsified results of a clinical trial comparing lumpectomy versus mastectomy in breast cancer treatment; and of hoaxes such as Secor and Walsh's analysis of the Sokal *Social Text* episode are popular in the rhetoric of science community, and with good reason. It is incidents such as these that reveal the irrevocable human-ness of science—when science is demonstrated, despite all the protestations to the contrary, to be associated with human error, arrogance and isolation, lying, cheating, greed, overconfidence, and mistaken assumptions. As such, these episodes are irresistible to researchers. Similarly, though no fraud was intended, the 1989 cold fusion episode at the University of Utah glaringly revealed the consequences of violating established rhetorical protocol and as such has enticed rhetoricians such as Thacker and Stratman.

Some work in the rhetoric of science discusses not scientific texts but the nature of the community of the rhetoric of science. This work is prominent for the same reasons that rhetoric and composition as a whole expends considerable energy on its disciplinary identity and status (see discussion earlier in this chapter). An example of such work is Harris's "Rhetoric of Science." The field, says Harris, consists of many different areas of inquiry, from analyses of scientific debates and close readings of important scientific texts to metacommentary on the field itself: why scholars should look for and study rhetoric in science, for example. The result of this wide range of interest is that the rhetoric of science is a somewhat fragmentary field, a situation that exists at least in part because science itself cannot be explained by a single theory or set of assumptions. But, at the most general level, Harris says that "rhetoric of science is the study of suasion in the interpretation of nature" (284), and it is a field that has a definite and unique realm of inquiry that can be distinguished from the sociology, psychology, history, and philosophy of science (although all of these approaches to the study of science, singly or in combination, have something valuable to offer). Harris posits a "fuzzy" (296) taxonomy for empirical investigations in the rhetoric of science that includes the rhetoric of technology, the rhetoric of religion in science, the rhetoric of scientific composition, the rhetoric of scientific language, the rhetoric of public science policy, and prototypical rhetoric of science. In the preface to the second printing of his landmark book *The Rhetoric of Science*,[17] Gross, similarly assessing the state of the field of the rhetoric of science, asserts that "Whether the rhetoric of science eventually attains disciplinary status depends in part on whether the next generation of practitioners can create a unique professional identity by founding and transforming scholarly societies and by building and improving doctoral programs" (ix). Later, Gross adds that disciplinary development "also depends on whether its intellectual achievements reach critical mass," (ix), and he laments that the rhetoric of science is merely "an aggregate of individual interests rather than a united effort of a group of scholars with a set of common goals" (ix). This statement echoes earlier concerns expressed by Harris, who states that the rhetoric of science is a "cottage industry [that] is something of a jumble" and that "has a lot of ends, most of them loose" (283).

Although some rhetoricians of science have branched out to examine laboratories, broader cultural context, and the formation and identity of the academic field of the rhetoric of science, much of the work in the field remains focused on textual analysis. Almost none of the work mentions material effects of scientific discourse[18] or the teaching of writing. However, most of the work has the pedagogical potential to help students recognize that scientific writing is rhetorical and that science is not value free. This connection is seldom made: only Graves, in a brief chapter at the end of her book *Rhetoric in(to) Science*, has suggested rhetoric- and composition-related pedagogical practices that students can apply specifically to the writing of scientific discourse (240–56), while Carpenter has presented similar arguments at the 2004 and 2005 Conference on College Composition and Communication.

For the rhetoric of science to achieve the disciplinarity that Gross and others seek, the questions of its relevance to undergraduate students and how to teach the rhetoric of science to them must be considered. The field's lack of visibility in undergraduate and, indeed, many graduate curricula limits the impact the rhetoric of science can have. Undergraduate and graduate students, as well as faculty in rhetoric and composition and "science studies" disciplines related to the rhetoric of science (e.g., sociology of science), cannot appreciate the contribution the rhetoric of science can make to the understanding of science as a culturally constructed, practiced, and maintained enterprise unless the rhetoric of science becomes known and valued by academicians other than the relatively small number of individuals who now populate the field. The rhetoric of science could go a long way toward establishing this viability by inviting the rhetoric and composition community as a whole to consider science in their research/teaching; this invitation can be much more appealing if carefully theorized and designed pedagogies are in place.

Medical Rhetoric

Medical rhetoric is another area in which scientific discourse receives a degree of critical attention within rhetoric and composition, although a focus on the IMRAD-based discourse of medical research remains a small part of the medical rhetoric domain. Doctor–patient communication, and more broadly, patient education materials produced by all kinds of healthcare information providers via oral, print, and electronic media, comprise a much larger portion of research in medical rhetoric, as does disability studies and writing as therapy. Such work is helpful because it enables its readers to better understand how science-related discourses operate in medical settings and how patients and their friends and families react to and understand medical information, to appreciate much more fully the material conditions of the disabled, and to recognize the role of writing as a healing art. However, this work does not generally allow readers to discover how medical procedures, for example, became accepted practice in the first place. It is removed from the locus of power with respect to epistemological and ontological operation in medicine: medical research journals. It is in this forum that claims are tested and evaluated. Even in the popular press, the influence of prestigious medical journals has been acknowledged: Dr. Marcia Angell, who was editor-in-chief of the *New England Journal of Medicine* during the late 1990s, was named one of the twenty-five most influential people in the United States by *Time* in 1997.

The study of medical research discourse and pharmaceutical writing offers the best opportunity in medical rhetoric to engage scientific discourse. Medical research, whether it is basic science, as in genetics or molecular biology, or epidemiological, such as a study of the 2003 SARS outbreak, or clinical, such as a drug trial, adheres strictly to the scientific method. Similarly, pharmaceutical discourse presents a golden opportunity to observe the production of knowledge and reality as it occurs. Researchers who investigate these texts (see, e.g., Bell, Walch, and Katz's analysis of a clinical protocol from pharmaceutical development) generally attempt to understand the discursive process that occurs from initial investigation of a potentially pharmacologically active compound to the submission of a completed new drug application to the U.S. Food and Drug Administration.[19] This enormously complex effort often takes years to complete, and it involves years of basic and then clinical research on the compound in question. Like the rhetoric of science, though, the study of the discourses of medical and pharmaceutical research does not have any impact beyond the small community of scholars who analyze these discourses.

Technical Communication

Technical communication would seem a natural area of rhetoric and composition for the study of scientific discourse. However, work in technical communication research and courses tends to focus more on technology than it does on science. A common—almost ubiquitous—writing assignment that students are asked to perform in technical communication courses, for example, is a documentation or process project in which students are asked to compose a set of instructions for the use of a CD burner or for the preparation of the perfect oysters Rockefeller. This documentation assignment is often welcomed by students as a refreshing alternative to the typical academic essay. However, this type of writing is associated much more strongly with technology fields such as computer science and engineering than with the physical, biological, and social sciences. Although some of the science majors that I have taught in my technical communication courses have written excellent documentation on laboratory procedures, such as how to operate an ultraviolet spectrometer, documentation will not be the most common or the most important type of writing that they will perform professionally. For science majors, the scientific research paper is far more crucial to their professional development; moreover, given its power, the scientific research paper is the most important genre for nonscience majors who take technical communication courses to study as well. How curious, then, that students in most technical communication courses do not write or read a scientific research paper.[20] The emphasis on technological environments in technical communication courses at the expense of scientific environments is not by itself problematic, but, to the extent that the course is also for science majors and for writing/English majors who seek to learn about scientific discourse, technical communication pedagogy emphasizes discourses associated with technology too intensely.

It could be compellingly argued that science majors learn how to write scientific research papers as part of their major coursework. Indeed, many science majors, even as undergraduates, are required to complete research projects and present their findings as part of a departmental seminar or poster session, and these students gain invaluable rhetorical experience. But this argument ignores the fact that other critically important genres such as the research proposal are a regular feature of technical communication courses, and proposals are also often covered in the major. Why, then, are proposals an integral part of technical communication but not the scientific research article? Additionally, the argument ignores the fact that many science majors acquire only a limited understanding of the scientific research article in their majors. While they do indeed learn about the craft of writing scientific research as part of their major—how to write a good abstract, how to write a good literature review, how to write a good methods section, and the like—they do not gain a more sophisticated appreciation of the rhetorical nature of scientific discourse, its development as a genre and its power and privileged position in Western culture.

Technical communication courses may have started to take a more pronounced turn toward theory at the undergraduate level, as demonstrated by, for example, the publication in 2003 of Peeples's *Professional Writing and Rhetoric*, which introduces undergraduates to some of the most important scholarship in the field. This trend reinforces the position of rhetoric and composition as an academic discipline and introduces it to students, many of whom perceive of writing courses (both first-year composition and professional writing) as simply service courses. A part of technical communication's turn toward theory should be a recognition of the importance of IMRAD scientific discourse, and there are signs that such a recognition is occurring. The winner of the 2003 Conference on College Composition and Communication Outstanding Dissertation Award in Technical Communication, for example, was a rhetoric of science study by Henze that focused on the emergence of ethnology in Britain in the first half of the nineteenth century.

Risk communication studies focus on the discourse that evaluates the level of risk that is associated with activities such as working in chemical plants and mining. Typically, these studies will examine how clearly the risk is explained and how to prevent injury or death to workers who perform the activities associated with the risk. Many risk communication studies *do* examine specific material effects of discourse on individuals, often in the form of warnings given to workers who work in environments that pose risk of injury or death. Ultimately, the discourses upon which communications of risk are in many cases based originally come from scientific research: the toxic effects of benzene, for example. Practitioners of risk communication studies have gained a fluency with the language associated with this research, even though they have not always scrutinized the IMRAD texts on which risk assessments are developed. Studying the texts that convey the risk to workers, then, they are poised just a short step away from the discourse that epistemologizes this risk and makes it real.

Like the rhetoric of science, though, risk communication scholarship does not generally reach students. Risk communication theorists should extend their inquiry to examine the scientific discourse associated with specific risks and think about how to teach both analysis and production of such discourse to their students. What an interesting project it would be, for example, for a risk communication theorist to trace the conception of risk from scientific research to the representation of this information to workers (*a la* Fahnestock in "Accommodating Science: The Rhetorical Life of Scientific Facts")—and to teach their students to do the same.

Conclusion

It is not uncommon for students in rhetoric and composition courses to read the *New York Times*, the *Wall Street Journal*, or the text of Supreme Court decisions. Why not the *New England Journal of Medicine*? The elements required for a meaningful engagement of scientific discourse in rhetoric and composition do exist, albeit in minute quantities. Science is recognized as a cultural institution. Scientific discourse is an object of rhetorical inquiry, as are discourses that are associated with science but that are not themselves IMRAD-based scientific discourse. The material effects of scientific and science-related discourse are being investigated. But the failure of rhetoric and composition to engage scientific discourse publicly and pedagogically has contributed to the continued, uninvestigated dominance of this genre and to its inaccessibility by the vast majority of the population. This dominance occurs at the expense of other equally valuable forms of knowledge production and truth claims that rhetoric and composition deems valid. Only by engaging scientific discourse can rhetoric and composition argue compellingly for the legitimacy of these other (more overtly rhetorical) epistemological and ontological operations. The key is to combine the best elements of the various movements discussed in this chapter: to examine closely the most powerful contemporary discourse and to practice using it in a literate way, to recognize its profound impact on individuals and society, and to understand the cultural context in which it operates. This challenge is undertaken in the next six chapters.

3 Scientific Discourse as a Cultural Studies Issue

I n the "Truth and Power" interview, Foucault almost off-handedly remarks that a study of scientific dissidence since 1945 needs to be undertaken (69). Offhand or not, Foucault pinpoints a large problem—that dissidence in science is rarely noticed. A recognition in the population at large that science is a place where arguments—sometimes heated—always and already occur would provoke a more realistic and balanced perception of science. Fortunately, some work of the type that Foucault seeks is being performed in the areas of cultural studies and science studies; these areas are the focus of this chapter.

Given the enormous extent to which science inscribes individuals and shapes culture, and given rhetoric and composition's unwillingness or inability thus far to make the study of scientific discourse a priority as described in the previous chapter, our task now is to seek a framework in which pedagogical strategies to engage scientific discourse in rhetoric and composition classrooms and research can be initiated and developed. This chapter argues that cultural studies-oriented pedagogies offer a readily available and sufficiently robust framework to study (in both critical and productive terms) scientific discourse in rhetoric and composition courses, while the next chapter looks at this integration as a literacy issue. Because discussions of cultural studies and literacy are already well established in rhetoric and composition, they provide the best potential way for the study of scientific discourse to be undertaken in our discipline.

For scientific discourse to undergo study within a cultural studies rubric, it is necessary to describe science as a cultural institution similar to language, education, law, religion, the media, the arts, and the entertainment industry, all of which are common enough areas of inquiry in rhetoric and composition courses. In these courses, students probe, interrogate, and potentially alter these cultural institutions by reading and writing about them. The purpose of this chapter, then, is to reframe cultural studies, which is already well-established within rhetoric and composition, so that it includes the study of science and acknowledges the field of science studies, of which cultural studies of science are an important part. This chapter also provides a demographic description of the cultural institution of science; included in these data is a comparison of some budgetary figures related to U.S. federal spending on the sciences and on the arts and humanities.

Cultural Studies of Science and Science Studies

In Western culture especially, science's impressive track record of success (e.g., with curing diseases, increasing agricultural yields, inventing new forms of transportation and communication, and the like) has resulted in a largely uncritical acceptance and expansion of its positivistic theoretical base and methodological and evaluative procedures (Atkinson 1). Therefore, science has become a powerful cultural institution—so powerful, in fact, that some theorists contend that it evolved into the religion of the twentieth century and the practitioners of science its clerics (Lewontin 7–16, Herndl 62).[1] Indeed, Herndl states that "the laboratory has become perhaps the most powerful site for the production of culture in our technological society" (77). And Sullivan notes that science "is an incredibly powerful orthodoxy in modern culture" (142). Of the discourses associated with cultural institutions, that of science is the most highly regarded. According to de Certeau, "the sciences are the operational languages whose grammar and syntax form constructed, regulated, and thus writeable, systems; the arts are techniques that await an enlightened knowledge they currently lack" (quoted in Longo 55).

As connections between science and culture have been identified over the past three decades, cultural studies has become recognized as a legitimate way to investigate science. According to Menser and Aronowitz, "the antidiscipline of cultural studies asserts that disciplinary rules are signifiers of a discursively constituted regime of truth complicated and implicated in power. And, against one of the hallowed mantras of modernity, cultural studies refuses to exempt technology, or especially, science from this assertion" (17).

Given the origins of cultural studies in Marxist theory and critiques of elitist and popular culture, cultural studies and science may at first seem incompatible. Science is not, after all, considered a blue-collar enterprise, nor is it typically associated with cultural production. In his cultural studies-based critique of an evolutionary biology paper in Selzer's *Understanding Scientific Prose*, Herndl admits as much but illustrates how the two can be joined constructively:

Because the contemporary movement called cultural studies was initiated by interest in working-class life and by the need to redefine
culture to include not only "high" literary culture but also working-
class or "popular" culture, a cultural studies analysis of science may
seem something of a stretch. Cultural analysis of science is relatively
new, a raid on the philosophy and history of science. Such an analysis
can take a variety of forms, but in the case of a scientific field like
evolutionary biology, the cultural analyst might detail the connection
between the knowledge developed by evolutionary biology and its
material and ideological conditions and consequences. More simply,
since cultural studies assumes that no undertaking, including science,
is autonomous and that any discourse is inherently ideological, cultural critics might ask how evolutionary biology participates in the
whole political and social process of organizing life and legitimizing
knowledge and power. (66)

With this observation, Herndl illustrates that knowledge production and,
more obliquely, consciousness formation are important aspects of the scientific enterprise and thus worthy of cultural studies analysis. In addition,
given that science is such a vast and influential institution, lab technicians
can be perceived quite convincingly as members of the working class, albeit
a well-educated working class. This claim is made, for example, in the case
of the Human Genome Project, in which the genetic code of human beings
is being unraveled. Although not his primary intent, Lewontin illustrates
the ruling-class–working-class dichotomy of science in his description of
the project: "The participation in and the control of a multibillion-dol-
lar, 30- or 50-year research project that will involve the everyday work of
thousands of technicians and lower-level scientists is an extraordinarily
appealing prospect for an ambitious biologist. Great careers will be made.
Nobel Prizes will be given. Honorary degrees will be offered. Important
professorships and huge laboratory facilities will be put at the disposal
of those who control the project" (51). Here, a clear class boundary-like
distinction is implied between "technicians and lower-level scientists"
and "those who control the project."

As cultural studies of science have gained momentum, they have become an increasingly recognized and important area of inquiry for a
loose confederation of scholars primarily in the humanities and social
sciences (but also biological and physical scientists such as Keller, Gould,
and Lewontin) who study science as a social and/or cultural activity.
This confederation, now known in a disciplinary sense as science studies, includes theorists from anthropology, sociology, philosophy, history,

feminist studies, and cultural studies (Hess 2). Ross states that "Today's burgeoning field of science studies is driven by assumptions and principles that are consonant with cultural studies" (173).

In 1997, Hess, an anthropologist in the Science and Technology Studies Department at Rensselaer Polytechnic Institute, described science studies as follows: "Science studies provides a conceptual tool kit for thinking about technical expertise in more sophisticated ways. Science studies tracks the history of disciplines, the dynamics of science as a social institution, and the philosophical basis for scientific knowledge. It teaches, for example, that there are ways for developing sound criteria for evaluating opposing theories and interpretations, but also that there are ways of finding the agendas sometimes hidden behind a rhetoric of objectivity. In the process, science studies makes it easier for laypeople to question the authority of experts and their claims. It teaches how to look for biases, and it holds out a vision of greater public participation in technical policy issues" (1). The rhetorical, cultural, and literacy emphases of this definition are unmistakable, and they represent new areas of inquiry for the study of science. Although at times frustratingly perceived as an "interdisciplinary Babel that can be confusing and intimidating" (Hess 2), science studies as an academic movement is gaining momentum and coherence. Indeed, nothing signals the coming of age of an academic discipline as much as the publication of its first reader, and the *Science Studies Reader* hit the shelves in 1999. Books labeled as introductions to the field also appear, and *An Introduction to Science and Technology Studies* by Sergio Sismondo was published in 2004.[2]

As the field develops, Hess suggests that the field of science studies is moving toward critical and cultural studies of science and away from philosophy and sociology (3); thus, cultural studies may be even more in the spotlight in the near future. Indeed, Hess devotes an entire chapter of his 1997 book to critical and cultural studies of science (referred to here collectively as "cultural studies of science") and their place in science studies. Cultural studies of science, says Hess, draws primarily on "anthropology, critical social theory, cultural studies, feminist studies, critical studies of technology, and the cultural history of science" (3). From Marxism, cultural studies of science has borrowed Lukács' notion of reification and Gramsci's delineation of the processes of hegemony. In addition, this budding area of inquiry is informed by conceptions of power adumbrated by Foucault and Bourdieu; feminist studies of gender, sex, androcentrism, essentialism, and Haraway's oppositional practices; race and science; critical and feminist technology studies involving such concepts as technological determinism, technological regularization, appropriate technology, and birth technologies; scientific revolution studies (e.g., those of Merton); ethnographically based anthropological studies; structuralism and poststructuralism; and a rapidly expanding movement known as public understanding of science and technology (often referred to by the acronym PUST) (Hess 114–44).

Most intriguing for rhetoric and composition, though, is perhaps the theoretical work of Latour. Latour grounds one of the central and most controversial issues of ontology in science studies—the degree to which scientific reality is socially constructed—in a text that is foundational to rhetoric: Plato's *Gorgias*.[3] Socrates not only plays the Sophists' foil in this work; he plays a "true scientist" (Latour, "Pandora's Hope" 11) as well, one who discounts Callicles' pragmatic observations regarding law and physical strength in favor of "the *power of reason*, 'the power of geometric equality,' the force which 'rules over gods and men'" (Latour 11, emphasis in original). Thus, Socrates represents a rejection of any type of social construction of knowledge, while Callicles acknowledges the role of rhetoric. Socrates argues that expert knowledge in the form of demonstration (i.e., science) trumps the body politic without exception (Latour 232). The beginning of the long, slow decline of rhetoric as an academic discipline is often associated with Plato, and it can be argued that the beginning of this decline corresponds exactly, as Latour points out, to the first separation of scientific knowledge from common, socially constructed knowledge. Rhetoric and science, then, can be said to share more than a little history—and a tumultuous history at that.

Like cultural studies, science studies has earned its share of criticism from those interested in preserving the status quo. As Nelkin points out, "Concerned about declining public support for science, some scientists are alarmed by efforts to demythologize their work. They have attacked science studies scholars as science bashers, alarmists, ideologues, or at best, foolish, faddish, muddled or left wing" ("Perspectives" 31). Probably the two most prominent examples of negative reaction from the scientific community are Paul Gross and Norman Levitt's *Higher Superstitions*, published in 1995, and the New York Academy of Sciences' 1995 well-publicized conference entitled "The Flight from Science and Reason" (35). Gross and Levitt lament that "the best-known [science studies/feminist] critics are accepted as legitimate historians and philosophers of science, in circles far wider than their feminist peers. They receive generous academic emoluments, large grants, distinguished lectureships, well-subsidized visiting positions, and tenured professorships at leading universities" (108).

Gross and Levitt target Haraway's work especially heavily; for example, they essentially dismiss her work as relativism that ignores basic physical laws (132–34). Haraway responds to them as follows: "Gross and Levitt . . . outrageously caricature the feminist science studies insistence on the contingency of 'reality' and the constructedness of science. . . . Obviously, neither I nor any other science studies person, feminist or otherwise, whom I have ever met or read, mean the 'laws of physics' get suspended if one enters a 'different culture.' That is a laughable notion of both physical laws and cultural, historical difference. It is the position Gross and Levitt, in deliberate bad faith or else astonishingly deficient reading, ascribe to me and other feminist science studies writers. My argument tries to avoid the silly oppositions of relativism and realism" (64). Gross and Levitt's assault, as well as Sokal's *Social Text* hoax, may also be a sign of unease on the part of some scientists and like-minded nonscientists, that is, an effort to staunch the flow of a healthy skepticism engendered by the promise of a scientifically literate populace.

The association of science studies with relativism is one of the most popular arguments advanced by opponents of the field. The "constructedness of science," however, is not equivalent to relativism, despite Gross and Levitt's claims to the contrary. Instead, it is a recognition that physical laws—while applicable across all cultures—are rooted in historical and cultural milieus. As Hess states, "scientific representations are both referential—maps or models of the world—and sociocultural—encodings of values, general cultural categories, interests, and so forth" (17). To illustrate this principle in a general sense, I ask my students if any of them knows, according to legend, what happened on that fateful day when Issac Newton sat down under the apple tree. Usually, one of my students will know the answer: an apple fell on Newton's oh-so-inviting head and gravity was "discovered." How then, I next ask my students, was this type of occurrence explained before Newton's epiphany? Certainly attempts were made to explain the causes of events such as these, weren't they? Ensuing discussion usually centers on religion or chance as causative agents, and the students often come up with great examples of other actions or phenomena that are explained in culturally contextualized ways.

Despite the resistance from those whom science studies makes nervous, cultural studies of science as a part of science studies is now responding to the challenge of illuminating, critiquing, and occasionally resisting the science hegemony. As Ross states, "This is the point at which the broad tradition of cultural studies meets up with developments in science studies—when a continuum of power is established between the interests of the state and the expressive, daily realm of rituals. . . . Where scientific reason is the dominant cognitive authority, its cultural and economic role in maintaining a social system of inequalities must be open to analysis and reform in ways that go far beyond internalist adjustments and purifications" (173–74). This work is important, then, because of the need to problematize the often clearly demarcated boundaries between science and society. Doing so can reveal alternative, marginalized ways of knowing as well as the extent to which subjects are inscribed by scientific practices and products.

Like Berlin's cultural studies, science studies provides for agency on behalf of the student and, in the case of science, all nonscientists. Hess describes several ways in which nonscientists and social science and humanities scholars have intervened in science on its most fundamental levels: policy-making and knowledge-making. "In several European countries," he points out, "citizen review panels provide a means of direct participatory policy making in which laypersons examine science and technology policy in the making. Although the result of these panels usually are nonbinding, citizen review panels do provide a potential mechanism for direct, participatory democracy in the science policy process and they do sometimes have an impact on national agendas" (151). In addition to these formal review panels, grassroots efforts involving the environment, cancer treatment, and AIDS treatment provide alternatives to those supplied by mainstream science (Hess 151). In terms of the involvement of nonscientist academics, Hess discusses several models in which scientists and engineers are partnered with social science or humanities scholars who perform some type of science studies research. Together, the researchers investigate a phenomenon, reform curriculum, and look for ways to improve the well-being of the community. The partnership works best, of course, when one of the partners does not possess a great deal more power or prestige than the other (Hess 151–52).

Knowledge Production in Science

Knowledge production in science is now undergoing analysis as a result of a cultural studies focus. This analysis is often performed with attention to the roles and practices of science within disciplinary, educational, corporate, and governmental institutions; these institutions form the cultural context in which scientific knowledge is produced (Winsor 127–28). As science has, since the beginning of the twentieth century, consumed greater and greater portions of economic, technical, and natural resources, the links between science and culture have become all the more apparent, and the notion of science as an impartial, disinterested cultural institution has receded (Lenoir 7). Cultural studies helps to frame knowledge production in science as an activity that cannot help but invoke culture in the interpretation and use of this knowledge.

The study of knowledge production in science can take several forms. Much of the work in this area has been done in sociology (e.g., Latour's *Science in Action*) (Winsor 128). It can range from questions of enculturation and range—how does a budding scientist learn what counts as common sense or "tacit knowledge" in his or her discipline and what counts as beyond the scope of that discipline—to how different research techniques emerge and take hold and differ along race, class, and gender lines (Traweek 51). Knowledge in science is thus shaped by interpretation, argument, and negotiation: even the work of distinguished scientists is sometimes met with hostility from other scientists whose worldviews are violated by new work (Winsor 128, 138). What counts as knowledge in science is continually contested.

One reason that the production of knowledge in science is becoming an increasingly important academic and economic issue is the tendency to view scientific knowledge as intellectual property. Because of the economic implications, the ownership of (and profit from) scientific knowledge is extremely relevant to cultural studies: it brings into focus the crumbling idealizations of disinterest and autonomy. Cultural studies can demonstrate that it is more difficult to view knowledge as objective when it is so obviously tied to economic gain. This recognition is relatively recent: according to Etzkowitz and Webster, "The Mertonian norms of science depicted scientists as unwilling to involve themselves directly in transforming research results into objects of monetary value. . . . Academic scientists who marketed their research were defined as deviant" (480). Not anymore. Since the 1980s, the authors continue, many scientists have openly commercialized their work, and, instead of being viewed as deviant, they are looked upon by their peers and by scientists in training as role models (Etzkowitz and Webster 480). The practice of marketing scientific knowledge is part of a global shift from an industrial, natural resources and land-based economy to an informational economy (Etzkowitz and Webster 481). Indeed, renowned scientists in an industrial economy received no such reward: "What is . . . perhaps most noteworthy about today's science is that many claims to 'credit' that previously would have been recognized only eponomously—as in 'Boyle's law' or 'Einstein's theory of relativity'—are recognized as belonging to a certain scientist, or team of scientists, because of the patent they hold on it—such as the

Cohen-Boyer patent on DNA cloning techniques. Gaining 'credibility' in science is increasingly tied to the ability to generate exploitable knowledge, making scientists more akin to 'economic' entrepreneurs" (Etzkowitz and Webster 487). It is, then, the scientist's ability to "sell" knowledge as much as to produce it that is important in the global information economy of the new century.

Science studies literature is replete with studies of scientists' vested interests in the knowledge they create. Not surprisingly, since information has become such a valuable commodity, headline-grabbing disputes over the ownership of knowledge have occurred. One of the most bitter and long-lasting disputes in recent memory was the fight between French and American scientists over the discovery of the AIDS virus. The argument was so contentious that it eventually had to be settled at the highest levels of government—by Presidents Mitterand and Reagan (Etzkowitz and Webster 488). The trend toward commercialization is especially evident in molecular biology and genetics, where arguments over how to assign "ownership" of gene sequences remain unresolved. The Human Genome Project has been criticized in this regard, and some theorists lament that the commodification of knowledge relating to the project is impeding its progress. According to Kevles and Hood in *The Code of Codes*, "expectation of profits discourages open discussion of technical detail during the critical R&D [research and development] phase before patent filing. It has been said that commercial considerations have interfered with the free exchange of results and ideas about genome research" (312). The European Community does not allow "on an exclusive basis" genome researchers or corporate entities to profit from work on the project, and Kevles and Hood argue that the knowledge gained from the project in the United States should likewise be considered within the public domain: "Genomic information—of human beings or any other organism—is what is in principle common property. It should be maintained as such as a matter of practical equity, since the mapping and sequencing of genomes will be—is already—the product of the ingenuity of a multinational community of scientists and of investments by many countries. Hard and imaginative thought needs to be given to means of preserving what is rightly common property while providing incentives for private development of research results for human benefit" (315). Despite Kevles and Hood's calls for the contrary, the prospect that genome-related knowledge will remain common property is remote. The ties among state agencies, corporate interests, and individual scientists in the production of knowledge are entrenched. Similarly, private companies, especially those in the pharmaceutical industry, now sponsor scientific research on their own products. Not surprisingly, many of these studies have found that the drug being studied works as advertised. This conflict of interest would have been considered unethical even as recently as twenty years ago and has been heavily criticized by some in the medical community, including the editor-in-chief of the *New England Journal of Medicine.*

The increased likelihood for scientists to market their work also represents an important issue for cultural studies theorists because much of the commercialization is taking place at the institutions in which these theorists work. Etzkowitz and Webster list three ways in which scientists, corporate interests, and universities capitalize knowledge:

- The licensing to corporations of research results on exclusive or nonexclusive terms by administrators
- The establishment of university offices to market intellectual property to industry
- The exchange of ideas for equity in a firm on the part of professors (497–98)

Most recently, close ties between the academy and industry have grown out of the establishment of engineering as an area of study at universities (Etzkowitz and Webster 498). The applied focus of engineering industry was replicated to some degree in academia by the maintaining of relationships between institutions such as MIT and corporations such as General Motors.

Although the recent emphasis on commodifying scientific knowledge may simply be a more explicit manifestation of an already existing practice (Etzkowitz and Webster 501), the degree to which institutions of higher education are increasingly subject to the goals of the state and industry is troubling to some. In a discussion of the development of nuclear magnetic resonance (NMR) technology, Lenoir states that the drive for profit was at times "equally distributed on both sides of the university boundaries" (291), that is, maintained by both corporate and university scientists. Lenoir explains that the effect of the drive can be monumental: the scientists who built the NMR, as a result of localized knowledge, also developed an entire methodology for interpreting spectra (290–91). In short, they created a worldwide industry.[4]

The Cultural Institution of Science: Demographics

So what does the cultural institution of science that is being examined by science studies look like? For one thing, it is enormously large and wealthy; indeed, science has come a long way from its initial struggle to survive in the latter half of the 1600s. In the United States, it is predominantly white and male, although this trend is changing rapidly in some areas, especially the biological sciences and medicine. And it is amazingly prolific and self-conscious. Using a survey and polling research apparatus that any national politician would envy, science carefully attends to its status as a powerful cultural institution, constantly watching numbers of college and university programs and degrees awarded, budgets, publications, and public perception, including public attitudes toward scientific research, federal funding of scientific research, and specific science-related issues such as genetic engineering. These data are readily available from the National Science Foundation and the American Association for the Advancement of Science.

While government support for science began with Charles II's charter of the Royal Society, state interest in science really took off when Louis Pasteur delighted nineteenth-century French milk producers by developing a cure for the anthrax poisoning that was decimating dairy herds (Aronowitz 19). For science, it's been a runaway success story since. The amount of money that the United States federal government currently spends on scientific (including medical) research is simply staggering. Figures from the National Science Foundation estimate that $103.1 billion were spent on scientific research and development in fiscal year 2004; this estimate includes funding for the research and development "plant" ("Info Brief").[5] Six federal agencies accounted for almost all (i.e., 96%) of the spending as follows:

- Department of Defense, $45.2 billion: 44%
- Department of Health & Human Services, $28.3 billion: 27%
- National Aeronautics and Space Administration, $10.7 billion: 10%
- Department of Energy, $8.5 billion: 8%
- National Science Foundation, $3.7 billion: 4%
- Department of Agriculture, $2.1 billion: 2%
  (National Science Foundation "Info Brief")

The Department of Defense share of the research and development funding fell to its 2004 level of 44% from 57% in 1990; the Department of Health and Human Services share has increased from 13% to 27% over the same period. Since 2000, however, the Department of Defense's budget has grown by an estimated 10.8% annually (National Science Foundation "Info Brief").

In contrast to the amount of money spent on science, the National Endowment for the Humanities (NEH) requested $152 million for fiscal year 2004 (*neh.gov*), while the National Endowment for the Arts requested $117.5 million for the same period (*nea.gov*). Put into perspective, the U.S. government spends nearly 383 times more money annually on science and technology research and development than it does on the humanities and the arts. In other words, the U.S. government devotes more money to science and technology in twenty-three hours than it devotes to the humanities and the arts in an entire year. "Public funding for science," says Sullivan, "dwarfs funding for the arts and humanities, largely because of the myth of scientific objectivity, because of highly publicized successes in medicine, and because of promised technological applications" (142). This trend shows no signs of abating.

In addition to recognizing how much money and resources are devoted to science by the state, studying *who* does science illustrates the power of the scientific institution. Science and engineering employ a total of approximately eleven million people in the United States (National Science Foundation Indicators 3–4). The number of jobs in science in technology, outside academia, increased 159% between 1980 and 2000. The fastest growing area is mathematics and computer science (623%), while physical science is the slowest growing (81%) (National Science Foundation Indicators 3–6). Especially in the physical and biological sciences, most scientists and engineers are white men, although women earned 36.5% of the doctorates in science and engineering in 2001, up from 28.7% in 1992 (National Science Foundation). Women are gaining the most ground in the biological sciences, where they earned 44.8% of the doctorates awarded in 2001, and the least in engineering (16.8%), physics (13.0%), and computer science (18.8%). In the social sciences, women earned 66.9% of the 2001 doctorates in psychology and 58.4% of the doctorates in sociology. In terms of comparison, women earned 49.9% of the doctorates in the humanities (National Science Foundation). Despite the progress women are making in numbers, a pay gap remains between the genders (Kennedy 265).

United States citizens and permanent residents, both women and men, earned a total of 16,382 doctorates in science and engineering in 2001, compared with 4,361 in the humanities. Of the science and engineering doctorates, 81% went to whites, 10% went to Asians, and a little less than 9% went to other minorities (African American, Latino, American Indian/Alaskan native), up from about 6% in 1992 (National Science Foundation). Non-Asian minorities represent 24% of the U.S.

population (American Association for the Advancement of Science). In addition, while funding for construction or renovation of academic scientific and engineering research facilities was up 8% nationally in 1992–93 compared with 1986–87, it declined nearly 90% during the same period at historically African American institutions (Davis). These colleges and universities awarded 27% of the bachelor's degrees in science and engineering earned by African Americans in 1990 (Davis); unfortunately, these graduates will often have a difficult time competing for jobs and graduate positions with alumni of institutions with more up-to-date facilities. The largest confederation of science and engineering societies is the American Association for the Advancement of Science, with 271 affiliated societies and academies comprising ten million members. The AAAS publishes the prestigious research journal *Science*.

In terms of the production of discourse, science is a force to be reckoned with. Thomson ISI (formerly the Institute for Scientific Information), a Philadelphia-based firm that tracks journal and author citations, lists a total of 7,808 journals in its Expanded Science and Social Science citation indexes, while the Arts and Humanities citation index follows only 1,121 journals, or about 1/7 of the total science and social science output. Both English-language journals and journals in other languages are monitored, although English is increasingly the *lingua franca* of science.[6] Thomson ISI collects an enormous amount of statistical information on academic publications, but one of its most well-known calculations derives from counting the number of times authors and journals are cited per year and calculating an "impact factor" for journals in an effort to determine how important a journal is in its field.

Conclusion

Despite the increasingly brazen displays of science's prioritization of financial reward rather than an idealistic and altruistic neutrality, scientific discourse retains its reputation for impartiality, truth, and universality. In a way, the increased transparency that is perhaps engendered by the trend of overt entrepreneurship in science is fitting because the very human motives associated with hoped-for financial gain are more clearly exposed; the agenda is less hidden than it is in a context of modernist science in which science is said to be immune from such temptations. However, this awareness has, in general, not been manifested rhetorically in the production or analysis of scientific discourse. Additionally, the impact of scientific discourse on individual agency and potential manifestations of individual empowerment with respect to science have not been articulated.

Rhetoric and composition, by making use of cultural studies of science and demographic data such as that described in this chapter, can make a difference in this respect. The work in cultural studies of science, like that in the rhetoric of science, is fascinating and valuable but ultimately insufficient because of its limited visibility and impact. It takes rhetoric and composition to put scientific discourse on the national agenda, to provide the visibility and access to undergraduates that science studies lacks. This challenge will not be without its detractors and difficulties but it is a challenge that must be undertaken nonetheless. By approaching science with the use of well-established as well as new cultural studies-informed methodologies, and by ensuring that rhetoric and composition become an integral part of the flourishing science studies movement, rhetoric and composition can help to assure that a much more scientifically aware populace participates in the all-important decisions about where and how to allocate increasingly strained resources. Decisions reached with the assistance of a citizenry that truly understands science's role in its culture will be all the wiser.

4 Scientific Discourse as a Literacy Issue

W e live in a scientific culture; to be scientifically illiterate is simply to be illiterate," says Harding (*Whose Science?* 55). The association of science and literacy is well recognized. Contextualizing the study of scientific discourse in terms of literacy focuses attention on its *public-ness* or lack thereof; it implies that writing or reading scientific discourse should become a familiar (but not uncritical) activity for the breadth and depth of society. As a public or civic discourse, then, scientific discourse falls within the province of rhetoric and composition; indeed, the discipline is obligated to highlight scientific discourse because of its dominance.

Halloran approaches scientific discourse as a literacy issue in the conclusion of his analysis of Watson and Crick's famous 1953 *Nature* paper positing the double helix structure of DNA. He calls for "emic"[1] criticism of scientific discourse, and he acknowledges the public and civic importance of the task: "That it should be done by scholars in rhetoric is suggested by the increased importance of scientific matters in the arena of public affairs, the traditional realm of rhetoric. Science is itself an increasingly public enterprise, both in the sense that the public supports it financially and in the sense that it offers monumental threats and promises to our well-being. Science also serves as a warrant for many of the arguments about traditionally non-specialized, civic questions—war and peace, ways and means for promoting the public welfare. *To understand public discourse . . . we must have some understanding of scientific discourse*" (81, emphasis added). Halloran's emphasis on the public character of scientific discourse suggests that, because science is a civic matter based on discourse, science and literacy are inseparable. In a similar manner, Zappen states that a contemporary rhetoric of science "must recognize the inseparability of the scientific community from public life and must educate each new member of that community" ("Historical Perspectives" 25).

A term related to scientific literacy that is undergoing much scrutiny is *scientific citizen*. It is not enough that we and our students understand scientific discourse. We must also participate as active, informed citizens in discussions about science that permeate our civic lives. Decisions at all levels and in all branches of government are made on the basis of scientific information. Citizens must be able to recognize the inevitably dubious nature of some of that information and the unmistakably rhetorical nature of all of it. They must be able to account for the conflicting testimony of dueling scientific experts in courts of law and before zoning boards. In the United Kingdom, exceedingly public, passionate debates chock full of competing scientific data about genetically modified foods have taken place, complete with *pathos*-laden labels like "Frankenstein food" (Irwin 1); in Ukraine, the combination of humanism, economic forces, and government action in response to the Chernobyl disaster comprise a "biological citizenship" (Petryna 5) with all the ramifications that accompany such a formation. In both of these locations, the debates incorporate highly technical scientific concepts and data, yet they also involve virtually unprecedented lay public participation. Thus, the term *scientific citizen* also implies that scientific literacy occurs not merely within an individual but instead in a community: "collective praxis," as Roth and Lee put it (33).

The scientific citizen is something of an ideal at this point, though. According to survey research from the National Science Foundation, "Americans are highly supportive of science and technology, but lack knowledge of them" ("Indicators" 7–4). Science and technology rank seventh—after crime, health, sports, community, religion, and local government and before national news, entertainment, international affairs, business and finance, consumer news, and culture and the arts—in a survey that asked Americans what type of news they followed most closely (7–5, 7–6). Also, a Pew study found that only 2 percent of news stories are about scientific research and discoveries (7–7), and science education is not held in high regard by the public (7–24). Finally, science expresses concern about its depiction in popular culture. According to a National Science Foundation report, "The charming and charismatic scientist is not an image that populates popular culture. For example, the entertainment industry often portrays certain professions such as medicine, law, and journalism as exciting and glamorous, whereas scientists and engineers are almost always portrayed as unattractive, reclusive, socially inept white men or foreigners working in dull, unglamorous careers" (7–25). The report also found that less than 2 percent of prime-time television characters were scientists (7–26) and that children who take a "Draw a Scientist Test" often render visualizations of scientists that include a lab coat, eyeglasses, facial hair, light bulbs (for sudden Eureka-like inspiration), and laboratory equipment. Sometimes the scientists look like Einstein or Frankenstein (7–27). Some of these features, the report implies, reflect negative stereotypes of scientists that even children seem to have internalized. (This perception may be changing because of television programs such as *CSI*; see chapter 2.)

Perhaps most surprisingly, the authors of the 2002 National Science Foundation *Science and Engineering Indicators* devoted an entire section of their report to the concern that the public is increasingly trusting in pseudoscience such as astrology, UFOs and alien abduction, extrasensory perception, channeling the dead, faith healing, and psychic hotlines. The report states that "belief in pseudoscience is relatively widespread" and that it is on the rise. The entertainment industry is depicted as the main culprit responsible for the popularity of pseudoscience, but the mainstream media also receives criticism because of regular examples of the "miscommunication of science" (National Science Foundation, "Indicators").

One of the primary reasons that the general public does not know about or follow science or increasingly looks to pseudoscience is because of the distance that exists between science and mainstream culture. Science was not always so estranged from the general public. In the beginning decades of modern science, in the late seventeenth century, scientific research often took place in private residences; often, a researcher began work on an experiment in private, and when he or she reached a point where the experiment was ready for public demonstration, moved to a public room in the house, where the experiment was performed in front of a group of invited guests enjoying the host's wine and cheese. Sometimes these private and public spaces were in the same building, as in the case of Robert Hooke (Shapin 496), a founding member of the Royal Society. In France, local farmers as well as visiting dignitaries watched Pasteur's experimental work on anthrax immunization for livestock; this work received extensive coverage from the local, national (i.e., Paris' *Le Temps*), and London newspapers because of Pasteur's celebrity status and because the work was performed as a result of a challenge to Pasteur by a rival scientist (Bucchi 6–7). Also in the nineteenth century, scientific debates that had before occurred via private letter now often took place in the pages of general public-targeted literary magazines. For example, in 1862, Lord Kelvin published his research on the age of the earth in *Macmillan's Magazine*; the article was an attack on geologists who thought the earth was much older than Kelvin did (Gregory and Miller, *Science in Public* 24). (The geologists turned out to be right.) Similarly, readers of *The Athenaeum* could follow debates about the Devonian geological era; the articles were technically dense and accompanied by "detailed stratigraphical sections" (Gregory and Miller, *Science in Public* 26). At that time, science was still under the auspices of natural philosophy and natural theology (i.e., science reveals the handiwork of God); as such, it occupied the same "cultural environment" as the arts and classics, making it "suitable for inclusion in literary publications" (Gregory and Miller, *Science in Public* 23).

Now, of course, scientific research is neither conducted in private residences nor demonstrated for public consumption. Says Shapin, "The disjunction between places of residence and places where scientific knowledge is made is now almost absolute. The separation between the laboratory and the house means that a new privacy [since the late seventeenth century] surrounds the making of knowledge whose status as open and public is often insisted upon. . . . Public assent to scientific claims is no longer based upon public familiarity with the phenomena or upon public acquaintance with those who make the claims" (498). The public does not witness scientific experiments, nor do they meet the scientists who conduct them. The general public does not, then, possess the means to assess claims made on the basis of scientific research because the spaces (both physical and textual) where such research is carried out are not public. Many nonmilitary and nonproprietary laboratories are not, of course, surrounded by a team of security guards, nor are they built in isolated or secret locations far from public view. Nonetheless, these spaces are not well known to nonscientists.

All of these indicators about the general public's distant relationship with science point to scientific discourse as a literacy issue; indeed, as pointed out above, scientific literacy has been a leading concern of the National Science Foundation for years. However, literacy in science circles has been under-theorized (see, e.g., Lee and Roth 405); it would benefit from the more thorough understanding of literacy developed in the humanities and social sciences. Another method to integrate scientific discourse and rhetoric and composition effectively, then, is to frame scientific discourse as a literacy issue similar to the discursive and technological literacies that are already well established areas of inquiry in the discipline.

Literacy and Scientific Literacy

This chapter focuses on scientific literacy, a highly contested term whose meanings have ranged "from mastery of basic knowledge to national technological superiority, from science viewed as a cultural imperative to that of a social responsibility, from science content to science attitude" (Shamos 85). Unfortunately, the term is regularly tossed around without sufficient rigor: for example, Johnson, a physicist, makes the statement that "Scientific literacy continues to be the emphasis of science instruction" (94) without defining scientific literacy. Definitions can also be vague, as with Shamos's statement that "at the very least scientific literacy means having some grasp of science, the main difference being in the level of scientific knowledge that should be requisite for said label" (86). Popular understandings of scientific literacy, though, are often framed in terms of accumulated specialized knowledge and demonstrated expertise in designing and carrying out experiments. For instance, Bruce reports a common understanding of scientific literacy as "mastery of the skills and knowledge associated with scientific practice" (293).

Typically, the first reply one hears when the term "scientific literacy" is spoken or written is how low it is. This lament is not without cause. In the United States, literacy in science is uncommon according to many authorities. For instance, Shamos, a leading physicist and science educator, estimates in a 1995 study that only 4–5 percent of adult Americans are "true scientific literates" (89), "nearly all being professional scientists or engineers" (90).[2] Shamos emphasizes that he does not expect a true scientific literate to have an enormous number of scientific facts committed to memory or to have the ability to solve quantitative problems (90). "Nevertheless," he states, "even this modest criterion puts scientific literacy beyond the reach of most educated individuals" (90).

Instead of proposing new conceptions of scientific literacy, though, some scientists see broad scientific literacy as largely unattainable. Shamos, despite his attention to scientific literacy, contends that all scientific literacy movements in the United States over the past several decades have failed and that current efforts to resolve the issue are futile (90, 158). Gross and Levitt, in *Higher Superstition: The Academic Left and its Quarrels with Science*, are similarly pessimistic, saying "we cannot hold high hopes. The historic record of American education in making the general public conversant with basic science has always been poor, except for a brief flurry of serious effort in the post-Sputnik era" (248).

Shamos does actually spell out a solution to the problem of scientific illiteracy, but it does not involve attempting to bring scientific literacy to the masses. Instead, he seeks to emphasize technology education rather than science education (201) and to encourage nonscientists to seek the advice of experts (i.e., scientists) when discussing scientific issues (200).

According to Shamos, "The only sensible solution to the problem lies in the judicious use of scientific experts, not as surrogates for the public in determining the proper course of action on science/technology-based social issues, but as advisors on the purely technical aspects of such issues, from which the public might hopefully reach better-informed judgments" (206–7). Shamos recognizes that experts are often "called into adversarial, even confrontational, proceedings" (207); thus, he also advocates the establishment of a "National Science Watch Committee" (consisting of scientists) to monitor science and to render opinions on the rightful use and significance of technology (212). Recognizing that conflicts of interest could easily arise, he calls for committee members to restrict themselves to "technical issues" and to "have no *recognized* political or social agendas" (213, emphasis added).

These suggestions are troubling for several reasons. First, while choosing one's experts wisely can be a valuable skill, it is no substitute for possessing an informed viewpoint of one's own. Second, focusing only on "technical issues" relieves scientists of any ethical obligations and thus fails to alter the status quo; in other words, currently, some scientists claim that they pursue knowledge for its own sake and that they do not bear any responsibility for how that knowledge is used. (To be fair, Shamos's mention of the "rightful use . . . of technology" seems to belie this focus only on "technical issues.") And third, even more worrisome than "*recognized*" political or social agendas are *unrecognized* ones.

Different forms of scientific literacy can be considered on a continuum of increasing theoretical robustness. At the least theoretically informed end of the continuum is "autonomous literacy" (after Goody). "Critical literacy" is in the middle. "Ideological literacy" (after Street) is at the most theoretically informed end. The primary variable on which the continuum is based is the extent to which the context of production, especially in terms of power relations and impact on identity, enters into the understanding of literacy. As demonstrated below, critical literacy assumes and encompasses autonomous literacy, and ideological literacy assumes and encompasses both critical and autonomous literacy. Ideological literacy is best suited for the kind of analysis and production of scientific discourse within rhetoric and composition.

Autonomous Literacy

At the autonomous end of the continuum, literacy is generally understood as competency in reading and writing. Such literacy is also called functional or basic literacy. "It is," state Morris and Tchudi, "the ability to encode and decode, to pick up a book and not only to call the words but also to say what they mean" (12). The definition used by the National Association of Educational Progress also fits here: "the ability to perform reading and writing tasks needed to function adequately in everyday life (filling out a driver's license application, reading a train schedule, writing a check, applying for a job, or reading an article in a newspaper)" (quoted in Winterowd 5). Keller-Cohen declares that autonomous literacy "is a feature of an individual and constitutes both a transferable bank of skills and/or body of knowledge that can be applied or utilized across situations" (8). This type of literacy is called "autonomous" because it depends on an individual's ability to grasp the "conventionalized" (or fixed) meanings of texts (Keller-Cohen 9). These meanings are presented as neutral and thus free of any political or other cultural bias.

The autonomous model is, of course, quite limited. Persons may be able to "function adequately" in terms of everyday activities, but there is no deeper understanding of ambiguity or of power relations. As Macedo, using the term "instrumental" instead of "autonomous," states, "The instrumental literacy for the poor, in the form of a competency-based skills-banking approach, and the highest form of instrumental literacy for the rich, acquired through the university in the form of professional specialization, share one common feature: They both prevent the development of critical thinking that enables one to 'read the world' critically and to understand the reasons and linkages behind the facts" (16). In this sense, literacy is understood as a means to perpetuate existing cultural norms and divisions. An individual is literate if she or he can contribute to that perpetuation. If we accept literacy as a process of enculturation or "normalization" (Downing, Harkin, and Sosnoski 11) that occurs in education, then research into the ways in which pedagogical practices can be altered to recognize and resist such tendencies becomes of paramount importance.

Definitions of scientific literacy that restrict themselves to, for example, understanding and practicing the experimental method reflect an autonomous view of literacy. Laboratory methods used in science are transmitted, context free. A person may, for instance, understand how to isolate an enzyme using various separation procedures but have no sense of the big picture: where the enzyme comes from, why it's being studied, who is interested in it, what its potential is. Such a perception of scientific literacy is posited by Morris and Tchudi, who state that it is "skill in experimentation, without any reference to writing" (x). This definition highlights motor skills and the ability to use scientific instruments rather than textual literacy of any kind.

Some scientists have moved away from a simple demonstration of laboratory-related or observation-related performative skills as a basis for scientific literacy; however, some of these scientists call instead only for familiarity with important scientific achievement in its place. Prominent examples of this Hirsch-like line of thinking are Brennan's *Dictionary of Scientific Literacy* and Hazen and Trefil's *Science Matters: Achieving Scientific Literacy*. The latter essentially explains several dozen scientific terms and concepts that the authors believe are important for the general public to understand. Hazen and Trefil define scientific literacy as "the knowledge you need to understand public issues" (xii). Unfortunately, this knowledge is mostly confined to a surface-level recognition of scientific vocabulary and principles that are explained on the basis that "the universe is regular and predictable" (1). Hazen and Trefil do, though, state that understanding science at a "deep level" is not a requirement of scientific literacy (1), an idea that deserves further exploration and elaboration.

By and large, the contemporary curricular structure of science education leaves little room for studying science as more than learning its experimental and observational methods. Many science educators whom I know, though, are sympathetic to and supportive of the desire for a broader sense of science literacy. However, given the amount of complex material that must be covered in a finite time span—pressure that is exacerbated in disciplines that rely on national accreditation or graduate/medical school expectations to maintain their reputation and even their existence—it is extremely difficult to incorporate a broader literacy. Labianca and Reeves, for example, report in the influential *Journal of Chemical Education* that writing across the curriculum (a pedagogical strategy that many would argue could help students develop a more sophisticated literacy) "has serious implications, for at its fullest implication, it can interfere with the main business of teaching science" (400), which most likely means learning scientific facts and laboratory procedures.

In fact, to solve the so-called science literacy crisis, which, as with discourse-based literacy crises, has occurred off and on over the past several decades, some scientists and science educators expect students to change (e.g., by taking more science courses) rather than science. However, efforts to draw students to science, they say, are complicated by science critics, mostly in the social sciences and humanities. Gross and Levitt, for example, complain that "practical measures for making discussion of scientific issues effectively more democratic by what should be the straight-forward process of extending scientific literacy are continually subverted by the intrusion of 'identity politics' into the pedagogy of science" (251).

This position reinforces autonomous scientific literacy and exacerbates a lack of appreciation for the complex relationships between scientific practices and the culture of which they are a part.

Critical Literacy

In the middle of the continuum is critical literacy. Generally, critical literacy acknowledges that knowledge-making and text-level interpretation play an important role in reading and writing—that literacy involves more than reading and writing with words that have fixed meanings. According to Calfee, critical literacy "incorporates a broader sense of understanding and insight, and the ability to communicate with others about texts whether these are written or spoken. It is the difference between understanding how to operate the lever in a voting booth versus comprehending the issues needed to decide for whom to vote and why" (27). Included here are definitions of literacy such as "a set of transferable skills that *restructure consciousness and enable analytic thought*" (Minter, Gere, and Keller-Cohen 671, emphasis added). Flower et al. define a critically literate individual as a person who "questions sources, looks for assumptions, and reads for intentions, not just facts" (5). Similarly, Rose views critical literacy as an activity that entails "framing an argument or taking someone else's argument apart, systematically inspecting a document, an issue, or an event, synthesizing different points of view, applying a theory to disparate phenomena, and so on" (188). Knowledge beyond that needed to read and write comes into play in this middle region: according to Brandt, "Knowledge is at the heart of literacy's value and power, its fundamental goal and most tangible product" (189). Thus, critical literacy can be defined as "the ability to move beyond literal meanings, to interpret texts, and to use writing not only to record facts but also to analyze, interpret, and explain" (Morris and Tchudi 12). Barton maintains that literacy is not defined "as specific abilities but as broad-based bodies of knowledge, including bodies of knowledge as arcane as academic disciplines . . . as well as sets of everyday practices as ordinary as reading labels on aspirin bottles" (408).

Also staking out some territory in the middle of this continuum is work by Geisler, who has studied the nature of expert academic literacy versus that of novice (i.e., student) literacy within a framework of expertise. Although she selects philosophical ethics as the site of her comparison, much of the early part of her book focuses on literacy in academia in more general terms. Among the attributes of literacy that look beyond knowledge of reading and writing, Geisler discusses the use of metadiscourse or hedging that literates use with their peers (14), the ability of literates to use different "repertoires" to discuss, for example, work with which they agree and work with which they disagree (17), and the potential for literates to not necessarily adhere to reader roles desired by writers (20–24). Additionally, Geisler asserts that literacy and learning do not necessarily go hand in hand because students can engage in writing tasks superficially, without the critical perspective that writing instructors generally associate with writing (50).

These attributes of literacy support Geisler's main argument that the cultural phenomenon of professionalization has come about because "expert" practitioners of a particular vocation such as science, in partnership with education, have created a "general public" that has been provided with some domain-specific knowledge but little awareness of rhetorical processes within and between these domains (see also above discussion on the distance between science and the public and the discussion in chapter 1 of Foucault's "specific intellectual"). Thus, the general public may have some knowledge and even some limited interpretive ability in law, science, and many other professions, but members of the general public do not typically know what to do when, for example, conflicts in science arise. The ongoing and often bitter controversy over what age women should begin annual mammograms illustrates this problem. Studies performed by radiologists (who make money from mammograms) almost invariably conclude that women should begin mammograms at age forty; studies by oncologists, on the other hand, often find that women do not benefit from mammograms until age fifty. Many women, even those who have consulted articles in medical journals or researched this issue in some other way, are caught in the middle and are often frustrated by this situation.

Although science educators typically use an autonomous literacy model in the teaching of science, some scientists have experimented with definitions of scientific literacy that are closer to the middle of the continuum, critical literacy. As a group, they are generally willing to concede that a "mastery" of scientific skills and knowledge is not necessary; rather, the possession of some knowledge and interpretive ability—especially the ability to identify the differences between science and other worldviews—is considered to be crucial. Although Shamos's solution to the scientific literacy problem reflects an autonomous approach, his initial definition of scientific literacy follows a critical model of literacy. He defines a "true scientific literate" (90) as follows: "At this level the individual actually knows something about the overall scientific enterprise. He or she is aware of some of the major conceptual schemes (the theories) that form the foundations of science, how they were arrived at, and why they are widely accepted, how science achieves order out of a random universe, and the role of experiment in science. This individual also appreciates the elements of scientific investigation, the importance of proper questioning, of analytical and deductive reasoning, of logical thought processes, and reliance on objective evidence" (89).

Another example of critical literacy involves a redefinition of scientific literacy because of alarm over the influence of religion-inspired opponents of science. In *Science, Nonscience, and Nonsense: Approaching Environmental Literacy*, Zimmerman, an evolutionary biologist, calls for a basic understanding of scientific logic and procedures so that individuals can distinguish between unsupported and un-testable declarations (Zimmerman singles out what he alleges as such statements from evangelical Christians arguing for Biblical creation) and scientifically verifiable hypotheses. "Our goal," he states, "should be to reach a level of sophistication sufficient to enable us to examine the specific hypotheses or types of claims made by those who, either purposefully or naively, are advancing anti-intellectual views. . . . Although differentiating between coincidence and repeatable, verifiable pattern is often a difficult task, just that sort of distinction is necessary for rational decision making. To accomplish [this task] requires at least a rudimentary understanding and appreciation of experimental design and statistics" (43). Zimmerman argues that this form of scientific literacy will promote environmental protection: "Once our schools start turning out scientifically literate individuals, they will be much more likely to be producing environmentalists at the same time, for it is difficult to be the former without being the latter" (xiii).

Despite their advantages over autonomous models of scientific literacy, both Shamos's and Zimmerman's conceptions of critical literacy are not without their shortcomings. While Shamos calls for a familiarity with the intellectual debates that led to the acceptance and staying power of scientific theories and illustrates the need for intellectual rigor and skeptical questioning—certainly a more complex view of literacy than that posited by autonomous models—his quest is hampered by modernist tendencies such as the assumption that science brings order to a random universe and that evidence is objective. Zimmerman's task is to help distinguish between the scientist and what he deems a scientist charlatan or carpetbagger; his suggestions are beneficial in this regard in that they call for a certain depth not considered in autonomous scientific literacy. Like that of Shamos, though, Zimmerman's model of scientific literacy remains trapped in a framework of modernist science in which rationality is associated only with experimental research, statistics, and universal patterns.

Biologists Uno and Bybee have suggested four levels of biological literacy—nominal, functional, structural, and multidimensional (553). Their fourth category, multidimensional biology, "represents a broad, detailed, and interconnected understanding of a subject in biology" (556). Arguing that the structural and multidimensional levels of biological literacy are preferable to the nominal and functional levels, Uno and Bybee suggest ways in which science teachers can integrate bioethics, the nature of science, and local science-related issues (556). Their suggestions perhaps represent the best model of critical scientific literacy because of the recognition of all science as ethical action and as locally situated and influential/influenced activity. Nevertheless, the model does not clearly illuminate the practices of science as a powerful cultural institution and the ways in which science impacts consciousness formation or empowerment.

Ideological Literacy

The best model for a scientific literacy that can be successfully incorporated into rhetoric and composition derives from the notion of ideological literacy. Ideological literacy emphasizes the "cultural embeddedness" of literacy and its "interactive and highly contextualized nature" (Minter, Gere, and Keller-Cohen 671). Another feature is consciousness of the potential of literacy to be used for both oppression and resistance. Thus, in addition to the functional reading and writing skills associated with autonomous literacy and the textual interpretation and explanation within a framework that comprises critical literacy, ideological literacy includes attention to how literacies operate within cultures to both dominate and empower. Alluding to this perception, Faigley asks, "Can we promote a literacy that challenges monopolies of knowledge and information?" (41). And Barton says that "literacy is now recognized as one of the means by which educational privilege, with its associated social and economic rewards, remains unequally distributed in contemporary society" (408). According to Keller-Cohen, two assumptions guide the ideological orientation toward literacy: "first, that literacy is a socially negotiated construct, dependent on the goals of the individual participants and society as a whole as well as the demands of the situation(s) in which literacy is put to use; second, that the production and interpretation of texts is a collaborative process to which implicit and/or real readers and writers contribute. How writers apprehend the context for or in which they write determines the shape the texts take; similarly, readers draw on a range of social factors—from the importance of a text in their home or community to their lived experience—to interpret texts. So, the meaning of a text does not emanate from the individual but rather from the ways social groups use texts" (9–10). Similarly, Knoblauch and Brannon's definition of literacy emphasizes the importance of social context: a literate must be able to "identify reading and writing abilities with a critical consciousness of the social conditions in which people find themselves" (79). Finally, Barton points out, drawing on Gee: "Literacy . . . is not simply what is said or written, but also what is expressed or assumed within contextual and ideological systems related to a particular event" (409). It is not equivalent to mere textuality (Brandt 190).

In addition to awareness of social context, ideological literacy carries with it the potential for resistance. For example, "dysfunctional literacy" (originally coined by Sledd), is "a subversive form of knowing and being that interrogates social meanings, instead of accommodating them" (Lunsford, Moglen, and Slevin 3). For Dorr, literacy "means the skill to recognize the cultural roles . . . representations play and to alter these roles in the service of achieving a more egalitarian, compassionate society" (138). An "ideological model" of literacy posited by Street and work by theorists such as Freire and Giroux also inform this type of literacy. The ideological model, as contrasted with a more rationalist and value-neutral autonomous model, recognizes that political and economic structures and local ideologies are inherent characteristics of any attempt to define or teach literacy (Street 96). Street describes the ideological model as an attempt "to understand literacy in terms of concrete social practices and to theorize it in terms of the ideologies in which different literacies are embedded" (95). Thus, an ideological model of literacy moves beyond a perception of literacy as merely a problem of understanding meanings of words or of technological determinism, that is, access to books and technology needed for writing (Street 96). An ideological model of literacy also challenges the authority of a text or speaker and disputes the association of written text and objectivity (Street 101, 102).

Interestingly, theorizing on ideological literacy has taken the counterintuitive turn away from specialization rather than toward it. In other words, literacy now involves the identification of context and boundaries and relations between fields of knowledge, not just the accumulation of information within specific disciplines. Macedo quotes José Ortega y Gasset, who, cautioning against fragmentation in science, states that "The specialist 'knows' very well his [*sic* throughout] own tiny corner of the universe; he is radically ignorant of all the rest" (19). Instead, then, theorists such as Orr contend that literacy "implies the ability to think broadly, to know something of what is hitched to what" (87). Ideological literacy may thus be associated more with a liberal-arts type of education that encompasses not only technical expertise and understanding of a scientific discipline that is provided by contemporary science education but also, in an equally prominent way, the role science plays and the mechanisms by which it operates in culture and on individuals—a task the humanities and the fine arts are better equipped to handle.

Several basic and often utopian assumptions about literacy have been questioned by theorists who work with ideological conceptions of literacy. One is the fundamental notion that literacy empowers people. Street explains that only certain forms of literacy—forms approved by those in power—are taught at any given time; the teaching of any form of literacy that has the potential to threaten the existing cultural hegemony is discouraged (Street 104). Graff adds, "Literacy *can* and *has been* employed for social control and for political repression as well" (70). Similarly, according to Keller-Cohen, "literacy is a hegemonic and counterhegemonic tool that creates and maintains power as well as offers an apparatus for resistance" (15). As these explanations indicate, literacy does not, then, necessarily result in increased authority, and it may reify existing power structures or even provoke strife rather than prevent it. As Ohmann notes, "Like every other human activity or product, [literacy] embeds social relations within it. And these relations always include *conflict* as well as cooperation. Like language itself, literacy is an exchange between classes, races, sexes, and so on" (226). Ideological literacy thus also carries with it an awareness of literacy itself as an institution and a tool that can be used for good or ill and that can potentially produce as many or more problems than it solves.

As such, literacy, a cultural institution all its own, is as subject to limitations, politics, and power struggles as science is. According to Göçek, "One crucial component in this social construction of literacy is the effect of the differential power of the individuals or groups engaged in the process. Each individual or group articulates their conception of literacy within the parameters of their own social experience. Their particular social realities and visions of society lead to different interpretations of literacy. This discrepancy becomes particularly significant across societies that have differential political and economic power" (269). Literacies that are defined by existing dominant economic and/or political cultural institutions may very well then have the primary purpose of preserving the status quo. An ideological literacy understands this tendency and attempts to ensure that it is not obscured and to provide a viable, stable forum for alternative visions of literacies.

The goal of an ideological scientific literacy would be to emphasize the counter-hegemonic potential of literacy in an effort to illuminate the political and economic interests of science in both historical and contemporary contexts. Scientific literacy, as Shamos points out above, has not been achieved by—allowed for—the vast majority of even well-educated adults; thus they are *subjected* to science. A significant increase in scientific literacy could enable people to gain awareness and power for potential engagement as they involve science-related issues. As Keller-Cohen states, "subjugated peoples can use literacy counter-hegemonically, as a form of resistance as well as a way to create alternative self-definitions" (16). Women, members of ethnic and racial minorities, and gays and lesbians have used literacy in this sense. Women and African Americans have especially used an ideologically informed scientific literacy to counter claims that the dominant institution of science has made about them. This type of literacy can, then, result in a more widespread understanding than scientific conclusions often reinforce existing cultural biases (Lewontin 10); in turn, this understanding can lead to a challenge to those biases.

An enterprise as powerful as science requires an equally powerful literacy, one that reflects a recognition of the role of ideology in science. According to Lewontin, scientific ideology can be understood as a dual process: "on the one hand, of the social influence and control of what scientists do and say, and, on the other hand, the use of what scientists do and say to further support the institutions of society" (4). These institutions not only include science itself but the vast array of other cultural institutions that look to science for validity and knowledge production. An ideological scientific literacy, then, could be characterized by the following:

- an understanding that science is fundamentally a discursive activity governed by rhetoric
- an understanding that science seeks to maintain its privileged status
- an understanding that scientific disciplines do not exist in isolation from each other or from broader issues of economics, history, and politics
- an understanding of the methodology of experimentation along with an awareness of its limitations and that it is but one way to create knowledge
- an understanding that all science is, as rhetoric, ethical action

- an understanding that science impacts individual consciousness in ways both similar to and likely different from other cultural institutions
- an understanding that the dominant institution of science can be interrogated and resisted when necessary

These criteria do not preclude knowledge of scientific facts or laboratory procedures; in fact, training in at least one science would enhance the ability of this model to engender the sophisticated understanding of science and culture for which this literacy strives. The criteria do insist, though, on a keen sense of the place of science in society and its operations with respect to identity formation.

Hints of several of the above criteria have appeared. For example, occasionally, concern about illiteracy caused by fragmentation arises, even in science. For example, despite their autonomous approach to scientific literacy, Hazen and Trefil report that "it has been our experience that working scientists are often illiterate outside their own field of professional expertise" (xiii). In the humanities, Harding, in a sweeping commentary, contends that "there are few aspects of the 'best' scientific educations that enable anyone to grasp how nature-as-an-object of knowledge is always cultural" ("Racial" Economy 1). Such educations essentially result in expertise in a narrow area of inquiry—the specialization that Ortega y Gasset warned against above.

Perhaps the most evidence of an ideological literacy in science appears in environmental studies. This discipline promotes several of the criteria for an ideological scientific literacy and provides a foundation on which such a literacy for other scientific disciplines can be built. In distinguishing this new form of scientific literacy from earlier perceptions, environmentalist David Orr, in *Ecological Literacy: Education and the Transition to a Postmodern World*, states that "Literacy is the ability to read. Numeracy is the ability to count. Ecological literacy . . . is the ability to ask 'What then?'" This question, Orr continues, "is . . . an appropriate question to ask before the last rain forests disappear, before the growth economy consumes itself into oblivion, and before we have warmed the planet intolerably" (85). Ecological literacy emphasizes connections between disciplines and resists specialization, thus acknowledging the concerns of theorists such as Milbrath, who states that literacy "should be interdisciplinary, drawing teachers and relevant knowledge from the natural and social sciences as well as the humanities" (277).

In addition to focusing attention on consequences of uncontrolled development, industrial pollution, and desertification (i.e., deforestation), some environmentalists have embraced a broader scientific literacy to discredit quick technological fixes and reliance on so-called junk science. According to Zimmerman, "acceptance of, and even a reliance on, pseudoscience has burgeoned at a time when science and technology are assuming an ever-increasing presence in our daily lives" (xi-xii). The point is, he says, that neither pseudosciences, such as astrology, mysticism, and the like, nor technology can be counted on to provide feasible solutions to the myriad problems faced by the earth's environment. This skepticism, along with the appreciation of state and corporate connections to the environment, contributes to a more complex and socially responsible scientific literacy.

Ecological literacy has been developed by these and other theorists in response to what is called the "human exemptionalist paradigm" (Milbrath 272) advocated by traditional science. This paradigm can be summarized as follows:

1. It is right and proper for humans to dominate and control nature.
2. Science and technology are powerful means for domination and control; their development should be emphasized; progress need never cease.
3. Acquiring material goods is the key to a good life.
4. The world is vast; there are plenty of resources, so we need not be concerned with running out.
5. Nature will absorb our wastes. (Milbrath 272)

This summary is rife with implications that an ideological literacy of science is equipped to address. Ecologists and environmental theorists have thus pushed for the development of such a model.

Conclusion

Rhetoric and composition can contribute significantly to an ideological scientific literacy for students. It is important that students be able to draw on this type of literacy during situations such as visiting a physician or attending a community meeting on environmental issues. Unfortunately, all too often, what is assumed and expressed in discursive events in which science is an issue and in which one of the participants is not a scientist is that this participant has little authority or recourse. She or he does not possess the power that an ideological scientific literacy can provide.

Because of the cultural dominance of science, an earnest, major move toward meaningful scientific literacy carries with it the potential for considerable power. An ideological scientific literacy movement spearheaded by rhetoric and composition would benefit from the experience that this discipline enjoys in issues of literacy, an experience that has pointedly allowed for and encouraged participation from multiple voices. As such, rhetoric and composition gains by establishing its place as a major part of the dominant institution of science, and science gains from the reinvigoration of fresh perspectives and ideas brought to it by the critical and public awareness brought to bear by the ideological literacy taught by rhetoric and composition.

Part 2

Texts and Scenarios

5 Popularizations of Science

cience popularizations have only recently begun to gain widespread critical attention and to be recognized as important components of the perception and practice of the contemporary cultural institution of science. Their importance is undeniable, even if popularizations are still not universally acclaimed by scientists themselves. Indeed, traditionally, some scientists—and nonscientists alike—utterly dismiss popularizations as watered-down translations of scientific theories and phenomena for simpletons, hardly worthy of the respect and prestige accorded to original research in which new knowledge is actually produced. But increasingly, science popularizations are being seen as a "player" in the scientific establishment of the Information Age. "The rhetoric of popular science" was the focus of a 2004 special issue of *Written Communication*. Popularizations in the form of books, websites, and magazines such as *Scientific American* and *Discover* do indeed influence scientific research agendas, methodologies, perceptions, and policies. In a study of the role of popularizations in the articulation of chaos theory, for example, Paul argues that James Gleick's 1987 bestseller *Chaos: Making a New Science* helped in "diffusing concepts of chaos theory within and across disciplinary boundaries in science itself" (33). (Paul's article is part of the special issue mentioned above.) This new perspective, then, acknowledges the rhetorical impact that popularizations can make not only on the general public, but on the institution of science as well.

I see histories of science such as Judson's *The Eighth Day of Creation*, which is about the discovery of the double helix structure of DNA, as one of many forms that science popularizations can take. However, I think that popularizations—historical and otherwise—differ from science biography, such as Knight's *Issac Newton: Mastermind of Modern Science*, in that the latter focus more on people than the activity of science. This difference is, though, often one of degree and not one of kind. I also distinguish science popularization from science journalism in that the popularizations often appear much later than journalistic accounts of science and are typically much longer, larger, and complex in scope. Additionally, good popularizations often present a more balanced view of science and scientists than that found in journalistic work or in either one of the above-mentioned history of science book titles would suggest appears in those works.

This chapter contains an analysis of three different types of scientific popularizations. The goal of the chapter is to demonstrate to rhetoricians and compositionists who wish to include science as part of their courses the range and usefulness of material available to them in addition to primary scientific literature. Indeed, in many ways, efforts to achieve a culturally informed, meaningful scientific literacy can be recognized and realized more quickly in popularizations than in original research; thus, they are a good place to either start or to introduce simultaneously with an original scientific research paper. For example, Bushnell has described the successes that he has enjoyed using science writing such as Junger's *The Perfect Storm* and Pollan's *The Botany of Desire* in undergraduate scientific and technical writing courses. He argues that "Science writing [i.e., popularization], unlike scientific writing [i.e., reports on original scientific research—primary scientific communication], is uniquely suited to articulating [the adventure of scientific discovery] in print" (257). While I take issue with Bushnell's dismissal of primary science discourse, I do agree that popularizations can be enormously helpful in learning about the issues and terminology associated with primary research, which can be unfamiliar and complex, and in contextualizing the primary research, enabling students and instructors alike to bring the big picture into focus. The pedagogical scenarios outlined in the final three chapters of this book make use of both popularizations and original research in an effort to describe and use in the rhetoric and composition classroom an entire body of discourse that is related to the topic presented in each chapter.

I classify the three popularizations that I have chosen to analyze on the basis of their "closeness" to the genre of the scientific research article. This classification scheme is, of course, only one of many such schemes that can be imagined, and I employ it because the scientific research article offers a useful, known point of reference. Additionally, each of the pedagogical scenarios presented in the last three chapters, while employing popular sources, is built around a central text that is taken from the primary literature, and instructors may find it helpful to think about popularizations related to the issue under study in terms of how close or distant they are from the primary text.

Science popularization texts can have limitations. The "horse-race framing" of important discoveries in some of these texts valorizes competition in science and obscures or altogether ignores important issues and nuances, as demonstrated by Charney's critique of *Longitude*, a popularization of the discovery of longitude by a seventeenth-century British clockmaker by Dava Sobel ("Lone Geniuses" 215–41). Popular science texts sometimes present science crudely and unproblematically and thus do not promote the depth of critical thinking necessary to engage science in a fully informed way—characteristics of what Fuller calls "cultivating science" (40). Fuller argues that "much popular science . . . does not make the technicalities of science accessible to this problematic and normalised concept of 'the people'; rather it is a discourse that enmeshes the 'facticities' of science with the master narratives of liberal bourgeois cultures" (38).

Perhaps an even larger problem, though, is that science popularization just isn't—well—it just isn't too popular to begin with. It tends to be consumed only by a few at the top of the cultural food chain. Fuller adds, "Much popular science has been foremost an attempt to construct dialogue between discursive elites, who for the main share cultural values" (39). Stephen Jay Gould, whose work Fuller analyzes, writes for the "perceptive and intelligent lay person . . . a low percentage of America, perhaps, but a high absolute with influence beyond their proportion in the population" (Fuller 40). Paul reaches a similar conclusion about *Chaos: Making a New Science*; although presented and perceived as a popular science text, the book has not been read by what Paul sees as the "public" (32–68). The arguments by both Fuller and Paul may be interpreted as saying that scientific popularizations appeal only to well-educated, upper middle-class or upper-class readers who have the time and money to enjoy science as a serious amateur hobby and who may also have a financial interest in science companies. In other words, these are people who can afford expensive telescopes (i.e., amateur astronomers) or trips to remote parts of the world (e.g., amateur anthropologists or amateur ornithologists) or significant investments in companies such as Eli Lilly, a major manufacturer of pharmaceuticals.

While this argument has merit, it is not entirely accurate to suggest that people of lower socioeconomic status do not follow and/or participate in science. Indeed, as McLaughlin-Jenkins has shown, the working class of late Victorian Britain maintained its own procedures for staying abreast of happenings in science (147–66). It is certainly plausible, though, that, given the increasing dependence of many scientific fields on sophisticated, costly technology over the past century, it is much more difficult for those with less financial means to play as active a role in science as they did during the late Victorian era that McLaughlin-Jenkins discusses. Because it is not performed in people's houses or discussed much in affordable, general circulation periodicals, science is not nearly as accessible as it once was. Nevertheless, scientists and others who attempt to popularize science to bridge the all-too-large gap between science and the general public deserve credit for their efforts, especially given the extent to which this work is sometimes scorned by their colleagues. At least some effort is made on the part of the popularization authors to invite nonscientists to play a meaningful role in the enterprise of science. Good popularizations have the potential to teach students to become culturally aware, literate writers and readers of scientific discourse.

Annotated Article Popularizations

The type of popularization that is closest to the scientific research article is the Annotated Article popularization. As the name suggests, an Annotated Article popularization contains the text of one or more original research articles as well as a contextual essay that attempts to explain the article in ways that are understandable to readers who are not scientists themselves or who are not members of the particular branch of science practiced by the authors of the article. The essay often also attempts to contextualize the article in terms of other research, especially research leading up to the article under scrutiny, and sometimes in terms of competing research as well.

A Century of Nature: *Twenty-One Discoveries That Changed Science and the World* is an excellent example of an Annotated Article popularization. The book is an edited collection of twenty-two original research papers (two announced the same discovery but were authored by different scientists) published in *Nature* from 1900 to 1999, along with commentary for each. The editors, Laura Garwin and Tim Lincoln, are both editors for the journal, and they selected the papers on the basis of (a) a list of classic papers that has existed at the editorial offices of *Nature* for many years, (b) discussions with "colleagues and advisors," and (c) a desire to reflect the wide scope of scientific disciplines (xii). Garwin and Lincoln, perhaps as a result of their occupational role as editors, recognize the discursive nature of science. They state that one needs to "consider the supreme importance of the scientific paper in the lives of scientists: in a very real sense, a discovery does not exist until it has been published, and validated by one's peers" (xiv).

Once the papers had been selected, the editors then "specially commissioned" prestigious scientists to write the commentaries—the editors refer to them as "explanatory essays"—for the famous papers in their respective fields (xiii). The editors explicitly requested that the scientists write these essays in narrative form to "give a flavor of what it feels like to experience the thrill (or, often, endure the frustration) of pioneering science," a sense that cannot be provided by the papers themselves or by textbooks (xiii). As will become evident later in this chapter, this effort to dramatize science is characteristic of all three popularizations of science that I have chosen. Popularizers of science seem to feel, then, that highlighting the human element of scientific research and discovery is of significant importance.

In the book, the explanatory essays, which contain short abstracts, references (primary scientific literature), and suggestions for further reading (other science popularizations), come before the famous papers; in a rhetorical sense, then, the explanatory essays set the stage for the papers by discussing some of the research that led up to the breakthrough discovery chronicled in the famous papers. The explanatory essays contain text boxes apart from the body of the essay that define key terms and concepts in two or three paragraphs. It is unclear whether these short definition compositions were written by the authors of the essays or by the editors of the collection. Each of the twenty-one sections begins with a page on which the year of publication is superimposed in large white text on a gray-tone reproduction of the first page of the original published manuscript.

By placing original research articles and explanatory essays side by side, and by listing (albeit separately) both primary literature and other popularizations, *A Century of* Nature helps to, if not blur the boundary between primary text and popularization, at least put them in the same arena. A nonscientist reader or even a scientist reading outside of his or her specialty area who finds that she can make sense of some of the famous primary texts printed in the collection may gain the confidence to read some of the suggested original research essays in addition to some of the other popular sources.

A relatively common popularization goal that this book reflects is one of promoting a more holistic view of science and highlighting its inextricable connections to culture at large. By discussing the series of events (i.e., experiments or other research) leading up to each discovery and by publishing papers from across the spectrum of the experimental and historical/descriptive sciences, the authors of the commentaries and the editors of *A Century of* Nature seek to provide readers with an appreciation of the range of work done in the sciences. Additionally, some of the commentaries attempt to place the discoveries that are chronicled in the papers in what amounts to an overview of the cultural context of which they are a part, by, for example, discussing the implications of the discovery in the years or even decades after its initial publication.

One notable characteristic of the collection of famous papers published in *A Century of* Nature is how short so many of them are. This feature makes this Annotated Article popularization an appealing choice for scientific literacy. The papers, while purely scientific, are brief enough so that they are not overwhelming. For example, papers on the discovery of neutrons (published in 1932) and the discovery of the new form of carbon named Buckminsterfullerene (published in 1985) take up only two and five pages, respectively; indeed, the explanatory essays that accompany the papers are longer than the papers themselves. Additionally, these short manuscripts often take the form of letters to the editor rather than traditional original research articles or reports; the authors and/or *Nature* editors of the time may have chosen this genre to publish the work as expeditiously as possible. Students may find these letters to be more accessible than longer traditional research articles.

The existence of these letters is reminiscent of early scientific discourse, which consisted of correspondence to and from Royal Society gossip Henry Oldenburg, the first editor of the first scientific journal in English, *Philosophical Transactions of the Royal Society*. Indeed, it is striking how many of these famous papers do not adhere to the typical IMRAD organizational scheme and objective tone that are characteristic of the genre. (For more on this point, see chapter 7.) Instead of a sense of certainty, many of the papers project a highly conjectural character that captures the sense of intellectual adventure in science and undermines the notion that it is made up of proven, unassailable facts.

The fifth paper of the collection is a letter to the editor published in 1939 by Austrian physicist Lise Meitner and her nephew, Otto Robert Frisch, that reports the discovery of nuclear fission, the process by which the nuclei of atoms are bombarded by neutrons and split into nuclei of elements with a different atomic number.[1] This transition releases energy; a chain reaction of such transitions is the basis of nuclear power-produced electricity and of the atomic bomb. The text of the letter is preceded by the headline "Disintegration of uranium by neutrons: a new type of nuclear reaction" (Meitner and Frisch 70). Three pages long in *A Century of* Nature, the letter was only about one page long in the issue of *Nature* in which it was published. The key passage in Meitner and Frisch's letter is as follows: "On account of their close packing and strong energy exchange, the particles in a heavy nucleus would be expected to move in a collective way which has some resemblance to the movement of a liquid drop. If the movement is made sufficiently violent by adding energy, such a drop may divide itself into two smaller drops" (71). The nucleus that Meitner and Frisch are discussing is that of uranium, and the energy addition results from neutron bombardment of that nucleus.

This passage appears about a third of the way through the letter. Preceding the passage is an account of recent work. After the proposed explanation, Meitner and Frisch justify their hypothesis on the basis of chemical and physical properties such as surface tension and radioactive decay and they reinterpret some of Meitner's earlier work on thorium in light of their new hypothesis. Overall, and with respect to the conjectural tone discussed above, their justification is highly speculative: indeed, it is not based on any laboratory research. Hedges like "seems," "possible," "may," "roughly," "should," "tend," "perhaps," and "probably" appear with frequency in the text (Meitner and Frisch 71–72). Additionally, Meitner and Frisch state openly that they are "puzzled" by the beta decay of uranium 239 (72).

The explanatory essay that accompanies Meitner and Frisch's letter is entitled "From nuclear physics to nuclear weapons" and is written by Joseph Rotblat, an emeritus physicist at the University of London and a 1995 winner of the Nobel Peace Prize for his work on nuclear disarmament. The commentary is slightly more than six pages long and contains two text boxes, the first on "The building blocks of matter" and the second on "Radioactivity" (64–65). Four references and five suggestions for further reading accompany the essay. Rotblat begins the essay by noting that the discovery of nuclear fission was prompted by the discovery of the neutron (63). This historical account is then continued; Rotblat describes subsequent research on neutrons, especially work that focused on the interaction of neutrons with protons. Researchers determined that bombardment of nuclei with neutrons led to atomic changes (64–65). It was Meitner and Frisch who realized that some of these occurrences were not simply minor changes to the nucleus of the existing atom: they were actually full-blown divisions of the nucleus.

The explanatory essay then shifts to cultural conditions surrounding the discovery and implications. In one paragraph, Rotblat explains that, at the time she and Frisch made the discovery of fission, Meitner was living in Sweden; she had left Austria to escape the Nazis' persecution of the Jewish people. Frisch was also in Scandinavia, in Denmark, where he

111

had obtained a position at the Niels Bohr Institute in Copenhagen. Frisch traveled to Sweden to spend Christmas 1938 with Meitner. Upon his arrival, Meitner shared a letter with him that she had received from Otto Hahn, a colleague with whom she had worked in Austria before moving to Sweden. In the letter, says Rotblat, Hahn discussed the difficulty he was having with the identification of the products resulting from the bombardment of uranium nuclei by neutrons. Meitner and Frisch went for a walk in the woods, and by the time they returned, they had decided that nuclear fission had occurred and that this mechanism accounted for the results that Hahn was observing.

Of course, Meitner and Frisch's paper would not have made *Nature*'s "most important" list without experimental verification. Rotblat explains that Frisch, upon his return to Copenhagen, performed experimental research that verified fission. The paper that describes this research was published in *Nature* a week after Meitner and Frisch's letter (66). After discussing some other notable discoveries (including his own) that followed close upon the heels of the discovery of fission, Rotblat spends a paragraph on electricity generated by nuclear power. He devotes the bulk of the remainder of the essay, though, to nuclear weapons, explaining the implications of World War II and the Cold War (67–68).

The explanatory essay renders the published account of the discovery of nuclear fission poignantly. Two Austrian Jewish scientists seek to escape Hitler's Holocaust and settle abroad. They take a walk in the beautiful Swedish woods on one of the holiest days of the Christian year and, while musing over a colleague's puzzlement concerning a mechanism of radioactivity, recognize a mechanism that would become the basis of a destructive power so vast that it could annihilate the human race. Sweden, of course, is the country that awards the Nobel Peace Prize, which is named after Alfred Nobel, the inventor of dynamite. In a final ironic twist, notes Rotblat, the name "fission" was "borrowed from biology, where it describes the division of living cells" (66). Life and death, creation and destruction, peace and war: all, this essay seems to demonstrate, are inexorably intertwined. Science is powerfully dramatized by the association of the original paper and explanatory essay.

Science Ethnography Popularizations

The second type of popularization that I wish to present is the Science Ethnography. This type of popularization explores in considerable descriptive and narrative depth an episode of scientific invention or insight or a narrative of development of a particular field of science. Unlike Annotated

Article popularizations, Science Ethnography popularizations do not include entire scientific studies. They do, however, quote liberally from the primary literature associated with the ethnographic setting under study; thus, while they are one step further removed from the scientific research article than Annotated Article popularizations in that they do not contain complete texts of the articles, they are closer than Armchair Scientist popularizations (the third type of popularization, which is discussed later in this chapter) in my classification scheme. A Science Ethnography popularization—as does any good ethnography—characterizes the specific people who perform the science and the influence of the cultures in which the science takes place, a characterization that primary scientific literature typically lacks. In this respect, while these ethnographies bear a passing similarity to the explanatory essay annotations that accompanied the *Nature* papers discussed above, they are orders of magnitude greater in terms of length and complexity.

In *Wonderful Life: The Burgess Shale and the Nature of History*, Stephen Jay Gould recounts the seismic shift that occurred in paleontology, evolutionary biology, and related fields during the 1970s and 1980s when researchers determined that fauna (i.e., animal life of a specific region or period) that had been collected early in the twentieth century did not tell the story that science and the public at large thought they did. The book is written in a nonfiction essay form and can be read by a motivated general reader, even one with little formal training in science. Gould does, however, quote extensively from primary sources and in fact builds the core of the book, chapter 3, around a sequence of original research articles published in the *Philosophical Transactions of the Royal Society* and other journals. These articles, contends Gould, are the manifestations of the monumental shift in the interpretation of the meaning of ancient fauna found at the Burgess Shale, a quarry in the Canadian Rockies near the British Columbia–Alberta provincial border.

The new interpretation quite literally turned the study of evolution on its fossilized head. Until the late twentieth century, the prevailing view of evolution of plants and animals was that a few elementary organisms, which had essentially been identified by 1900, evolved into the multitude of diverse species that we know today. Starting in 1909, the eminent American scientist Charles Doolittle Walcott, a geologist and secretary (i.e., director) of the Smithsonian, gathered a significant and, at the time, unique collection of fauna from the Burgess Shale. These fauna date from the Cambrian period, which occurred about 530 million years ago during the Paleozoic era (Gould, *Wonderful Life* 55, 71). Despite some puzzling features displayed by the fauna, he placed them into the existing categories that were based on the elementary organisms, thus perpetuating the well-entrenched, nineteenth- and twentieth-century tree-like model of evolution in which an entire broad canopy of diverse, complex branches grows over time from one main trunk (i.e., the small number of original, elementary organisms). However, a group of scientists who re-examined the fauna and analyzed specimens collected since Walcott's expedition found, over a period of about seventeen years from 1971 to 1988, that the fauna were unique: they did *not* belong in any categories to which Walcott had assigned them. In fact, the range of variation exhibited by the fauna was nothing short of astonishing. Little by little, they began to understand that, rather than present-day Earth containing a vast diversity of species compared with earlier epochs, the planet now contains only a *fraction* of the diversity that it once possessed. The process of evolution has not, then, been one of diversification—but of decimation.

The scientist who initiated the reinterpretation of the Burgess Shale fauna is a Cambridge paleontologist, now emeritus, named Harry Whittington. Gould explains the shift as follows: "Harry Whittington and his colleagues have shown that most Burgess organisms do not belong to familiar groups, and that the creatures from this single quarry in British Columbia probably exceed, in anatomical range, the entire spectrum of invertebrate life in today's oceans. Some fifteen to twenty Burgess species cannot be allied with any known group, and should probably be classified as separate phyla. Magnify some of them beyond the few centimeters of their actual size, and you are on the set of a science-fiction film; one particularly arresting creature has been formally named *Hallucigenia*. For species that can be classified within known phyla, Burgess anatomy far exceeds the modern range" (*Wonderful Life* 25). What happened, apparently, is that millions of years ago there were many, many more categories of organisms than scientists thought. Most of these categories have, for one reason or another, been wiped out. The few remaining categories have each evolved into many different species, to be sure, but the overall resulting variety falls far short of what would have populated the Earth had species of other early categories survived (25). The planet contains more species than ever before, but these species are simply slight variations on a small number of "basic designs" rather than the much larger number of primitive designs demonstrated by the Burgess fauna (47). Finally, while some of these basic organisms may have enjoyed a Darwinian "edge" that may have helped to ensure their survival while other species perished, Gould believes that continued existence and eventual flourishing of the few basic organism designs that evolved into today's species has much more to do with luck or contingency than it does with survival of the fittest (50). Additionally, the rate of evolution has not been a smooth, even progression over time; instead, multicelluar life appeared quite suddenly after 2.5 billion years of single-celled organisms that did not seem to "advance" (at least as we understand the term in terms of traditional evolution) in any meaningful way (60).

In many ways, from the perspective of a rhetorician of science, *Wonderful Life* is an exemplary popularization. For example, even as he quotes from the primary literature, sometimes at considerable length, Gould makes observations about the genre. At one point, for instance, Gould notes the "conventional passive voice of technical monographs" (89). ("Monograph" is the term that Gould uses for original scientific research articles published by the scientists he discusses.) In other instances, Gould notes anomalies that occur in the primary literature authored by Whittington and his colleagues—rhetorical moves that are unusual for the genre. For example, in one monograph, notes Gould, Whittington recounts a personal anecdote (albeit in passive voice) about laughter during a presentation he made at a conference (124–25); in another, he makes overtly emotional statements (167). Such overt acknowledgement of emotion is rare in primary scientific discourse. In his analysis of a paper by Conway Morris, one of Whittington's graduate students, Gould declares that "personal pride and passion come through beneath the stylistic cover-up" (147).

Gould performs many the same kind of tasks in his account of the reinterpretation of the Burgess Shale data that rhetoricians, compositionists, and other humanists and social scientists would do in theoretical work, case studies, and ethnographies, thus bringing to science the same type of inquiry as that employed by rhetoricians of science and other science studies scholars. First, Gould clearly connects science to cultural norms and expectations. As early as the preface, he comments on "the traditional attitudes (or thinly veiled cultural hopes) that the Burgess Shale now challenges" (*Wonderful Life* 15). The specific cultural hope to which Gould refers is that of humankind being at the top of a linear, ladder-like, knowable evolutionary heap—"a comfortable view of human inevitability and superiority" (28). He shows just how entrenched this conception is by quoting from a 1988 *Science* editorial that postulates a linear, vertical evolution with humans at the top. Gould describes this point of view as "motley and senseless" (43). (At this point, the work of Whittington and his colleagues had been widely known and accepted for nearly a decade, which is why Gould critiques the *Science* editorial so energetically. The editors of the United States' leading scientific journal, he implies, should have known better.) Gould demonstrates that this hope is present not only in science, but in other cultural institutions as well. He quotes passages from Pope's *Essay on Man* (28), Khayyám's *Rubáiyát* (43), Twain's impressions of his first visit to the Eiffel Tower (45), and Frost's *Design* that advocate *homo sapien's* position at the pinnacle of creation. Second, Gould incorporates the works of famous figures such as Aristotle (50), Tolstoy, Vonnegut, and popular authors to explain the important concept of contingency and its role in evolution (285).[2] (Inexplicably, however, although Gould's use of these works seems to imply that they play a crucial role in his—and his reader's—understanding of some of the central concepts of the book, they are not cited in the bibliography. Only scientific publications are listed.) Finally, Gould argues that "ideological constraint" played a decisive role in Walcott's misinterpretation of the Burgess fauna (244) and that, more generally, "Reality does not speak to us objectively, and no scientist can be free from constraints of psyche and society" (276).

In another move that we would typically associate with humanities-oriented postmodernism, Gould interrogates heroic narratives that surround the initial discovery of the Burgess Shale. Legend had it, apparently, that while at the Burgess Shale with his wife and children, who typically accompanied and worked with him on his summer expeditions, Walcott's wife's horse slipped and in doing so turned up a rock that contained the first Burgess fauna to be recognized. This event happened, of course, at the end of the last day of the field season as snow fell, and Walcott could not follow up on the discovery until the following summer, when it took a full week to locate the actual source of the fauna. Gould states that this sequence of events is pure fiction. On the basis of daily, detailed diary entries made by Walcott, Gould reconstructs the discovery of the Burgess Shale as a much more methodical, mundane experience (70–75).

Another feature of good science popularization is the notion that complex material can be clearly explained by someone willing to put forth the time and energy to do so and understood by a reader willing to do the same. Gould expressly commits himself to this notion when he says "Words, of course, must be varied, if only to eliminate a jargon and phraseology that would mystify anyone outside the priesthood, but conceptual depth should not vary at all between professional publication and general exposition" (16). A corollary of this idea for Gould, then, is that this material can be comprehended by individuals who are not specialists in the field from which the material is derived. As Gould puts it in a discussion of why "overblown, rapturous" descriptions of nature are not needed for the average reader, "Audiences do not need such a crutch. The 'intelligent layperson' exists in abundance and need not be coddled" (260).

For the most part, Gould strives to meet the ideal he characterizes. He defines key terms and uses description and analogy in an effort to clarify and illuminate the content. For example, at one point Gould describes an organism called *Dinomischus* as "sessile (fixed and immobile)" and as appearing "much like a goblet attached to a long thin stem" (149). Gould employs a "grab-bag" analogy to try to explain what he sees as the random nature of evolution (see, e.g., *Wonderful Life* 215). He also introduces paleontological "jargon" with explanation; for example, in chapter 3, when Gould contemplates how and why a few species survived the massive Cambrian decimation while most others didn't, he hypothesizes that the surviving species may have had an anatomical advantage, and he mentions the scientific term: "This idea of survival for cause based on anatomical deftness or complexity—'superior competitive ability' in the jargon—has been the favored explanation, virtually unchallenged, for the reduction of Burgess disparity, and indeed for all episodes of extinction in the history of life" (234). (As Gould notes, this argument has, more recently, been subject to an increasingly vocal chorus of doubts.) At other points in the book, Gould falls short of the ideal: for instance, "placental" carnivores and "predacious" are not defined (298), nor are "metazoan" animals (313) and "chordate" (321).

Gould himself is a deliberate writer, who at times reflects deeply on the cognitive and material effects of word choice, etymology, and definition. In a footnote that occupies half a page, he justifies his use of "decimation" as his choice of a term to describe evolution in place of the conventional theory of increasing diversity. He discusses his initial choice, "winnowing," and explains that he later decided against using this term because "all meanings of winnowing refer to separation of the good from the bad" (*Wonderful Life* 47), and Gould contends that morality has nothing to do with the evolutionary history of Earth. Gould settled on "decimation" because of its connotations of randomness (from the Latin *decimare*, or "to take one in ten") and of large magnitude of destruction, which reflects contemporary usage of the word. Gould argues that both of these connotations are reflected in the new view of evolution articulated by Whittington and his colleagues. In addition to carefully considering this nosological conundrum, Gould takes a full page to distinguish between "diversity" and "disparity" (49) and between "homology" and "analogy" (213). He muses on the power of words, especially those that are part of scientific discourse, saying in response to a passage written by Conway Morris and Whittington that "Phrases that we intend as descriptions betray our notions of cause and ultimate meaning" (235). In this same paragraph Gould asks the reader to "consider the weight of such phrases as 'destined to be supplanted'" (235). He even comments on the complexities of translation, complete with a reference to Milton's *Paradise Lost* and Haydn's oratorio *Creation*.

Gould comes across as a remarkably open writer. At several points in the book he includes metadiscourse more typically associated with the humanities that provides the reader with a particularly candid account of Gould's thought processes about the book, about science, about history, about (scientific) journalism, and about human nature. Before discussing the crucial monograph that he sees as tipping the scales toward the new view of evolution, for example, Gould writes the following: "I now come to the fulcrum of this book. I have half a mind to switch to upper case, or to some snazzy font, or to red type, for the next page or two—but I desist out of respect for the aesthetic traditions of bookmaking. I also refrain because I do not want to fall into the lap of legend. . . . My emotions and desires are mixed. I am about to describe the key moment in this drama, but I am also committed to the historical principle that such moments do not exist, at least not as our legends proclaim" (129). Gould spends almost another entire page ruminating on the implications of describing a eureka moment. Later in the book, he acknowledges that he himself made mistakes in his work on interpreting the story of the reinterpretation of the Burgess Shale and explains how he came to realize his mistakes and how he attempted to rectify them. For example, Gould says that he underestimated the value of the work of Briggs, another of Whittington's graduate students who contributed significantly to the reinterpretation (*Wonderful Life* 158–59). Lastly, Gould employs a *dissoi logoi* approach to his own arguments: he plays "devil's advocate" (*Wonderful Life* 209) against his own conceptual foundation of decimation and contingency, raising and then refuting other points of view. In a similar way, he looks at possible alternative evolutionary histories at the end of the book (292–323).

Gould also considers the power of visual rhetoric, for which he uses the term iconography. In *Wonderful Life*, Gould chides scientists for underestimating the influence of icons, stating, "Every demagogue, every humorist, every advertising executive, has known and exploited the evocative power of a well-chosen picture. Scientists have lost this insight somewhere along the way" (28). He includes a number of illustrations that demonstrate the traditional view of evolution with humankind at its pinnacle. The most famous of these is the "march of progress" illustration, which Gould claims is "*the* canonical representation of evolution" worldwide, used in advertisements, public relations campaigns, and editorial cartoons (31–35).[3] This illustration is the one that, on the left side, shows a profile view of a chimpanzee or other primate species in stride and then subsequent profiles of four or five gradually taller, more upright male figures from left to right, the right-most figure being a modern-era man walking purposefully and confidently. Other versions of this icon have been racist as well as sexist (29). Additionally, Gould discusses visual representations of the traditional "cone of increasing diversity" view of evolution contained in popular 1980s evolution textbooks, illustrations that are taken for granted despite the fact that, as Gould puts it, "the geometric possibilities of evolutionary trees are nearly endless" (38).

Like many popularizers and historians of science, Gould seeks to illuminate the always-existing connections between science and the culture of which it is a part by humanizing the scientific enterprise by including biographical detail. Gould describes Walcott, his family, and his colleagues especially well, perhaps because they are for the most part long deceased. Gould claims that, in the sixty years after his summer trips to the Burgess Shale, little work was performed on the fossils that Walcott brought back to Washington because (a) Walcott intended to do the work himself but was too caught up with administrative duties at the Smithsonian and (b) Walcott's wife "was quite possessive" (111) and actively discouraged anyone else from examining the specimens. Gould describes an "acerbic" comment by one of Walcott's contemporaries as remarkable because the colleague was "the most mild-mannered of men" (111). Later in the book, Gould discusses Walcott's blatant prejudice against Germans and how he used this bias to railroad a prominent German-American anthropologist (255–57).

Conversely, although he provides some biographical detail, Gould does speak not negatively of his contemporaries Whittington, Conway Morris, Briggs, and others. For example, he describes Whittington's childhood, including such details as his ability to visualize objects in three dimensions as evidenced by his success with model cars and airplanes and the British equivalent of an Erector set (101). (This talent would become vital as Whittington pursued a career in geology and paleontology.) Gould even takes pains to point out that Whittington's conservative nature was, in Gould's opinion, "crucial and favorable" (125) in terms of the success of the revision of evolutionary history. That being said, Gould does lean toward disagreeing with Whittington about the classification of one organism, saying that Whittington was "probably wrong" (171).

To reinforce the notion that science is nothing more, and nothing less, than an all-too-human activity, in the third chapter, which is the core of the book, Gould presents the entire shift from the traditional to the revised view of evolution as a drama in five acts, a drama that is complete with fascinating, fully developed characters. Again, as with decisions pertaining to terminology, Gould mulls over various methods of exposition before settling on drama. At the beginning of chapter 3, he writes, "After considering many possible modes of composition, I finally decided that I could present this information in only one way. The revision of the Burgess Shale is a drama, however devoid of external pomp and show—and dramas are stories best told in chronological order" (81). Gould bases the five acts of his drama on five of what he sees as the seminal published research articles that led to the reinterpretation, and he notes the potential limitations of this approach, saying "Does such a procedure distort or limit the description of science? Of course it does. Every scientist knows that most activities, particularly the mistakes and false starts, don't enter the published record, and that conventions of scientific prose would impart false views of science as actually done, if we were foolish enough to read technical papers as chronicles of practice. Bearing this self-evident truth in mind, I shall call upon a variety of sources as I proceed" (82).

Nevertheless, Gould's decision to tell the story of the Burgess Shale as a drama brings to most readers' minds characteristics that are associated with this art form: narrative, dialogue, emotion, conflict—in short, all the events and characteristics one typically associates with being human.[4]

Gould speculates on the effects that the institution of British education and Western culture at large had on the reinterpretation of the Burgess Shale. Two graduate students who studied at Cambridge under Whittington, Simon Conway Morris and Derek Briggs, performed much of the work that contributed to the shift. Gould attempted to discern if and how they worked together in an attempt to determine how to write his play. Specifically, he wondered if Whittington, who is "meticulous and conservative, a man who follows the paleontological straight and narrow, eschewing speculation and sticking to the rocks" (83) had any confrontations with Conway Morris, a "fiery Young Turk, a social radical of the 1970s" (83). In Gould's interviews with them, Whittington, Conway Morris, and Briggs contend that they never worked as a coherent team. Gould maintains that this recollection is most likely true because of the nature of the British graduate system, in which doctoral students take no coursework and work completely independently of their faculty advisors, only meeting with them to decide on a topic to research and then occasionally to inform them of progress (83).

Gould discusses the culture of science throughout the book and places these discussions within the saga and/or implications of the Burgess Shale discovery and reinterpretation. He talks about the apprenticeship practices of science and the role of undergraduate teaching (140–41) and comments on Harvard's decision to categorize science courses by methodological approach (i.e., experimental sciences such as chemistry versus historical, narrative-based sciences such as geology, cosmology, and evolutionary studies) (277–79). This step was taken by Harvard administrators in an attempt to break the grip of institutional disciplinarity and help erase the boundaries—and hierarchy—between the hard and soft sciences. Such action is vital for science to answer fundamental questions such as "Why can humans reason?" that need to be investigated just as much by historical scientists such as physical anthropologists as they are by experimental scientists such as neurologists (Gould, *Wonderful Life* 281). This action is part of a larger mission by Gould to use *Wonderful Life* to argue for equal validity of paleontology as compared with experimental sciences, especially physics, and to honor Darwin as the "greatest of all historical scientists" not only because of his work on evolution, but also because of his "development of a different [from experimental science] but equally rigorous methodology for historical science" (282).[5]

To my knowledge, no better description of a Kuhnian paradigm shift exists anywhere in scientific discourse, be it original research or popularization, than in *Wonderful Life*. By the mid 1960s, it was clear, even to Gould, who was a graduate student at the time, that Walcott's work on the Burgess Shale fauna was superficial at best (*Wonderful Life* 76). The Burgess Shale had always been regarded as a highly significant paleontological site, and Whittington, fifty years old and chair of the geology department at Cambridge, decided to devote a year or two to update Walcott's work. Whittington spent two summers (1966 and 1967) at Burgess collecting specimens, but much knowledge production work that led to the reinterpretation was actually done later with specimens that Walcott had collected many years previously. These specimens were stored at the Smithsonian (Gould, *Wonderful Life* 80, 141–43), and Whittington and his graduate students obtained and studied them starting in 1973. Whittington's planned two-year effort turned into more than a decade of work.

Whittington began his Burgess Shale work on an organism called *Marrella* because a large number of fossils of this creature had been collected. Whittington found that he could not resolve the puzzling features of *Marrella* in the same way that Walcott did, and he found himself in a bind:

> Consider . . . the dilemma that Whittington faced as he began to compose his monograph on *Marrella*. He took for granted the old view that fossils fall within major groups and that life's history moves toward increasing complexity and differentiation. Yet *Marrella* seemed to belong nowhere. . . . Today, this situation would cause no problem. [Whittington] would simply smile and say to himself—ah, another arthropod [i.e., an insect, spider, or crustacean] beyond the range of modern groups, another sign that disparity reached its peak at the outset and that life's subsequent history has been a tale of decimation, not increasing variety in design. But this interpretation was not available in 1971. The conceptual cart could not push this lead horse; in fact, the cart hadn't even been constructed yet. (Gould, *Wonderful Life* 120)

Because the "conceptual cart" was not even a flicker in anyone's mind at the time, including Whittington's, he dismissed his suspicions, acquiesced to the prevailing ideology, and played it safe—just this once. He placed *Marrella* into one of the traditional, already existing paleontological categories of organisms, Trilobitoidea, a type of arthropod. This placement agreed with Walcott's earlier work on *Marrella*. Whittington published a monograph entitled "Redescription of *Marrella splendens* (Trilobitoidea) from the Burgess Shale, Middle Cambrian, British Columbia." Later, Whittington recalled composing this title with reluctance and discomfort, and, after sending the final draft of the manuscript to the journal that published it, he immediately regretted the decision (*Wonderful Life* 121).

Whittington next tackled an organism called *Yohoia*, again noting features that were inconsistent with previous work that had also resulted in a placement into the Trilobitoidea category. This time, after completing his work and writing the monograph, Whittington did not include the name of a category in the title of the monograph, as he did with *Marrella*. Instead, he mentioned only the much more specific genus name. However, the formal taxonomic chart, a rhetorical feature of paleontological monographs, requires the identification of a category to which the genus belongs. In this chart, Whittington listed "Trilobitoidea" as the category but added a "fateful" question mark, thereby manifesting the first shred of doubt about the traditional story of evolution (*Wonderful Life* 124).

According to Gould, it was Whittington's work on a third Burgess organism, *Opabinia*, that finally pushed him over the paradigmatic edge. This animal had always been classified as another arthropod on the basis of features visible on the two-dimensional Burgess fossils that scientists had been studying since their collection decades prior. However, Whittington had perfected a technique to study the organisms in three dimensions by carefully unlayering the shale in which the animals were fossilized. With the use of this technique, Whittington found that *Opabinia* did not in fact contain appendages that are required for an animal to be classified as an arthropod. In his monograph on *Opabinia*, entitled "The enigmatic animal *Opabinia regalis*, Middle Cambrian, Burgess Shale, British Columbia," Whittington, for the first time, expressly contradicted earlier work (*Wonderful Life* 131–32). On the basis of this work and the initial work of one of his graduate students (145), Whittington did not place *Opabinia* into any category, and, from that point forward, worked within a new network of interpretation of which a primary assumption was that Burgess Shale fauna often represented brand new types of organisms that had never been studied as such (see also *Wonderful Life* 164). Work on later organisms by Whittington, Conway Morris, and Briggs would confirm this new interpretation (164–72). Gould is unrestrained in his praise of Whittington's third monograph, saying that "I believe that Whittington's reconstruction of *Opabinia* in 1975 will stand as one of the great documents in the history of human knowledge. How many other empirical studies have led directly on to a fundamentally revised view about the history of life?" (136).

Although Gould narrates the gradual realization of the new model of evolution in a linear chronology, he insists that the conversion was complex: "The pathway had not been smooth and direct, clearly marked by the weight of evidence and logic of argument. Intellectual transformations never proceed so simply. The flow of interpretation had meandered and backtracked, mired itself for a time in variety of abandoned hypotheses . . . , but finally moved on to explosive disparity" (*Wonderful Life* 172–73). Gould talks about dissent within the scientific community over Whittington's conclusions (see, e.g., 108).[6] He also describes mistakes (see, e.g., *Wonderful Life* 148 for a "beauty" by Conway Morris, *Wonderful Life* 193 for another by Conway Morris that also involved Briggs, and the footnote on page 129 for a brief account of errors made by Italian paleontologist Simonetta). Indeed, the entire episode on which the book is based rests on a fundamental miscalculation by Walcott.

In several passages in *Wonderful Life,* Gould describes the collaborative and cross-cultural nature of contemporary scientific practice. Despite the assertion that Whittington, Conway Morris, and Briggs did not work as a formal team, Gould leaves little doubt that a productive synergy emerged even as they worked independently on their Burgess-related projects. For example, both graduate students employed methodologies developed by Whittington (see, e.g., *Wonderful Life* 197). And, although most of the initial work on the Burgess fauna was done by English (Whittington and Conway Morris) and Irish (Briggs) scientists, scientists from other countries, especially Canada, joined the effort (see, e.g., *Wonderful Life* 224). Since the mid-1980s, work on fauna similar to that found at the Burgess Shale has become a worldwide phenomenon, and some of the most compelling research, according to Gould, has been performed by a pair of Chinese paleontologists working in China (*Wonderful Life* 226).

In an especially revealing analysis of Whittington, Conway Morris, and Briggs's earlier published manuscripts from the 1970s as compared with work from the 1980s, Gould finds that all three scientists use words such as "primitive" and the idea that only the strong organisms survived much less frequently in the more recent monographs. In the 1980s publications, the scientists instead openly acknowledge the role of "good fortune" (*Wonderful Life* 237) in determining which species survived. Of the shift, Gould notes the following: "All three architects of the Burgess revision began with the conventional view that winners conquered by dint of superior adaptation, but eventually concluded that we have no evidence at all to link success with predictably better design. On the contrary, all three developed a strong intuition that Burgess observers would not have been able to pick the winners. The Burgess decimation may have been a true lottery, not the predictable outcome of a war between the United States and Grenada or a world series pitting the 1927 New York Yankees against the Hoboken Has-Beens" (*Wonderful Life* 238). This change represents a profoundly humbling shift in how many human beings view how and why we got here.

Although Gould praises one of Whittington's monographs as potentially one of the most important works on evolution ever published, *Wonderful Life,* with its exploration of the historical and more broadly cultural contexts associated with the Burgess Shale since its initial discovery, may in fact have much more impact. It will reach a much wider audience than the monograph, the additional papers related to the shift, and even paleontology textbooks that teach the new interpretation to students who take courses in the subject. *Wonderful Life* may also, then, significantly influence the field of paleontology in particular and science more broadly.

Armchair Scientist Popularizations

The last type of popularization that I would like to discuss is what I refer to as the Armchair Scientist popularization. The Armchair Scientist popularization is the most distant from the scientific research article. Armchair Scientist popularizations summarize current scientific research and positions on a particular topic. They do not quote original research. Popular magazines such as *Scientific American, Discover, New Scientist,* and *Psychology Today* and television programs such as PBS's *Nova* are typical examples of this type of popularization. Consumers of Armchair Science popularizations are generally not practicing scientists, or perhaps scientists who work in a field other than the one they are reading about or watching. In this respect, they are similar to other armchair amateurs of note—armchair quarterbacks and armchair orchestra conductors. They have a serious interest in the activity, and they may even dabble in it as participants, as do the armchair quarterback in an occasional pick-up touch football game with friends and the armchair orchestra conductor as a member of a community band or orchestra, chorale, or church choir. Most often, though, football or music is not the armchair amateur's primary occupation.

Despite the fact that the armchair quarterback and the armchair orchestra conductor do not work professionally in these fields and may lack playing experience and, in the case of the armchair orchestra conductor, formal study and/or degrees in music, armchair amateurs frequently feel that they have enough knowledge to occupy the role of an informed critic. The armchair quarterback will announce to anyone within earshot that she or he would have called an end around rather than a play action pass because the end around play would have picked up more yards. The armchair orchestra conductor will declare that the tempo at which an oboe concerto is being conducted is too fast and the dynamic contrasts too subtle. The armchair amateurs may participate in spirited face-to-face or, especially in the case of football, online debates with friends and colleagues who share their passion. They may even register their opinions with the football team or orchestra itself.

Unlike that associated with armchair quarterbacks or armchair orchestra conductors, the critical function of Armchair Scientist popularizations is typically not emphasized. The Armchair Scientist consumer is thought of as one who reads or watches for informational purposes and who celebrates the science being performed—and science in general—with little if any kind of interrogation. I think that this lack of emphasis needs to change, and, for that reason, I have chosen an Armchair Scientist popularization that overtly places science consumers in the role of critic to present in this section. The Taking Sides textbook series (e.g., *Taking Sides: Clashing Views on Controversial Issues in Health and Society*) published by Dushkin (a subsidiary of McGraw Hill) contains edited collections representing almost all disciplines, including many of the sciences; these collections consist of paired essays or opposing Congressional testimony, accompanied by commentary by the editor(s) of the specific volume, that argue yes and no positions on a given question. For example, Issue 10 in *Taking Sides: Clashing Views on Controversial Environmental Issues* is "Will Hydrogen End Our Fossil Fuel Addiction?" The "Yes" essay is "Hydrogen: Empowering the People," written by Jeremy Rifkin and published in *The Nation*. The "No" essay is "Gas and Gasbags . . . Or, the Open Road and Its Enemies" by Henry Payne and Diane Katz and published in *National Review*. Issue 11 in this volume is "Should Existing Power Plants Be Required to Install State-of-the-Art Pollution Controls?" and contains as its "essays" transcripts of testimony to a U.S. Senate committee in July 2002 by Eliot Spitzer ("Yes") and Jeffrey Holmstead ("No"). Issue 6 in *Taking Sides: Clashing Views on Controversial Issues in Human Sexuality* is "Do Schools Perpetuate a Gender Bias?" The "Yes" essay is "Girls Still Face Barriers in Schools That Prevent Them from Reaching Their Full Potential" by Janice Wienman. The "No" essay is "In Fact, the Public Schools Are Biased Against Boys, Particularly Minority Males" by Judith Kleinfeld. Both essays were published in *Insight on the News*.

While the series does have an unmistakable *Crossfire*-like eristic character, the existence of two positions is a big step up from the single position that in armchair popularization science has too often been presented as the only point of view worthy of consideration. The series invites the motivated reader to evaluate the validity of arguments, weigh evidence, and consider further research before reaching a conclusion, if one is to be reached at all. In a sense, the back and forth provides some semblance of the drama of science.

Issue 13 in the *Taking Sides* environmental volume is the necessity—or lack thereof—of population control as an important component of environmentalism; it is a potentially provocative topic for traditionally aged college students, many of whom will become parents in future years. Like all the issues in the *Taking Sides* series, the topic of population control is framed as a question: "Is Limiting Population Growth a Key Factor in Protecting the Global Environment?" (Easton 214). The entire chapter is seventeen pages long and includes a short "Issue Summary" by the editor of the volume, Thomas A. Easton, a "Yes" essay entitled "Rescuing a Planet Under Stress" from *The Humanist*, a "No" essay entitled "Body Count" from *National Review*, and a one-page "Postscript" by the editor. Immediately preceding the Issue Summary is complete bibliographic information for the Yes and No essays, written by Lester R. Brown and Stephen Moore, respectively. The Issue Summary itself historicizes the notion of population control, starting with the eighteenth-century British economist Malthus's observation that population increased exponentially while food production increased linearly, and then introduces a few important texts on the topic (none of which are primary literature from science), notes the opposition of some religious organizations, and mentions initiatives sponsored by the United Nations and the World Bank. Easton clearly favors population control: he calls a projected world population of eight billion by 2025 "frightening" and states that the international efforts bring "hope" (Easton 215).

Brown's "Yes" essay, published in 2003, draws an analogy between resource consumption/carbon dioxide production and endowments/"bubble" economies, claiming that the bubble must eventually burst and lead to prohibitively high prices for food (216–17). This bubble economy, says Brown, is due in large part to overpopulation and other "mega-threats" such as the AIDS epidemic, which has already significantly reduced life expectancy in sub-Saharan Africa; overuse of water resources; climate change; erosion; and desertification (217). Brown explains that the world population has increased from "2.5 billion in 1950 to 6.1 billion in 2000" and lists consequences of this proliferation, including huge increases in demand for grain, water, and fossil fuels (218). Food is already becoming a national security issue, argues Brown (219).

Brown calls for a "massive mobilization" to prevent disaster (220). The first order of business is to stabilize the world population at 7.5 billion (Brown 221); the world must also turn to hydrogen, solar power, and wind instead of carbon for energy and stabilize water tables and soil (Brown 221–22). Brown returns to his economic arguments at the end of the essay, saying that the steps he proposes would cost a total of $62 billion (223). He also links his argument to terrorism, arguing that spending money on education, health care, family planning and reproductive health services, prevention strategies for AIDS, and food aid such as school lunch programs "would more effectively undermine the spread of terrorism than a doubling of military expenditures" (223). The final two paragraphs return to the theme of the bubble economy and the choices that the world must make (Brown 223).

The "No" essay, written by Stephen Moore and published in 1999, opens with an attempt to discredit Malthus, an important and challenging task given that, according to Moore, "the population control movement is gaining steam" (224). Moore discusses what he sees as vast amounts of money and other resources committed to population control by the U.S. government and the United Nations (225) and American billionaires such as Ted Turner, Warren Buffet, and Bill Gates (227). He calls the results of population control "morally atrocious" (225). China's one-child policy, says Moore, has resulted in forced late-term abortions and child neglect in orphanages, and these abuses are now being reported in other countries that are pursuing population control (225–26). Moore calls the "overpopulation crisis" a "hoax" and refutes arguments that we will soon reach the Earth's "carrying capacity" (227), noting that birth rates and incidents of famine have declined significantly (228). Problems that the Earth faces are not, claims Moore, a result of overpopulation, but a symptom of poor government (228–29). Moore ends his essay by arguing that the population control movement "poses a serious threat to freedom" considering that the decision to have children and how many to have "are the most private of all human choices" (229). In the final paragraph, Moore brings the essay full circle by noting that Malthus himself later reversed his stance on population control (230).

Nonscientists of all sorts will likely find the Issue Summary and "Yes" and "No" essays familiar in form and eminently readable. The "Yes" and "No" essays are overtly persuasive, short, nontechnical texts. Students may notice that the *logos*-centered "Yes" essay contains a large number of compelling statistics pertaining to resource consumption but talks about population control—stabilization—only in the abstract. The *pathos*-centered "No" essay, on the other hand, vividly describes awful mistreatment by those charged with enforcing population control policies but sidesteps the issues of resource consumption and environmental degradation. Although the essays neither take the form of original scientific research nor draw on it directly, they are indeed scientific: both contain data from a multitude of scientific studies, albeit uncited ones.

Conclusion

As often the most readable (for a lay audience) and most openly argumentative form of scientific discourse, students may find popularizations to be a way into primary scientific discourse and the culture of science at large. Indeed, especially after reading an Annotated Article popularization or a Science Ethnography popularization, nonscientists may gain a large measure of confidence upon realizing that they can read and understand much of what happens in the primary literature. Armchair Scientist popularizations provide the same kind of assurance but on a broader level: they enable readers to grasp basic scientific concepts and, perhaps more importantly, to witness argument in science.

Popularizations of all sorts, unlike the primary literature, *invite* public participation in science. *The Double Helix*, published in 1968, was quite a phenomenon and can be regarded as the first highly influential contemporary popularization of science. The book is James Watson's autobiographical account of the discovery of the double helix structure of DNA in the early 1950s. On the basis of objections by Watson's collaborator Francis Crick and others, Harvard University Press refused to publish the book, despite agreeing earlier to do so. This decision prompted a storm of criticism, including pointed commentary from the Harvard student newspaper. Watson published the book elsewhere. This popularization, far from being a simple explanation of the discovery of the double helix that could by digested by nonscientists, in fact has had a profound impact on science itself *because* it invited nonscientists to see how science really works. It showed the people, the passion, and the politics. The three popularizations profiled in this chapter accomplish such a mission, with *Wonderful Life* doing the best job. Other science popularizations have this potential as well.

6 Scientific Discourse of Another Culture

I n some of my technical and scientific communication courses, I ask my students to compare Western and non-Western medical discourses in an effort to illuminate Western assumptions about science and medicine. This strategy has proven to be successful, especially when students compared U.S. National Cancer Institute information about standard Western treatments for lung cancer with information from an Asian company promoting herbal treatments for lung cancer (Zerbe 191–94). With the use of such a comparison, assumptions about Western and non-Western medicine and scientific research are brought to the surface, where they can be identified and discussed (Hess 143).

Although Western science dominates worldwide, it is useful to remember that in its inception, it was established as and remains to this day an ethnoscience (see chapter 1) just as other culturally localized sciences are. It was an integral part of European colonial expansion, which is one of the reasons why it has become virtually ubiquitous, along with the ultimately pragmatic fact that it has often worked, producing enormously beneficial life-saving, labor-reducing knowledge. Harding notes that the cultural context of a science is both a "toolbox" and a "prison house" (*Is Science Multicultural?* 61). The recognition of Western science as an ethnoscience does not mean that it lacks rigor or is unsuccessful; on the contrary, both rigor and success have been hallmarks of Western science because of the "tools" of Western culture that it has used. Indeed, the institution of Western science reminds us that despite the fact that complete objectivity is an unobtainable ideal, scientists (and all researchers) should strive to be as thorough and fair as they can and to expect the unexpected. What such a recognition can bring about, though, in terms of a "prison house" is an awareness of blind spots: an understanding that nature can be conceptualized in other ways, that local knowledge and practices have much to contribute to scientific research agendas, and that making the benefits of science available to all is an immensely complex task.

This chapter presents a comparison of Western and traditional Chinese strategies for weight loss, a topic of concern to many students as well as instructors (bulimia and anorexia remain serious health problems, especially for college-aged women) and an issue of increasing importance as obesity becomes more pronounced, even in children. Weight loss is also a good topic on which to focus because even within the Western scientific community, it is the subject of fierce and unusually public debate (for example, see the March 13, 2006, issue of *Newsweek*, which features a cover story on Diet Hype and mainstream media's inability to capture the complexity of the research and debate).

The pedagogical scenario presented in this chapter is to have students read and discuss several studies on diets from the *New England Journal of Medicine* and excerpts from a book that describes a traditional Chinese method of weight loss. Generally, American students, not to mention most other Americans, with the possible exception of those who live in communities where Asian medicine enjoys legitimacy, will immediately dismiss the non-Western approach to science and medicine as unsubstantiated folklore, fantasy, or New Age psychobabble. One of the goals of the pedagogical tactic discussed here, then, is to illuminate and discuss the reasons why this knowledge is greeted with such derision while Western assumptions about knowledge and science are accepted, often without any question. For this part of the scenario, students would research cultural context surrounding the weight-loss industry in the United States. Finally, students would be asked to use the dissonance caused by the comparison of the Western and Chinese weight-loss methods to propose or conduct, depending on whether the project is more oriented toward physiological or social science, a research project that would test one or more of the questions or assumptions associated with the comparison.

Reading and Discussing Science on Weight Loss

Contemporary American culture clearly and constantly valorizes a body image that displays little if any fat. This image is associated with health, endurance, ruggedness, and athleticism, among other positive qualities, while being overweight is associated with slovenliness, a lack of intelligence, a lack of sexuality, and poor physical condition. It is little wonder, then, that weight loss continues to be a major concern of American culture. We are bombarded with books, videos, infomercials, Web advertisements, and spam that claim to have the latest and greatest secret to weight loss; this weight loss will, apparently, lead to a longer, healthier life as well as a better self image. It is absolutely possible, even likely, we are told, that we can look like our favorite thin supermodel (woman or man) or movie star.

Despite the continuous litany of "new" and "better" ways to shed unwanted pounds, weight loss in Western society basically comes down to four fundamental strategies. The first of these is reducing fat intake, and this strategy comprises the foundation of most Western diets as well as prescription medications such as Xenical, which inhibits fat absorption in the body. Fat is targeted for good reason; 1 gram of fat contains twice as many calories as 1 gram of protein or 1 gram of carbohydrates do (*WebMD.com*). The second strategy is to reduce calories; by consuming fewer calories, the body is forced to use energy already stored in the body in existing fat cells. So-called Very Low-Calorie Diets—the Grapefruit Diet and the Hollywood Diet are examples—typically call for the consumption of between 800 and 1500 calories per day (*WebMD.com*). Both low-fat and low-calorie diets are often undertaken with the assistance of appetite suppressants such as Didrex, Tenuate, Sanorex, Mazanor, Adipex-P, or Meridia. The third strategy, the subject of recent controversy, is to reduce carbohydrate intake while increasing protein consumption: the Atkins diet. The theory behind the Atkins diet is that significantly reducing carbohydrate intake forces the body to enter a different metabolic state, called ketosis, in which it burns existing fat for energy instead of the usual source, glucose from carbohydrates (*WedMD.com*). Many food and beverage manufacturers quickly jumped on the Atkins bandwagon when the diet first became popular in 2003; they developed product variations (e.g., Michelob Ultra) that contain fewer carbohydrates than the normal product. Finally, the fourth strategy is to increase exercise, which burns calories. As such, we are told to invest in home gym equipment such as Bowflex, to watch exercise programs on TV or buy videos, or to join health clubs. These four strategies, while they are manifested in a wide variety of ways, are *the* methods to achieve weight loss in Western culture.[1] Methods that do not depend on one or more of these strategies are often rejected as wishful hocus pocus, especially those that seem to espouse an approach that involves no sacrifice or physical effort.

The four strategies are the product of decades of scientific research. Most recently in the annals of Western weight loss, the Atkins diet has been the "hot" topic, and students would be asked to read a pair of randomized studies in the May 22, 2003, issue of the *New England Journal of Medicine,* which found that dieters lost more weight, at least initially, with the Atkins diet as compared with a more traditional low-fat, low-calorie diet. The first study followed 132 dieters with severe obesity for six months; of the 79 who completed the study, the Atkins dieters lost an average of 5.8 kg versus 1.9 kg for the traditional dieters. In addition, the Atkins dieters experienced, on average, a greater decrease in the amount of triglycerides (a type of fat implicated in heart disease and atherosclerosis) in the blood (Samaha et al. 2075–77). The second study followed 63 dieters for one year. As in the first study, of the 37 dieters who completed the study, the Atkins dieters lost more weight after six months than the normal dieters did: a 7 percent decrease versus a 3.2 percent decrease in body weight. However, at twelve months, the difference in weight loss was not statistically significant; in fact, dieters in both groups regained some of the lost weight, and there was less difference between the two groups (Foster et al. 2083–85).

In stark contrast to the focus on fat and carbohydrate metabolism and calorie burning of Western science, Chinese tradition maintains that regular breathing exercises, combined with a diet that has not been scientifically tested, can lead to weight loss. The yoga-like breathing exercises are called Chi Kung, and a description of this practice is found in a quite readable book entitled *Oriental Secrets to Weight Loss, Beautiful Skin and High Energy*, written by Han Yu and translated from Chinese to English by Sidney Yuan. This book is available from Yutopian Enterprises (yutopian.com) in Santa Monica, California; the original book in Chinese was published by the Qinhua University Press. Chi Kung is, says one of its practitioners, "a precious treasure which has evolved from thousands of years of Chinese culture" (Yutopian 85), and students would be asked to read the preface, chapter 2 ("Theory Behind Chi Kung Weight-Reduction and Its Comparison with the Pure-Diet Approach), chapter 3 ("The Chi Kung Weight Reduction Exercise"), chapter 5 ("Statistical Results of the Chi Kung Weight-Reduction Exercise"), chapter 6 ("Diet During the Exercise Program"), and appendix 1 ("Feedback From Readers").

The Chi Kung program calls for three thirty-minute sessions per day; the regimen can be attenuated somewhat once a person has lost the desired amount of weight. Each session involves three exercises. The first exercise reduces the amount of fat in the body, while the second and third alleviate negative aspects of dieting—low energy and hunger pangs, respectively (Yutopian 13). The first exercise is called the Frog exercise (another name is the Jade Cicada exercise) and requires the practitioner to "tune" the body, heart, and breathing while in a sitting position. During the breathing portion of the exercise, when inhaling slowly, the practitioner needs to concentrate on his DanTian, an interior area of the body slightly below the navel but toward the back of the abdomen. The practitioner inhales to 70–80 percent of full capacity, pauses for two seconds, inhales to 100 percent capacity, and exhales slowly through the mouth, concentrating now on the air coming out of the DanTian. The exercise concludes with a self-administered face and scalp massage. The "theory" (i.e., Western science explanation) behind the Frog exercise, according to the author, is that it improves circulation by forcing stagnant blood from internal organs such as the liver to all points throughout the body, thereby providing oxygen and nutrients. This process speeds metabolism, including the burning of fat (Yutopian 18–28).

The second exercise is the Lotus Seat exercise. The practitioner sits cross-legged on the floor or in a chair and relaxes by tuning the heart. Next, the mind is focused on slowly inhaling and exhaling, then just exhaling, and then nothing at all; the practitioner tries to achieve a "state of stillness." The exercise is ended with the face and scalp massage. The theory of this exercise is that it mimics REM sleep, which is the most restful of sleep stages, and thus provides the body with more energy (Yutopian 30–35).

The third exercise is called the Surfing exercise, and it can be performed standing, sitting, or lying down. The practitioner places one hand on the chest and the other on the abdomen. While inhaling, the chest is expanded and the stomach is contracted; while exhaling, the opposite is done. Unlike the first two exercises, the breathing rate is supposed to be faster than normal—about twice the normal rate. The exercise eliminates hunger pangs, and the author states that he is unsure of the physiological mechanism. He speculates that the opposing expansion and contraction motion (which on the outside of the body looks like undulating waves of ocean surf, hence the name) forces the stomach to pump its acid into the intestine, where it does not stimulate hunger, as it does in the stomach (Yutopian 35–39).

The exercises are supposed to be accompanied by a diet; the author lists a fast-paced diet, an intermediate-paced diet, and a slow-paced diet. The intermediate-paced diet is described as follows (note that 50 grams roughly equals 1 ounce):

Breakfast: ½ lb of milk or 1 egg
Lunch: 1 egg, 50 grams lean meat, 100 grams vegetables, 30 grams starch
Dinner: 30 grams starch, 100 grams vegetables, 30 grams lean meat (Yutopian 68)

By Western standards, this diet is demanding in that the allowed portions are miniscule; the fast-paced diet is even more so. The diet can be stopped after the practitioner has reached the desired weight, but the exercises should continue, along with attention to what is eaten.(72).

Like the Atkins diet, Chi Kung has, its proponents claim, been studied in detail. One chapter of the book is devoted to "Statistical Results of the Chi Kung Weight-Reduction Exercises," and tables and graphs frequent its pages. The author cites two studies, one of 106 people for five months in 1988 and a larger, longer second study of 1,056 people for a two-year period from 1989 to 1991. The results of both studies were similar (Yutopian 56). Participants lost, on average, 4.2 pounds during the first two days of using the Chi Kung program (Yutopian 49). Over time, 63 percent continued to lose weight, albeit at a slower rate, and "a majority of the participants lowered their weight to the ideal value" (Yutopian 51). The most noticeable weight reduction occurred in the abdomen (Yutopian 51), and in the second study, the author measured fat content in this area and reported a decrease in fat thickness (Yutopian 56–57). In addition to monitoring weight, the author checked body chemistry and reported a decrease in blood pressure for some of the participants who had hypertension and a decrease in GPT (a substance in the liver) in a person whose level was too high (Yutopian 51, 54, 60).

Discussion of Chi Kung, compared with the Western diets analyzed in the *New England Journal of Medicine*, may center on the "science" of the different approaches. Many students, even those who are not science majors, will likely insist that the Western-type science provided in support of Chi Kung is, to borrow one of my students' terms, sketchy. (The author states that more detailed statistical information about Chi Kung is available in an earlier edition of the book [49], but because there is no indication that this earlier edition was published in English, students may have difficulty verifying this assertion and obtaining the information for analysis.) They will have a point. Many of the numbers don't "add up," and data are often inconsistent. For example, in the first study, in which the authors claim 106 people participated, one of the tables of data lists the following:

Days into exercise	2	3	5	7	10	14	30
No. of people	102	17	10	50	8	18	9

(Yutopian 49)

For whatever reason, the number of participants is never more than 102—not 106—and even this number drops dramatically immediately after the commencement of the study. Indeed, it appears that only nine participants were followed for the thirty days. While it is technically correct that 102 people "participated" in the research, many Western readers would interpret that to mean that the participation lasted for the duration of the study. Additionally, although the author states that the first study lasted April through August, most results (with the exception of one table that contains data for six people) are presented for only thirty days. Similarly, the second study is said to have lasted for two years, but results are only presented for ninety days. In the diet chapter, the author includes fruit in a table that summarizes the three diets even though no fruit is listed in any of the textual descriptions of the diets. Many other examples of inconsistency according to the standards of Western science can be found.

Students may ask questions about the methodology of the studies discussed in the Chi Kung book so that they can compare them to that used in the Western studies on the Atkins diet. The concept of the double-blind randomized case-control study will likely be a topic of discussion; it is the gold standard, methodologically speaking, of clinical (i.e., people-based) research in Western science. It works like this: study participants, who have already been screened for potentially confounding variables (i.e., those that could bear at least partial causal responsibility for the effect being investigated) such as gender, age, health history, smoking history, and pregnancy, are randomly placed into either the case group, which receives the experimental treatment, or the control group, which receives the standard treatment. Neither the researchers nor the participants know to which group the participants have been assigned. The experiment is conducted and only after data are obtained are the group assignments made known. The goal of such a study is to prevent any kind of preconceived bias on the part of the researchers or perceived psychological advantage or disadvantage on the part of the participants.

Students may note that it is impossible to conduct a true double-blind study with respect to diets because participants will know what they are eating. (In a study of a new medication, for example, a double-blind study is common because the experimental medication taken by the case group participants can be manufactured to look exactly like the standard medication or placebo that is taken by the control group participants.) Thus, an excellent discussion may ensue about research validity: how do researchers construct studies in such a way that they can be confident that the effects (in this case, weight loss) that they observe are in fact caused by the variable (in this case, diet) under investigation?

Students may object to other practices used in the Chi Kung book because they do not fit the Western scientific norm. The students will be unimpressed by the Qinhua University affiliation from an *ethos* standpoint because they haven't heard of the institution; it is not American.[2] (How do they know what kind of reputation this university has in China?) They will have problems with documentation of sources: the author cites some American studies on obesity but provides no references. (Why do students think references are necessary? Why might the author have chosen not to use them?) They may well be horrified by the use of first-person testimonials in conjunction with scientific data, despite the subordination of the former as an appendix. These testimonials affirm Chi Kung's success as a weight-loss method and also credit the program with alleviating hepatitis, an irregular heart beat, a slipped disk, impotence, swelling and aching of the legs, and hypertension. (What decisions *do* students make on the basis of testimonials? Have they made any dieting or weight-loss decisions on the basis of testimonials?) Similarly, students may protest the author's note in the preface, which states that this new edition of the book has been completely revised on the basis of practitioners' suggestions. (Would "practitioners" possess knowledge and experience that might be of value? Why or why not?) Finally, typographical errors are evident throughout the book. (The mistakes are not major. Why are they an issue? What does a student's noticing of them tell that student about her or his own perceptions of writing—and of science?)

At one point in the book, the author Wu directly criticizes Western medicine and explains why Chi Kung is better: "From the point of view of Western medicine, obesity is a result of imbalanced internal secretions. They [Western physicians or nutritionists] recommend diets or using medications to suppress your appetite, reduce the absorption of nutrients in your body, or in some cases even create diarrhea. In the long run, this can do more harm to your body than good. Chinese medicine stresses the treatment of the organ functions by correcting the abnormal behavior and restoring the normal functions. This Chi Kung exercise program emphasizes restoring the original body functions of the overweight people and maintaining those functions" (Yutopian 71). Students may find it unusual to see such direct criticism of Western science and medicine. They may engage in an interesting discussion based on this excerpt about whether Western approaches to weight loss do indeed have the potential to cause harm and about how the philosophies of Eastern and Western medicine differ. For example, the idea that harm must be done in order to achieve a later, greater good—as in the case of Western diets and cancer treatments such as chemotherapy—seems unreasonable in traditional Chinese medicine. Additionally, students may try to glean the more holistic approach of Chinese medicine as compared with the more fragmented Western approach by noticing that Chi Kung emphasizes entire organs rather than Western medicine's typical cellular or molecular stance necessitated by the study of specific secretions.

They might also note, however, that the author states that readers of the book should consult their physician before beginning the program (Yutopian 5). He also notes that individual results will vary (19). Finally, Wu lists people who should not use Chi Kung: people with heart disease, ulcers, and others (73); this list is contained in a chapter devoted to Frequently Asked Questions.

Cultural Context of the U.S. Weight-Loss Industry

The next step in this pedagogical scenario is to ask students to investigate the U.S. weight-loss industry. This research will enable students to recognize why and how weight loss is such an important issue for many Americans to begin with. The students will most likely collect financial statistics on the weight-loss industry, find out who patronizes the industry, determine how the industry reaches consumers, decide to what extent the industry is subject to government regulation, locate historical information on the industry, and discuss the health issues associated with the weight-loss industry. This part of the scenario follows and extends the work of Strickling, who in 1999 offered a composition course at the University of Texas that focused entirely on the weight-loss industry. This section presents an overview of this industry that is based primarily on the following sources:

> Federal Trade Commission
> Laura Fraser, *Losing It: False Hopes and Fat Profits in the Diet Industry*
> Marketdata Enterprises
> *Bodypositive.com*

In 2002, U.S. consumers spent $40 billion on diet and weight-loss products, programs, and retreats. This amount is expected to grow at a 5.8 percent annual rate (Marketdata Enterprises). The top four categories break down as follows:

> $14.56 billion   Diet soft drinks (Marketdata Enterprises)
> $13.52 billion   Health clubs (Marketdata Enterprises)

| $5–6 billion | Over-the-counter diet aids: pills, herbal supplements, teas (Fraser 82) |
| $1.20 billion | Commercial weight-loss centers (Marketdata Enterprises) |

Consumers also spend substantial sums on diet/exercise cassettes, books, and videos (Marketdata Enterprises). The industry is presented as an excellent investment opportunity; searching for and publicizing these opportunities seems to be the mission of Marketdata Enterprises. Additional investment may make the industry even more powerful.

Issues of gender, race, and class are prominent in the weight-loss industry. According to Strickling, "The great majority of these consumers [who purchase weight-loss products and services]—more than 80%—are women. Since men are as likely as women to be obese, why is it that 95% of the members of Weight Watchers, and over 75% of Nutri-System customers are women? It has been suggested that women respond to a 'tyranny of slenderness' that requires them to bring their bodies into conformity with an idealized female 'norm.'" ("E309K Syllabus"). And, although most of these women are white (Fraser 143), the weight-loss industry has begun to target women of color. According to Fraser, the industry is "reaching out . . . to African American and Latina women, and to a lesser extent, men. . . . African American and Latina women are more likely to be overweight than white women, several studies have shown, and are less likely to attend commercial diet groups, so the diet companies see them as a lucrative potential market" (143). One of the reasons that women of color do not diet as much is because they have more self-confidence with their bodies, whatever their shape. Fraser adds: "If the diet companies have anything to do with it, women of color will change their largely positive attitudes about body size. Many Weight Watchers and Jenny Craig ads now feature black women, encouraging them to become as neurotic about their weight as upper-middle-class white women" (143). Fraser refers to upper-middle-class women specifically because concern about weight is "more closely correlated with class than race—professional black and Latina women tend to be thinner and have higher rates of eating disorders than poorer women—[thus] diet company advertisers are especially targeting upwardly aspiring minority women with the message that they're not going to make it in the professional world unless they lose weight" (144).

The U.S. weight-loss industry is largely unregulated except for prescription medication, which must be approved by the Food and Drug

Administration.[3] Most of the industry, though, falls under the purview of the Federal Trade Commission because of its advertising. In the autumn of 2002, the Federal Trade Commission (FTC) published a "Report on Weight-Loss Advertising: An Analysis of Current Trends." In the study, FTC researchers and attorneys studied three hundred weight-loss advertisements from print (magazines, newspapers, direct mail), television (infomercials), radio, and Internet sources that appeared between February and May 2001. The advertisements were for dietary supplements, hypnosis, meal replacement, diet food, diet plans/programs/centers, wraps, transdermal products, and "other" (Federal Trade Commission 9). The following types of claims were coded; the percentage demonstrates the prevalence of the type of claim in the three hundred advertisements:

- Consumer testimonials (65%)
- Before-and-after photos (42%)
- Rapid weight-loss claims (57%)
- Lose weight without diet and exercise claims (42%)
- Long-term or permanent weight-loss claims (41%)
- Representations that the user will not fail no matter how many times he or she has failed before (34%)
- Clinically or scientifically proven claims (40%)
- Endorsements by medical professionals (25%)
- Money-back guarantees (52%)
  All-natural and/or safe claims (44%) (Federal Trade Commission 4, 7)

The FTC researchers concluded that "The use of deceptive and misleading claims in weight-loss advertising is rampant" (Federal Trade Commission 30). Nearly 40 percent of the advertisements that they analyzed made a claim that "almost certainly is false," while 55 percent made a claim that was "very likely to be false" or lacked "adequate substantiation" (Federal Trade Commission 30). All of this hyperbole or outright prevarication is occurring even though the FTC initiated more actions (81) against weight-loss companies in the 1990s than it did in the previous six decades combined (72) (Federal Trade Commission 26); these actions are necessary because the volume of weight-loss advertising has skyrocketed since 1992. The report states that in seven mainstream women's magazines, the number of weight-loss ads increased 129 percent from 1992 to 2001 (Federal Trade Commission 21).

The FTC report also faults the media for not exercising stricter control of the advertisements that they disseminate, criticizing not only supermarket tabloids but also mainstream magazines and newspapers such as *Let's Live, Cosmopolitan, Redbook, Women's Day, Women's Own, Ladies Home Journal, Family Circle, First for Women*, the *Atlanta Journal-Constitution*, the [Denver] *Rocky Mountain News*, and *USA Today*. The three mainstream television networks, ABC, CBS, and NBC, as well as *Good Housekeeping Magazine*, are mentioned as notable exceptions: these outlets will not broadcast or print ads that make unrealistic or unsubstantiated claims about weight loss.

Calls for accountability on the part of the weight-loss industry have been made. Body Positive, an organization that attempts to counter the pervasive and unrelenting myth of an ideal body, recommends that all weight-loss plans and programs be required to provide the following information:

- The percentage of all participants who complete it.
- The percentage of those completing the program who achieve various degrees of weight loss.
- The proportion of that weight loss that is maintained at 1, 3, and 5 years.
- The number of participants who experienced negative medical effects as well as their kind and severity. (Body Positive)

At present, little if any information of this type is available to interested consumers.

The U.S. weight-loss industry depends on the immense cultural power of "thin," and students may be interested in the construction and maintenance of this norm. The current fixation with thinness has its origins in the 1880s (although Puritan morality railed against fatness long before this decade, equating it with sinful gluttony), and the thin ideal completely took hold by the 1920s. As Fraser notes, before this turn-of-the-century shift, "a man with a thick gold watch swaying from a big, round paunch was the very picture of American prosperity and vigor. . . . [A] beautiful woman had plump cheeks and arms, and she wore a corset and even a bustle to emphasize her full, substantial hips. Women were sexy if they were heavy. In those days, Americans knew that a layer of fat was a sign that you could afford to eat well, too, and that you stood a better chance of fighting off infectious diseases than most people. If you were a woman, having that extra adipose blanket also meant you were probably fertile, and warm to cuddle up next to on chilly nights" (16). Medicine and science, in step with cultural mores of the time as always, supported the ideal: gaining weight—instead of losing it—was recommended by the nation's most eminent physicians. And fat was considered essential for a "balanced personality," for prevention of "nervous disorders," and for child bearing (Fraser 19, 23).

Paradoxically, though, while being fat projected an image of health and physical vitality with respect to reproduction, corsets were a must for Victorian women because they were considered so frail "that they needed help staying upright" (Fraser 24). Corsets were also an economic image builder. A woman who wore a corset was severely restricted in her movement, which was fine because she was not required to do any work; the servants took care of it. Another paradox was that, while women were supposed to be plump, they were not supposed to eat. As Fraser explains, "Refraining from food was a sign that one was wealthy enough not to have to worry about when the next meal would come. It was also a sign of propriety: any appetite for food was equated with an unladylike appetite for sexuality" (25). Indeed, women rarely ate in public.

As with many issues in the United States, the confluence of a number of economic, racial, and gender factors contributed to the shift to thin. First, as fatness was a sign of prosperity, it marked a class difference. As food became more abundant for people in all socioeconomic classes through improved agriculture, distribution, refrigeration, and preservation, though, fatness ceased to be a distinction. Similarly, immigration to the United States around the turn of the century brought large numbers of new residents who were "genetically shorter and rounder" (Fraser 17) than earlier American immigrant groups; these new immigrants were, for the most part, not members of the upper or middle classes. The availability of food and immigration trends resulted in a role reversal: "Well-to-do Americans of Northern European extraction" notes Fraser, "wanted to be able to distinguish themselves physically and racially [many of the new immigrants were Italian and Greek], from stockier immigrants. The status symbols flipped: It became chic to be thin and all too ordinary to be overweight" (18).

A strong case of Europe envy also contributed to the shift. Romanticism in Europe brought with it something of a fad for thinness. Literary elites—Keats, Shelley, Byron, Emily Brontë, and Chekhov among them—were all thin. With the exception of Byron, all of these authors had tuberculosis, which accounted at least partially for their thinness; nevertheless, many members of the European public, and then the American public, sought to emulate these celebrities (Fraser 18).

With respect to gender, the shift to thinness has been linked to the broadening of women's roles in society: as women started to become part of the workforce, the "plump and reproductive physique . . . began to seem old-fashioned next to a thinner, freer, more modern body" (Fraser 19). Essentially, slenderness was a symbol of women's freedom. Over the forty years from 1880 to 1920, two progressively thinner fashion icons (as compared with the earlier Victorian ideal) cemented the thin ideal for women. The first was the Gibson Girl, an early 1890s creation of illustrator Charles Gibson, who admired European women who had begun to enjoy "genteel sports" such as croquet and tennis (Fraser 27) and golf, cycling, and yachting (Pyke quoted in Fraser 29). Gibson Girls "were tall, slender, and had an air of freedom and vitality about them that was utterly fresh. The women, who were all variations on one type, had upswept hair, dainty facial features, rather broad shoulders, a tiny waist, and a vigorous build. They were the first women to appear in magazines who looked strong enough to swing a tennis racket" (Fraser 27). The Gibson Girl had a huge impact on women in the United States because her creation "coincided with the development of mass-circulation magazines and advertisements, and she was the first mass-marketed ideal image to appear in newspapers and advertisements everywhere" (Fraser 31). Her image was used to help sell not just fashion, but almost anything women would buy.

The second icon, which gained popularity in the 1910s and 1920s, was the Flapper. Thinner than the Gibson Girl, the Flapper "was an impulsive, flirtatious, jazz-dancing young woman who had utter disdain for anything old-fashioned" (Fraser 33), especially the Victorian physical and moral ideals of her parents. The Flapper desired to be thin, with short hair, and to be active. Although no specific image of a Flapper existed, F. Scott Fitzgerald is credited with much of her popularity: the typical Flapper was thought to look a lot like his wife Zelda. The Flapper's more pronounced thinness, as compared with the Gibson Girl, is attributed to a number of factors: first, the Flappers presented an image of sexual freedom that Victorian women did not. Her clothes showed more of her figure, and she smoked and drank. However, the image was constrained by her slenderness: "Her androgynous look made her appear less overtly sexual than a full-bodied, hourglass-figured woman would have looked in the same slinky clothing," says Fraser (36). Conversely, the fuller-figured Victorian woman could afford to display physical sensuality (i.e., her curves) because she was assumed to be asexual (36). The second factor that contributed to Flapper thinness was the "light and streamlined" aesthetic of modernism. According to Fraser, "This aesthetic was reflected in the speed of automobiles, the angles of abstract art, the design of new products, and the images of mass media. Everything was straight, quick, and lean" (37).

As with the fat ideal, science and medicine were associated with the shift to thin, albeit with resistance. It was during this time that physicians, as part of the quantification obsession of modernism, first began to calculate ideal weights, develop diets and exercise programs, and devise treatments, many of them absolute quackery, for losing weight. Examples included diet bath powders, arsenic, shoe inserts, and chewing all bites of food thirty-two times (FTC 1, Fraser 54). The calorie was defined, and counting calories became an almost instant imperative (Fraser 55). However, the shift to thinness was not universally supported by the period's medical community. Dr. Woods Hutchinson, one of the leading American physicians of the late nineteenth and early twentieth centuries, lamented, "Adipose, while often pictured as a veritable Frankenstein, born of and breeding disease, sure to ride its possessor to death sooner or later, is really a most harmless, healthful, innocent tissue. . . . The longed-for slender and boyish figure is becoming a menace, not only to the present, but also the future generations" (quoted in Fraser 16–17). Dr. Hutchinson's pleadings, though, were futile amongst the overwhelming cultural onslaught of thinness.

Despite the pervasiveness and power of the "thin" ideal over the past one hundred-plus years, obesity is today common in the United States and is viewed as a significant health problem by medical and government authorities:

> Obesity claims more than 300,000 lives each year, and is linked to at least five of the 10 leading causes of death. It costs society an estimated $100 billion annually, and affects those in all age groups, ethnicities, and income/education levels (*Centers for Disease Control and Prevention*).

> An estimated 64% of Americans are considered overweight or obese, up from 56% in the early 1990s (*National Center for Health Statistics*).

> According to a study published in the *Journal of the American Medical Association*, almost one-third (31%) of U.S. adults are obese. In 1994, the rate was 23%; in 1980, it was 15% (*National Center for Health Statistics*).

> More women (33%) are obese than men (28%). The study also reported that 50% of black women are obese, compared with 40% of Mexican-American women and 30% of white women. Among men,

there wasn't a significant difference in obesity based on race or ethnicity (*National Center for Health Statistics*). *(Jennycraig.com)*

Fraser, however, is having none of it. "I realized that we need to view the science about obesity with as much skepticism as we do other kinds of weight-loss hype," she states (Fraser 12). Fraser points to a long-term, widely publicized 1995 study on weight that concluded that even 10 to 20 pounds over a woman's "ideal" weight is dangerous to her health. According to medical research standards, the study was well done: 115,195 women were followed for sixteen years. The researchers found that, generally speaking, the women who were the most thin when the study began in 1976 lived longest. For a 5' 5" woman, the ideal weight—at which no risk of premature death was established—was said to be 120 pounds; a weight of between 120 and 149 pounds for the same woman, though, was associated with a 20 percent increased risk of premature death. As weight increased, so did the risk of premature death (Fraser 12). The lead researcher, Manson, stated in a press release that "Even mild to moderate overweight is associated with substantial risk of premature death" (quoted in Fraser 12).

Fraser, though, criticizes the study on several counts: first, despite the large size of the study, only 4 percent of the study participants died, and only about a third of these women had never smoked. Fraser argues that smoking could have been a major factor in women who made up the other two-thirds of this group. The study also failed to account for exercise. Additionally, Fraser disputes the significance of the percentages. According to the study, that 5' 5" woman who weighed between 161 and 175 pounds was subject to a 60 percent increased risk of premature death. However, Fraser says, "the death rate was so low to begin with that 60% more than almost nothing was still almost nothing" (13). Finally, Fraser notes that Manson had a potential conflict of interest: she "was a paid consultant to Interneuron Pharmaceuticals, Inc., the company that developed the diet drug dexfenfluramine" (14).

Writing Science about Weight Loss

The discussion of the various Western diets and science, Chi Kung, and the U.S. weight-loss industry should, in the spirit of *copia*, provoke a large number of ideas for writing. At this point, students would be asked to write a paper in which they propose (for a physiological experiment) or conduct (for a social science experiment) a research project that would analyze at least one of the issues brought up in the discussion. The possibilities are many, but three are presented below:

A Comparison Study

Many students may be curious about whether Chi Kung really does work, especially in comparison to a traditional Western diet. The easiest way to determine the answer to this question is for the student to propose a comparison study in which one group of people tried one of the conventional Western diets while the other used Chi Kung. The student would need to explain how she or he would set up two groups of people who are trying to lose weight, one that uses a conventional diet and one that uses Chi Kung. The subjects would need to be randomly assigned to each group (the student would need to explain how this selection would be accomplished), and other variables—most notably age, gender, pregnancy, tobacco, alcohol, or drug use; and amount of exercise—would need to be controlled. The student would need to explain where and how these subjects would be recruited, whether or not they would be compensated, that they had been fully informed of the study's objectives and risks, and how long the study should be. Subjects using the conventional diet would need to maintain their normal levels of stress, be it job related, family related, or otherwise related. The members of the other group, if they did not already know how to perform Chi Kung, would need to be taught this technique and instructed when and where to perform it. The methods for collecting data would need to be spelled out; for example, the student would need to decide if the weight data would be self reported. The student would also need to report what results were expected to be obtained. The results of such a study would need to be analyzed to determine statistical significance. Finally, the student would need to propose possible limitations of the study. For example, if the weight is self reported, how can the student be sure that the results are accurate? Additionally, would any of the subjects have jobs that involve physical labor, which could affect that person's weight? Should this question be addressed when considering the exercise variable?

An interesting variation on this study would be to conduct an experiment in which one group used the Chi Kung program as described in the book, while the other practiced Chi Kung with either just the diet or just the exercises. Such research may narrow down a cause-and-effect mechanism for the diet.

A Possible Physiological Mechanism for Chi Kung

One possible link between Western science and Chi Kung that students may establish may be the enzyme cortisol, which has been studied extensively in the United States and other Western countries. This enzyme is released by stress, and it causes the body to store fat, especially around the waist (*WebMD*). Presumably, Chi Kung reduces stress and thus may contribute to weight loss because the body finds it unnecessary to produce cortisol. This hypothesis, which could be used to both test the efficacy of Chi Kung as a weight-loss method and attempt to determine a physiological mechanism if weight loss does indeed occur, could be tested by proposing an experiment in which levels of cortisol and weight are monitored in a group of case subjects who engage in Chi Kung and in a group of control subjects who do not. A student who proposed such an experiment would need to point out that people who enrolled in the study would have to be randomized to the case or control group (and would need to explain how such randomization would be assured) and that variables such as age, gender, pregnancy, tobacco, alcohol, or drug use; amount of exercise; and diet would need to be controlled. The student would need to explain where and how these subjects would be recruited, whether or not they would be compensated, that they had been fully informed of the study's objectives and risks, and how long the study should be. Control subjects would need to maintain their normal levels of stress, be it job related or family related or from some other source. Case subjects, if they did not already know how to perform Chi Kung, would need to be taught this technique and instructed when and where to perform it. The methods for collecting data would need to be spelled out; for example, would weight data be self reported or would the subjects be weighed when they came to the research facility to have their cortisol level measured? And for that matter, the student would need to find out how cortisol levels are measured (typically from venous blood samples drawn at different times of the day because cortisol levels vary) and to determine how often the measurement should take place and at what time of the day (presumably, soon after the case subjects completed a Chi Kung session). The student would also need to report what results were expected to be obtained. The working hypothesis would be that people who engage in Chi Kung will have lower cortisol levels and thus lose weight, maintain their weight, or gain weight more slowly compared to the control subjects. The results of such a study would need to be analyzed to determine statistical significance. Finally, the student would need to propose possible limitations of the study. For example, cortisol is not the only enzyme that affects weight. Should other enzymes such as fatty acid synthase be identified and measured? Additionally, the production of enzymes by the body can differ across ethnic groups. Should this question be considered?

Cultural Specificity of Chi Kung

Another potential writing assignment is the extent to which Chi Kung works for Chinese people because of other Chinese cultural practices; conversely, then, Chi Kung would not work well for most Americans (unless they live in a community in which traditional Chinese culture is prevalent) because American cultural practices are different. Because it is unlikely that a typical American would adjust his or her lifestyle to accommodate such a drastically different cultural practice, the hypothesis goes, Chi Kung may not do any good for the American because it is not accompanied by other actions that are necessary for its success.[4] For this kind of a study, the student would need to set up a two-part experiment. In the first part, a group of people who live a fairly traditional Chinese lifestyle and practice Chi Kung[5] would be compared with a group of people who live a fairly typical American lifestyle and practice Chi Kung. For this part of the study, the student would need to assign members to the two groups. Variables such as diet and exercise would not be controlled because cultural differences need to be exploited, but other variables such as age, gender, and pregnancy would need to be controlled.

Assuming that the results demonstrated that the members of the traditional Chinese group lost more weight compared to the members of the typical American group, the student would then need to choose an area of cultural practice in which pronounced differences exist between traditional Chinese and mainstream American culture. The goal of this second part of the study would be to determine which factor(s) contribute to the success of Chi Kung in traditional Chinese culture. One such area could be the use of the bicycle. While the exercise variable would be controlled in the Comparison and Possible Physiological Mechanism experiments described above, it is likely that members of either group in those studies do not get as much regular exercise as a person who lives a traditional Chinese lifestyle, who may ride twenty or more miles a week on a bicycle. To test this hypothesis, the student would need to compare two groups of people, both of which use Chi Kung. The members of both groups would live a traditional Chinese lifestyle with one exception: members of one of these groups would not ride bicycles, while members of the other would ride bicycles daily (or perhaps weekly or monthly) for a fixed distance and at a relatively constant pace, perhaps to and from work. For this part of the experiment, as in the first part, the student would need to form the groups and to control for age, gender, and pregnancy; in addition, because the focus is on exercise as a factor, diet would need to be controlled.

For both parts of the experiment, the student would need to assure awareness of the study's goals and risks on behalf of its participants and compliance with the study procedures as well as determine how long the study should last. The student would also need to explain how the data would be collected and what results would be obtained. The results of such a study would need to be analyzed to determine statistical significance. Finally, the student would need to propose possible limitations of the study. For example, the proposed design does not account for possible genetic factors with respect to weight.

7 Classics

Astrategy that can contribute a great deal to a more sophisticated understanding of scientific discourse as a cultural phenomenon and promote an ideological scientific literacy is to study some of the scientific research article genre's classics and attempt to determine why these texts command such wide respect. For the same reasons students read primary rhetorical, philosophical, literary, historical, and political texts that significantly impact culture—*De Oratore*, *Discourse on Method*, *Macbeth*, *The Vindication of the Rights of Women*, the Declaration of Independence, *Uncle Tom's Cabin*, the Gettysburg Address, *The Communist Manifesto*, and the Letter from a Birmingham Jail—they should also read science "classics" like Watson and Crick's "A Structure for Deoxyribose Nucleic Acid" and other critically important examples of primary research in science. Like the texts from other disciplines, these scientific discourses have profoundly influenced the material reality in which we live. They should, then, receive the same level of recognition and undergo the same kind of scrutiny that the first group of texts does—and do so in rhetoric and composition courses.

Part of the process should involve questions of why and how the text being studied became part of the scientific canon, following the work of theorists such as Ohmann, who examined the publication and canonization of *Catcher in the Rye*. Scientific discourse that becomes thought of as "classic" often achieves this status because the discourse represents a Kuhnian paradigm shift; so, for example, Watson and Crick's publication of "A Structure for Deoxyribose Nucleic Acid" in 1953 quite literally gave birth, as Halloran puts it, to a brand new field—molecular biology—changing biology from a still largely descriptive science (e.g., botany, wildlife biology) to a primarily experimental science. To be sure, though, some classics—literary or otherwise—are not recognized immediately; in fact, they may be ignored or even scorned when first published. Undoubtedly there exist virtually unknown scientific texts that are potentially important. These texts may languish for many reasons:

they may have been written by people who lack the credentials needed to establish *ethos* in the scientific community, they may have been published in an obscure journal and/or in a language other than English, or they may have involved a scope or methodology considered to be beyond the province of science. As they read a text that has been declared a classic, upon its publication or later, students may wonder what other classics have yet to be discovered.

This chapter seeks to examine a text that is not widely known outside of the field of its publication and yet that contains a potentially important message that should be accorded the same kind of exposure and study as the well-known political and literary texts mentioned above. The pedagogical scenario in this chapter, then, is to work through this text and try to fully understand what is novel about the ideas presented in it, to determine why it is a "classic," to illustrate the effects of the text on culture and identity, and to examine some cultural practices that are associated with the text. As for writing science, students will be asked to propose and support an experiment or idea that would represent a paradigm shift similar to the one this "classic" article articulates—to think outside the box.

Reading and Discussing an Environmental Science Classic

Science classics have undergone extensive rhetorical analyses in the rhetoric of science literature; for this reason, they are excellent candidates for study in a rhetoric and science classroom. However, in this chapter, recognizing the immensely valuable efforts to expand and complicate all types of canons, I want to present a work that has not achieved quite the same level of fame (and, hence, rhetorical scrutiny) as the classics mentioned above or the famous papers published in *A Century of* Nature (see chapter 5). The work is "The Strategy of Ecosystem Development," by Eugene P. Odum, who held an endowed chair at the University of Georgia, founded the Institute of Ecology, and helped to establish the contemporary environmental movement and refute the exemptionalist paradigm referred to in chapter 4. Published in *Science* in 1969, "The Strategy of Ecosystem Development" has, over time, earned something of a reputation as a minor classic, especially in environmental studies and ecology communities. It has been reprinted in at least two collections of foundationally important texts in environmental studies: *Classics in Environmental Studies* and *Foundations of Ecology*.

"The Strategy of Ecosystem Development" presents "ecosystem" as a legitimate unit of analysis, proposes a model of ecosystem aging and rejuvenation by examining factors that influence the rise, reign, and fall of ecosystems, and attempts to demonstrate the impact of humankind on the life cycle of ecosystems. As students read and discuss this article, at least four issues can be considered. First, like many other scientific classics, "The Strategy of Ecosystem Development" complicates the IMRAD genre to an extent: it doesn't adhere to the IMRAD organizational scheme too closely. Paradoxically, then, some of the genre's classics are texts that break some of the genre's most basic rules. Although based on a great deal of previous scientific research like a typical scientific research report, the article was originally presented as a speech in, presumably, a much more condensed form at the 1966 Ecological Society of America meeting at the University of Maryland; Odum was president of the organization when he gave the speech. Unlike a typical IMRAD article, this text does not contain a literature review at its beginning; instead, references are scattered fairly evenly throughout the text. Additionally, the article contains no easily discernable Methods, Results, and Discussion sections.

Second, the article represents a good choice for analysis because it clearly articulates inextricable links among science, nature, and human society; indeed, a subtitle-like sentence (which, interestingly, takes the place of an abstract) below the title of the article states that "An understanding of ecological succession provides a basis for resolving man's conflict with nature" (Odum 262). In looking at human society, Odum focuses on links to the political process especially. Seeing these links, students will then be better prepared to establish them in scientific texts in which the connections are less apparent or even suppressed.

Third, the text demonstrates the epistemological potential of writing in a scientific context: in a manner similar to that of Lavoisier, who in the course of drafting and revising his eighteenth-century reports finally got the mechanism of respiration right (Holmes 220–35), Odum writes to come to a more complex understanding of ecosystem development. His tone is highly speculative and informal and at times apocalyptic—again, all anomalies in scientific discourse. Words and phrases like "perhaps," "theoretically," "so far as I know," "believe," and "may be presumed" are sprinkled liberally throughout the article, and Odum uses exclamation points, engages in hyperbole, and even asks a rhetorical question at one point.

Fourth, and finally, closely associated with the speculative tone of "The Strategy of Ecosystem Development" is an attempt to frame an entirely new research agenda for ecologists and not just settle for the infinitesimal step forward that is typical of Kuhn's normal, puzzle-solving science. At least two avenues are pursued here. First, Odum wants ecologists to look at entire ecosystems, not just small portions of them. Second, Odum wants ecologists to take advantage of research and techniques in other areas of biology, especially experimental branches like molecular biology and genetics, to better understand ecosystem development.

The beginning of the article establishes the importance of the topic to humanity and makes observations about the contemporary state of scholarship in ecology:

> The principles of ecological succession bear importantly on the relationships between man and nature. . . . Most ideas pertaining to the development of ecological systems are based on descriptive data obtained by observing changes in biotic communities over long periods, or on highly theoretical assumptions; very few of the generally accepted hypotheses have been tested experimentally. Some of the confusion, vagueness, and lack of experimental work in this area stems from the tendency of ecologists to regard "succession" as a single straightforward idea; in actual fact, it entails an interacting complex of processes, some of which counteract one another. (Odum 262)

At this point, in the late 1960s, much of biology was still a field science that relied on observation. Odum recognized that much of the scientific community, especially chemistry and physics, instead used methodologies that relied much more on experiment—a conscious construction of an environment and manipulation of variables within that environment—rather than simply observe phenomena. Odum correctly surmised that biology would also need to head in this direction.

Students may start to recognize some of the elements that set this article apart and establish its status. First, unusually for a biological science outside medicine or physiology, the article establishes a direct link between humanity and physical reality; in fact, as demonstrated throughout the paper, humanity is an integral part of the world's ecology and cannot escape the responsibilities and consequences pertaining thereto. Indeed, as soon as the second paragraph in the article, Odum writes "As viewed here, ecological succession involves the development of ecosystems; it has many parallels in the developmental biology of organisms, and also in the development of human society" (262). Such an idea—that humanity is inextricably tied to the laws of nature, not above them—was still relatively new for American culture in 1969; *Silent Spring* had just been published a few years before, and pollution control legislation was just getting off the ground. Second, Odum discusses what he sees as methodological and conceptual shortcomings in ecology; these problems are, presumably, going to be addressed in the article. Indeed, toward the end of the introduction, Odum announces his purpose directly: "It is the purpose of this article to summarize, in the form of a tabular model [see table 1], components and stages of development at the ecosystem level as a means of emphasizing those aspects of ecological succession that can be accepted on the basis of present knowledge, those that require more study, and those that have special relevance to human ecology" (262). The use of the verb "summarize" indicates that this article will tend to look more like a review than it does an original research article; thus, students may question why this article is so important since it does not appear to break any new ground. An answer to such an inquiry could be the following: Odum is working at the "ecosystem level" and not at a simpler level (e.g., just trees, just streams, or just wildlife). No one had done that before. An ecosystem, according to Odum, "is considered to be a unit of biological organization made up of all of the organisms in a given area (that is, 'community') interacting with the physical environment so that a flow of energy leads to characteristic trophic [i.e., related to nutrition] structure and material cycles within the system" (262). In a sense, then, Odum is defining an entirely new biological unit of study and implying that previous work in ecology has been too fragmented; he implies that researchers have not been able to obtain accurate results or draw correct conclusions because of this fragmentation. Thus, Odum presents a new research agenda for ecological research.

Odum explains his concept of ecological succession, or development, in terms of three parameters:

> (i) It is an orderly process of community development that is reasonably directional and, therefore, predictable. (ii) It results from modification of the physical environment by the community; that is, succession is community-controlled even though the physical environment determines the pattern, the rate of change, and often sets limits as to how far development can go. (iii) It culminates in a stabilized ecosystem in which maximum biomass (or high information content) and symbiotic function between organisms are maintained per unit of available energy flow . . . [i.e.,] increased control of, or homeostasis with, the physical environment in the sense of achieving maximum protection from its perturbations. (262)

He also continues to link the issue of ecological succession to humanity, saying that an ecosystem's goal of "maximum protection" can conflict directly with humanity's goal of "maximum production" (262–63).

Table 1. A tabular model of ecological succession: trends to be expected in the development of ecosystems.

Ecosystem attributes	Developmental stages	Mature stages
Community energetics		
1. Gross production/community respiration (P/R ratio)	Greater or less than 1	Approaches 1
2. Gross production/standing crop biomass (P/B ratio)	High	Low
3. Biomass supported/unit energy flow (B/E ratio)	Low	High
4. Net community production (yield)	High	Low
5. Food chains	Linear, predominantly grazing	Weblike, predominantly detritus
Community structure		
6. Total organic matter	Small	Large
7. Inorganic nutrients	Extrabiotic	Intrabiotic
8. Species diversity—variety component	Low	High
9. Species diversity—equitability component	Low	High
10. Biochemical diversity	Low	High
11. Stratification and spatial heterogeneity (pattern diversity)	Poorly organized	Well-organized
Life history		
12. Niche specialization	Broad	Narrow
13. Size of organism	Small	Large
14. Life cycles	Short, simple	Long, complex
Nutrient cycling		
15. Mineral cycles	Open	Closed
16. Nutrient exchange rate, between organisms and environment	Rapid	Slow
17. Role of detritus in nutrient regeneration	Unimportant	Important
Selection pressure		
18. Growth form	For rapid growth ("*r*-selection")	For feedback control ("*K*-selection")
19. Production	Quantity	Quality
Overall homeostasis		
20. Internal symbiosis	Undeveloped	Developed
21. Nutrient conservation	Poor	Good
22. Stability (resistance to external perturbations)	Poor	Good
23. Entropy	High	Low
24. Information	Low	High

Table 1. Odum's tabular model of ecological succession showing six categories of variables (i.e., "attributes") in young (i.e., developmental) and mature ecosystems. From Odum, Eugene P. "The Strategy of Ecosystem Development." *Science* 164 (1969): 262–70. Reprinted with permission from AAAS.

Odum then explains the bioenergetics of ecosystem development by examining the ratio of total photosynthesis (P, energy production) to community respiration (R, energy consumption). In young ecosystems, this ratio is greater than 1; that is, photosynthesis produces more energy than is used by the community (the "biomass," B, which is small at this point). As the ecosystem matures, succession occurs, and the ratio approaches 1: the rates of production and consumption equalize into a steady state equilibrium. Additionally, as the ecosystem matures, the biomass increases. As Odum describes the process, "Theoretically, then, the amount of standing-crop biomass supported by the available energy flow (E) increases to a maximum in the mature or climax stages" (263).

In the next section of the article, Odum compares bioenergetics data collected from a laboratory-constructed, 100-day aquatic microecosystem to that from a hypothetical 100-year forest ecosystem. He concludes that the succession that occurs in both follows a similar trajectory, one that leads to a high-biomass, low-production ecosystem (see fig. 1). Odum concedes that generalizability of laboratory-produced data may be problematic but insists that the comparison cannot be ignored: "While direct projection from the small laboratory microsystem to open nature may not be entirely valid, there is evidence that the same basic trends that are seen in the laboratory are characteristic of succession on land and in large bodies of water" (263).

Next, Odum moves from bioenergetics to community structure and describes the changes in food chains that occur as an ecosystem matures. The chain is "simple and linear in the very early stages of succession, as a consequence of low diversity" (264). The chain takes the form of plant–herbivore–carnivore. Later, however, "food chains become complex webs in mature [ecosystem] stages, with the bulk of biological energy flow following detritus [i.e., loose organic matter that results from disintegration] pathways" (Odum 264); mechanisms such as "the development of indigestible supporting tissues (cellulose, lignin, and so on), feedback control between plants and herbivores . . . , and increasing predatory pressure on herbivores" help the ecosystem maintain a more complex and diverse biomass. These mechanisms, Odum contends, have not been investigated. The effects, though, are clear: less grazing occurs in these later ecosystem stages, and the effects of the physical environment, while never unimportant, are mitigated to a degree. With respect to humanity's impact on such complex webs and mechanisms, Odum states that "Severe stress or rapid changes brought about by outside forces can, of course, rob the system of these protective mechanisms and allow irruptive, can-

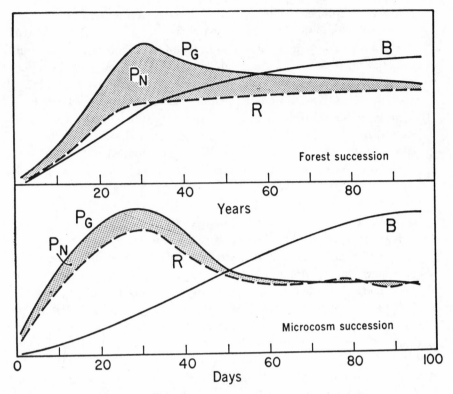

Figure 1. Odum's comparison of changing bioenergetics from a laboratory-constructed, 100-day aquatic microecosystem (i.e., microcosm) and a hypothetical, 100-year forest ecosystem. P_G is gross production, P_N is net production, R is total community respiration, and B is total biomass. From Odum, Eugene P. "The Strategy of Ecosystem Development." *Science* 164 (1969): 262–70. Reprinted with permission from AAAS.

cerous growths of certain species to occur, as man too often finds to his sorrow" (264).

Odum then moves on to address what he calls the most controversial issue in ecosystem development: diversity. After comparing several different diversity indices and critiquing a commonly used one, Odum suggests that "While an increase in the variety of species together with reduced dominance by any one species or small group of species (that is, increased evenness) can be accepted as a general probability during succession . . . , there are other community changes that may work against these trends" (264). These changes include "an increase in the size of organisms, an increase in the length and complexity of life histories, and an increase in interspecific competition that may result in competitive exclusion of species" (264). Odum says that little research has been done at the ecosystem level on the variety of species in a given community; he again mentions what he sees as the too-narrow focus of current ecological research, saying "Data are so far available for segments of the community (trees, birds, and so on)" (265). Additionally, Odum asserts that little work has been done on the above-mentioned changes or on other changes that can occur, such as an increase in "biochemical diversity" (264). Biochemical diversity was a brand new idea for ecologists in 1969; they were used to operating in the field, not the laboratory. Finally, Odum calls for the cause-and-effect relationship between diversity and stability of an ecosystem to be "investigated from many angles" (265).

The heart of Odum's analysis of diversity, though, is whether it is desirable ecologically. Odum leans toward the affirmative, saying, "It seems safe to say that, as succession progresses, organic extrametabolites probably serve increasing important functions as regulators which stabilize the growth and composition of the ecosystem. Such metabolites may, in fact, be extremely important in preventing populations from overshooting the equilibrial density. . . . If it can be shown that biotic diversity does indeed enhance physical stability in the ecosystem, or is the result of it, then we would have an important guide for conservation practice" (265). Given the extent to which humanity is subject to the laws of nature, then, it should not escape our attention that diversity might be a biological as well as a moral imperative. Indeed, at the end of the section, although not addressing human diversity directly, Odum nonetheless asks rhetorically, "Is variety only the spice of life, or is it a necessity for the long life of the total ecosystem comprising man and nature?" (265).

At this point, students may ask questions about the current state of world, national, or local biodiversity. Connections could be made to issues of animals on the brink of extinction and those that have been saved from this fate, arguments for and against endangered species laws, poaching, and introduction of non-native insect or animal species in an effort to solve a local agricultural or livestock problem. Related to this last issue is the extent to which biodiversity can be "managed" by human beings. Finally, a potentially fascinating idea to discuss is human diversity. One need look no farther than Native Americans' first contact with European explorers and settlers to understand the devastating consequences of lack of exposure to other cultures' pathogens. The smallpox virus and other diseases that Europeans brought to the Americas killed millions of Native Americans even before they had cast eyes on a European.

The next ecological succession factor that Odum addresses is nutrient cycling; nutrients that are analyzed include nitrogen, phosphorous, and calcium. Here, Odum concludes that "Mature systems, as compared to developing ones, have a greater capacity to entrap and hold nutrients for cycling within the system." He suggests that nutrient cycling also varies considerably according to geography: "Theoretically, as one goes equatorward, a larger percentage of the available nutrient pool is tied up in the biomass and a corresponding lower percentage is in the soil or sediment. This theory, however, needs testing, since data to show such a geographical trend are incomplete. It is perhaps significant that conventional North Temperate row-type agriculture, which represents a very youthful type of ecosystem, is successful in the humid tropics only if carried out in a system of 'shifting agriculture,' in which the crops alternate with periods of natural vegetative redevelopment" (265). Odum ends the section by noting that rice paddies provide "much better nutrient retention" in these areas (265).

Selection pressure is the last issue Odum considers; it refers to environmental pressures that have significant influence on which species flourish in a given ecosystem. In young ecosystems, Odum says, conditions are uncrowded; thus, "Species with high rates of reproduction and growth . . . are more likely to survive" (266). In contrast, in more crowded, mature ecosystems, species with "better capabilities for competitive survival" dominate, even if they have a "lower growth potential" than the fast-multiplying species that do well in earlier stages. Odum then considers the impact of genetic changes on selection pressure, again drawing the attention of ecologists to molecular biology and genetics. He notes that "in most well-studied seres [a series of sequential ecosystems], there seem to be a few early successional species that are able to persist through to late stages. Whether genetic changes contribute to adaptation in such species has not been determined, so far as I know . . ." (266). (In asking these questions, Odum brings up several of the points that Gould will discuss twenty years later in *Wonderful Life*. See chapter 5.) As in many of the other sections of his article, Odum does not move on before connecting this issue to humanity, and in this instance, he drops the speculative tone in favor of a much more urgent and somewhat apocalyptic one, saying "Certainly, the human population, if it survives beyond its present rapid growth stage, is destined to be more and more affected by such selection pressures as adaptation to crowding becomes essential" (266). Students may consider that in 1969, the world population was less than 4 billion; in 2006, it was 6.5 billion—an increase of over 50 percent.

Summarizing his position on ecosystem succession toward the end of the article, Odum states, "While one may question whether all the trends described are characteristic of all types of ecosystems, there can be little doubt that the net result of community actions is symbiosis, nutrient conservation, stability, a decrease in entropy, and an increase in information. . . . The overall strategy is . . . directed toward achieving as large and diverse an organic structure as is possible within the limits set by the available energy input and the prevailing physical conditions of existence (soil, water, climate, and so on)" (266). Even the summary, though, ends speculatively: "The intriguing question is," Odum ponders, "Do mature ecosystems age, as organisms do? In other words, after a long period of relative stability or 'adulthood,' do ecosystems again develop unbalanced metabolism and become more vulnerable to diseases and other perturbations?" (266). The question challenges fundamental assumptions, such as the one that ecosystems are essentially cyclical: in a forest, for example, trees grow old and die or are destroyed by fire, and new trees take their place—or so we think.

Until this point in the article, Odum has linked his ideas of ecological succession to humanity clearly but briefly. Now, however, Odum devotes an entire section of the article to "Relevance of Ecosystem Development Theory to Human Ecology" (266). Odum's goal in this section is to illustrate a direct conflict between the goals of humanity, as he sees them, and the goals of nature as manifested by ecological succession. According to Odum, humanity tends to regard nature as a site of production, and its goal is to maximize that production per unit area—a "high P/B efficiency" (266) in which energy production is quite high relative to total biomass. Nature, on the other hand, if Odum is right about ecological succession, moves in the opposite direction, toward a high B/P ratio. In other words, biomass is high, but energy production is low in a mature ecosystem. Odum makes the point that high biomass/low energy production ecosystems are also vital to humanity's survival, however, saying "man does not live by food and fiber alone; he also needs a balanced CO_2–O_2 atmosphere, the climatic buffer provided by oceans and masses of vegetation, and clean (that is, unproductive) water" (266); these necessities are best provided by mature ecosystems that have not been altered by humanity to achieve high production. He adds, "Many essential life-cycle resources, not to mention recreational and esthetic needs, are best provided man by the less 'productive' landscapes. . . . The landscape is not just a supply depot but is also the *oikos*—the home—in which we must live" (266).

Odum maintains that ecosystem life-cycle processes, such as the consumption of carbon dioxide by plants and the subsequent release of oxygen via photosynthesis, have been "more or less taken for granted" (266) but can no longer be ignored because humanity has reached a point in terms of sheer numbers and influence at which it can interfere—by chance or design—with these processes to its peril. New research must be conducted, Odum argues, that recognizes the distinctiveness of ecosystems and assumes humanity to be "a part of, not apart from, the environment" (266). He sees a major shift in terms of the environmental effects of materialism from earlier centuries, when humanity had very little, to the present, when humanity has too much, and research must determine when too much of something threatens our well being. For example, Odum says, "concrete is a 'good thing,' but not if half the world is covered with it. Insecticides are 'good things,' but not when used as, they are now, in an indiscriminate and wholesale manner. Likewise, water impoundments have proved to be very useful man-made additions to the landscape, but obviously we don't want the whole country inundated! Vast man-made lakes solve some problems, at least temporarily, but yield comparative little food or fiber, and, because of high evaporative losses, they may not even be the best device for storing water; it might better be stored in the watershed, or underground in aquifers" (267). Odum then singles out dams for a more focused critique.[1]

At this point, perhaps taking advantage of his proximity to Washington, D.C., where he presented this text as a speech, Odum goes beyond a research agenda to discuss institutional and government action that he thinks needs to be taken. This move can be seen as yet another way in which Odum attempts to link the science he discusses to humanity directly. Of government, Odum remarks that it is "so fragmented and limited in systems-analysis capabilities that there is no effective mechanism whereby negative feedback signals can be received and acted on before there is a serious overshoot" (267). Odum calls for government to take more interest in and control of the environment; he also suggests that nongovernmental organizations, such as those associated with the soil conservation movement, become more active (267).

Odum spends the rest of the article proposing two solutions to the conflict between humanity and nature that would, in his estimation, create a win-win situation. These solutions should, he states, be used in landscape planning and wilderness management. The first solution, pulse stability, involves wide-scale moderation: the goal is "to provide moderate quality and moderate yield on all the landscape" (267). Pulse stability can be achieved by periodically using an "acute physical perturbation" to keep the ecosystem in a middle state between youth and maturity. A process like this one occurs naturally in many ecosystems—the Everglades, for example. There, seasonal changes in water levels, as well as occasional forest fires, maintain the balance that this ecosystem needs to stay healthy. Odum notes that humanity already utilizes these techniques: "Alternate filling and draining of ponds has been a standard procedure in the fish culture for centuries in Europe and the Orient. . . . Rice culture is another example. The rice paddy is thus the cultivated analogue of the natural marsh or the intertidal ecosystem" (268). As for fire, Odum observes that humanity "uses fire deliberately to . . . set back succession to some desired point" (268). He cautions that many of humanity's interventions with respect to pulse stability are "too sudden, too violent, or too arrhythmic for adaptation to occur at the ecosystem level, so severe oscillation rather than stability results" (268). Greater care must be taken, and ecologists must work within an ecosystem's parameters rather than trying to completely recreate the ecosystem.

Another aspect of pulse stability that should be pursued, says Odum, is detritus agriculture. Detritus agriculture can be practiced with both crops and fisheries and involves the cultivation of plants and fish that do not attract predators or disease, both of which must be fought by chemical means (e.g., insecticides) that end up poisoning the food and the environment. Detritus agriculture does not provide as high of a yield in the short term as traditional agriculture, but its long-term protection of the environment makes up for any initial disadvantage. Odum notes that detritus agricultural practices are already in use in the "production of silage by fermentation of low-grade fodder" and in Asian fish cultures (268).

The second solution that Odum proposes is compartmentalization. In this model, young, high-production ecosystems and mature, high-biomass ecosystems in a given area are established separately, but the overall desired balance is maintained in the area as a whole. In practice, the entire area would actually consist of four types of ecosystem compartments: the high-production and high-biomass compartments mentioned already, a compromise middle-stage compartment as explained above in the pulse stability section, and an urban–industrial compartment (Odum 268). Parameters such as size and capacity would be continually adjusted in the compartments to assure the health of the entire area; such adjustment could be achieved with zoning. However, says Odum, current zoning practices are inadequate: "While the principle of zoning in cities is universally accepted, the procedures now followed do not work very well because zoning restrictions are too easily overturned by short-term economic and population pressures. Zoning the landscape would require a whole new order of thinking. Greater use of legal measures providing for tax relief, restrictions on use, scenic easements, and public ownership will be required if appreciable land and water areas are to be held in the 'protective' categories" (268–69). This new form of zoning should not be restricted to land, says Odum. The oceans should be permanently protected areas because of their role as the "biosphere's governor. . . . Eutrophication [i.e., the process by which a body of water becomes nutrient rich but oxygen poor] of the ocean in a last-ditch effort to feed the populations of the land could well have an adverse effect on the oxygen reservoir in the atmosphere" (269).

At the conclusion of the article, Odum attempts to accomplish three things: first, he again looks outside of science to other areas—law and education, in this instance—for help in saving the environment. He says: "I urge law schools to establish departments . . . of 'landscape law' and to start training 'landscape lawyers' who will be capable not only of clarifying existing procedures but also of drawing up new enabling legislation" (269). Odum's name—landscape law—didn't stick, but his idea certainly has: environmental law is now well established at many law schools. Of education, Odum contends that it, "as always, must play a role in increasing man's awareness of his dependence on the natural environment. Perhaps we need to start teaching the principles of ecosystem in the third grade" (269). Indeed, environmental studies has become an established part of curricula at all levels of education. The second task Odum tries to complete is to reestablish a sense of urgency without sounding alarmist.[2] He again uses a measured yet urgent tone to reinforce the urgency of land and water conservation, but this time he adds an economic metaphor. He states "Until we can determine more precisely how far we may safely go in expanding intensive agriculture and urban sprawl[3] at the expense of the protective landscape, it will be good insurance to hold inviolate as much of the latter as possible. Thus, the preservation of natural areas is not a peripheral luxury for society but a capital investment from which we expect to draw interest" (269). The third task Odum endeavors to accomplish is to cement the link between nature and humanity. He points out to his readers that restrictions on land use are an "analogue of a natural behavioral control mechanism known as 'territoriality' by which many species of animals avoid crowding and social stress" (269). In this vein, Odum's final paragraph is worth quoting in its entirety:

It goes without saying that the tabular model for ecosystem development which I have presented here has many parallels in the development of human society itself. In the pioneer society, as in the pioneer ecosystem, high birth rates, rapid growth, high economic profits, and exploitation of accessible and unused resources are advantageous, but, as the saturation level is approached, these drives must be shifted to considerations of symbiosis (that is, "civil rights," "law and order," "education," and "culture"), birth control, and the recycling of resources. A balance between youth and maturity in the socio-environmental system is, therefore, the really basic goal that must be achieved if man as a species is to successfully pass through the present rapid-growth state, to which he is clearly well adapted, to the ultimate equilibrium-density stage, of which he as yet shows little understanding and to which he now shows little tendency to adapt. (269)

In this paragraph, Odum abandons the less formal tone used in earlier sections of the article, preferring instead third person, declarative sentences, and a more demanding tone (e.g., with the use of "must") and avoiding hedges and exclamation points. Additionally, he sounds a warning for the final time by questioning whether humanity will ultimately survive; his assertion that we are unlikely to adapt seems to indicate that Odum is pessimistic about our chances.

Cultural Context of Population Control and Zoning

The implications of Odum's article are substantial, and a large number of cultural issues can be considered in addition to the close analysis of the text itself. Among these issues is overpopulation because, given Odum's arguments, it is quite possible that humankind's growth will draw the conflict between human beings and their wants and the ability of the earth's environment to sustain these desires to a head. Students may want to discuss why birth rates are low and still falling in the North American, European, and Asian/Pacific industrialized countries as compared to countries in other parts of the world. They may want to investigate United Nations sustainable population movements or even ZeroGrowth, an American organization that seeks to stop increases in population and resource utilization. Additionally, in terms of resources, they could look into the economic development plan of a state, region, or country to assess its impact on the environment. For example, China hopes to quadruple its economy by 2020, an ambitious plan that Klaus Toepfer, head of the United

Nations Environmental Program, contends is environmentally disastrous. According to a CNN report on the matter, "if China had the same density of private cars as, for example, Germany, it would have to produce 650 million vehicles—a target that environmentalists say the world's supply of metal and oil would be unable to sustain" ("U.N. Official"). Also, says Toepfer according to the CNN report, China's growth plans "can only occur if developed nations radically change their consumption habits to free up scarce resources for the world's poor" ("U.N. Official").

As this topic relates to Odum's article, students may want to debate a tension that crops up in the text. That tension is the extent to which human population, like plant and animal populations, is subject to the physical limitations of a given ecosystem (i.e., environmental determinism)—one of Odum's foundational assumptions. What is distinctive about the assumption with respect to Odum's text is that this assumption is associated with issues that are among the most fundamentally basic of humankind's day-to-day activities. Unlike the spraying of DDT, for example, an absolute poison as Carson so eloquently demonstrated in *Silent Spring*, the activities that Odum discusses—reproduction, farming, storing water for drinking, and building shelter—are vital to the survival of humanity. What a paradox it is that these very activities may also in fact doom the race!

Students may also want to investigate zoning; this issue lends itself to local or even institutional inquiry if, like mine, the students' institution is expanding and seeks zoning approvals or exemptions. Students could, for example, procure a copy of local zoning rules and determine to what extent these rules are relaxed and for what reasons. Additionally, the practice of zoning itself could be called into question; does it promote or hinder environmental protection? In the United States, strict separation of residential and commercial districts forces people to drive because most municipalities do not have good public transportation; thus, air pollution is a consequence. Cities like Santa Monica, California, have attempted to address this problem by providing for some limited commercial use in primarily residential districts. According to one Santa Monica planning document that defines this type of combination-use area, "The C2 District is intended to protect and enhance neighborhood commercial areas by promoting the concentration of businesses that provide convenience goods and services used frequently by local residents. This District provides for a scale and character of development that is consistent with pedestrian-orientation and which tends to attract and promote a walk-in clientele. Development within this District should maximize human scale elements while providing a sensitive transition between these uses and neighboring residences, including the provision of adequate and properly sited parking facilities" (*Santa-monica.org*). This particular policy is quite progressive, but even now, it is still a long way from what Odum envisioned in the late 1960s. For example, only one of the many types of zoning districts in the Santa Monica regulations deals with parks, and it is not nearly as specific as many of the other zoning ordinances are. However, according to Odum, we should be zoning undeveloped land just as carefully as developed land, and we need to preserve undeveloped land at all costs. Finally, students could try to flesh out additional zoning implications of Odum's article. For example, are residences included in Odum's urban-industrial compartment and not in other compartments? And what would the zoning of the ocean look like?

A third area that students might look into is the successes and failures with regard to humanity's attempts to manage the environment. Odum essentially likens humanity's actions to those of a bull in a china shop when it comes to environmental intervention: clumsy, violent, and destructive. Students may look into local sites such as parks, artificial lakes, dams, and wildlife refuges as well as investigate local initiatives such as land conservation, tree planting, recycling, insect and weed control, and pollution control efforts and determine the goals and results of these endeavors. A dam, for example, may be erected to provide a recreational boating and fishing area. Is this area in fact used for such purposes? To what extent? Are there conflicts between power boaters, sailors, and jet skiers? What are the environmental consequences of the dam on land, plants and trees, wildlife, air, and waterways? In other words, what would the site look like had the dam not been built? What kinds of different activities could have taken place in the area?

Finally, students may want to consider, more broadly, how the science discussed in Odum's article differs from traditional Western science. It is, for example, much more situational than traditional Western science in its discussion of many different kinds of ecosystems. Although not directly stated, Odum strongly implies that a huge variety of ecosystems exist on the basis of geography, topography, and biology. Second, Odum's characterization of ecosystems reveals them to be incredibly complex webs of interrelationships, not easy-to-understand, linear cause-and-effect entities. In effect, then, Odum's science is much more holistic and chaotic than traditional Western science, and it acts as a harbinger of the postmodern science movements (e.g., chaos theory, string theory) that enjoy increasing recognition and popularity in the early twenty-first century.

Writing Science about the Evolution of a Scientific Community

For the past several semesters, I have asked students in my first-year composition course to write what I call a Crystal Ball paper. For this assignment, I ask my students to identify and explore what they see as the most significant scientific or technological achievement of the next twenty years and to include a discussion of the implications of this achievement on humanity in terms of daily life, law, education, religion, and the like. For a course that I am envisioning that investigates science more closely, students would write a similar kind of text, but one that focuses more on proposing a new research agenda for a specific scientific community. To this end, students would, like Odum, list and discuss what they see as topical or methodological shortcomings in the community, outline a research agenda, and establish links between the science, the object of inquiry, and human culture. The students may consider, like Odum, adopting a speculative tone while at the same time attempting to convey a sense of urgency, especially with respect to issues that society must consider in light of the changes that are occurring in the scientific community under study.

An assignment such as this one stretches students' imaginations and can be fun and challenging to write. For example, a student may choose to write about the physical science of acoustics. Upon researching this subject, the student would learn that scientists in this field concentrate on the following topics:

- What sound is
- How sound moves, and other properties
- Why sounds feel different in different rooms
- How sounds are produced by different instruments
- How to soundproof rooms
- How to protect your ears from damage (Doyle)

The student may also discover that acoustical research focuses almost exclusively on indoor environments such as concert halls and stadiums, where many types of performances that must consider sound production are put on. Perhaps fresh from a summer landscaping job, the student may argue that acoustics needs to turn its attention to the outdoors. The student has been subjected to a cacophony of lawn mowers, weed whackers, hedge trimmers, leaf blowers, lawn edgers, and chainsaws for several months, and wonders if this could have caused hearing damage. The student proposes that acoustic scientists establish a new research agenda that investigates the amount of noise produced by lawn and garden equipment and ways that this noise can be minimized.

Even indoors, the traditional focus of acoustic science, a student who is perhaps a musician could attempt to move the field in a new direction. Because acoustical science puts a great deal of effort into measuring transmission, frequency, amplitude, direction, absorption, reflection, and duration of sound waves, the field could benefit from studying the interaction of sound waves and the surfaces they hit. Doing this would require interdisciplinary work; the student could suggest that acoustical scientists join forces with materials scientists, who study the surface properties of materials; in this way, acoustical scientists could gain a more complex understanding—at the molecular level—of what happens when various kinds of sound waves hit the surfaces of different kinds of materials. All of this work could be made urgent, for example, if the community in which the student lives or the college or university the student attends is planning to build a new concert hall or other type of performing arts space.

An interesting variation on this assignment would be to ask students to propose an entirely new branch of science instead of arguing for a new direction in an existing science. For such a paper, the student would need to name the science, demarcate its basic realm of inquiry, explain its methodology and tools, and justify its importance. The science could be a new branch of an existing social, physical, or biological science, it could be a new interdisciplinary science, or it could be a new science altogether. For example, a student could propose a new branch of physics called ethnoastronomy. In this field, scientists would investigate and test explanations for astronomical phenomena from non-Western cultures. Such research is important because these explanations may hold clues to astronomical phenomena that Western astronomers have not considered. In a manner similar to ethnobotanists, who study non-Western, plant-based medicinal treatments for illnesses, ethnoastronomers would spend time with members of non-Western cultures to learn their cosmological tradition (much of it oral, not written); the different perspectives on the development and operations of the earth, solar system, galaxy, and beyond offered by non-Western cultures may provide a wealth of ideas for the ethnoastronomers to ponder. The student may note that, unlike the social and biological sciences, which have steadily increased their incorporation of non-Western ideas in recent decades, physics remains a staunchly Western discipline. Explanations of astronomical phenomena from non-Western cultures, as well as the many sophisticated ancient cultures, are indeed studied, but as folklore, not as science.

8 You Are What Science Says You Are

One of the most effective and immediate ways for students to learn how science constructs individual identity is for them to study what science says about them in particular. For this purpose, social science studies of college students can demonstrate what kinds of questions are being asked and what kinds of conclusions are being drawn about them—not about distant galaxies, subatomic particles, or Antarctic lichens, but *them*. In this way, students can begin to understand that their identities are not only shaped by popular culture, education, law, religion, and other cultural institutions, but by science as well.

Students may be surprised to find out that they are indeed the subject of *scientific* study that is unrelated to marketing or educational assessment, and this discovery may motivate them to attempt to discern the cultural and ideological assumptions that underlie the research. A good place to find science-based characterizations of college students is in the college student health field. Almost all U.S. colleges and universities employ health care providers and counselors for their students. These professionals work with college and university students on a daily (and sometimes nightly) basis and perform a great deal of interesting research with this population. One of the leading journals in the field is the *Journal of American College Health*. The January 2003 issue of this journal contained a study entitled "Self-Reported Drinking-game Participation of Incoming College Students" by Borsari, Bergen-Cico, and Carey; this study is exactly the type of analysis that draws conclusions about the students who populate our writing courses, conclusions that can impact them in profound ways. The study appeals especially to students in first-year writing courses, since the population being studied in the analysis is incoming college students.

Reading and Discussing Science about Drinking Games

Students would be asked to read the relatively straightforward and short (five-page) study, perhaps with a suggestion that they read the textual content as critically as possible and not get too bogged down with the statistics (there are not many) that occasionally crop up in the study. Essentially, the study examines experience with, motivations for, and predictors of drinking game participation among incoming college students. At the beginning of the article, Borsari and his coauthors provide some background material pertaining to drinking games, noting that they "have a history dating from the fifth century B.C." (149), introduce some slang terms such as "slamming" drinks (i.e., drinking very quickly), and explain why drinking games are popular. The four motives for participating in drinking games listed by Borsari et al. are purported "social advantages, such as lowering inhibitions and facilitating friendship and camaraderie" (149), getting drunk quickly, attempting to get others drunk, and competing (149). The next part of the introduction establishes a link between frequent participation in drinking games and alcohol-related health problems; the authors conduct a literature review and conclude that "drinking-game participation appeared to contribute uniquely to students' increased risk for alcohol-related problems, especially if the participants drank heavily during the games" (150). In the remainder of the introduction, Borsari et al. establish the gap that their research attempts to address: whether incoming U.S. college students have been exposed to and participated in drinking games *before* matriculating. The authors note that all studies of U.S. students and drinking games conducted previous to the publication of their work had included only college students and that their study may have implications for the design and implementation of educational sessions on the risks of drinking game participation that would be held during orientation programs for incoming college freshmen.

To conduct their study, Borsari et al., over three consecutive summers, anonymously surveyed three cohorts of incoming first-year students who attended voluntary university orientation programs. Each cohort "represented approximately 20% of the incoming [freshmen] class" (150), and the researchers obtained informed consent from the student participants, as well as parental permission for the students who were under eighteen years of age (150, 151). All incoming students were informed of the study at a mandatory assembly during the orientation; at this assembly, the researchers asked for volunteers to participate. The authors created a measure called the "College-Bound Student Health Risk Behavior Survey" to use for the study. The two questions specific to drinking games were the following:

- Participation in drinking games (at least 1 time per week; 1–3 times per month; once per year or less).

- Reasons for playing drinking games (to get drunk, to meet other people, to control others, or to get someone else drunk). Borsari et al. 150)

The final sample size was 1,041 students, or 77% of the original cohort (Borsari et al. 151).

Results indicated that 63% of the students had "played drinking games in their lifetimes" and of these 792 students, "20% reported playing once a week, 47% once or twice a month, and 33% less than once a year" (Borsari et al. 151). The motives associated with drinking game participation in order of priority were "to get drunk quickly" (55%), "to socialize and meet people" (53%), and "to control others or get someone else drunk" (21%) These percentages were consistent across gender lines (Borsari et al. 151).

The article next presents predictors of drinking game participation, which were determined by answers to other questions in the survey instrument that sought demographic information or data concerning alcohol and drug use. The results were calculated as odds ratios (ORs). The first statistically significant predictor that Borsari et al. list is gender; the researchers state that "men were half as likely (OR = 0.52) as women to report participating in drinking games" (151). They quickly qualify this finding, however, indicating that "this counterintuitive finding appeared to be an artifact of excluding participants with incomplete data" (Borsari et al. 151), most of whom were men. Once those participants with incomplete data were considered, the difference between the genders was less pronounced; the OR of men to women was 0.77 (Borsari et al. 151). Other statistically significant predictors were, as shown below, related to age of first alcohol consumption, binge drinking, frequency of alcohol consumption, and marijuana use:

- Age: "Students who started to drink between the ages of 13 and 15 years were nearly 3 times as likely (OR = 2.79) to play drinking games as students who started to drink after the age of 16" (Borsari et al. 151).
- Binge drinking: "Those respondents who binged 1 to 3 times in the past month were 4 times as likely (OR = 4.0) to have played drinking games as those who reported no binge episodes . . . students who binged 4 or more times were nearly 12 times as likely as moderate drinkers to have played drinking games (ORs of 11.43 and 11.6, respectively)" (Borsari et al. 151).

- Frequency: "Students who consumed alcohol 1 to 3 times in the past month were twice as likely to have played drinking games as those who did not consume as much (OR = 1.84). Respondents who drank 4 to 9 times in the past month were 3 times as likely to have played (OR = 2.67)" (Borsari et al. 152).
- Marijuana use: "Students who reported marijuana use in their lifetimes were more than twice as likely (OR = 2.3) to play drinking games as those who reported no use" (Borsari et al. 152).

Associations of drinking game participation with inhalants and other types of drugs were not found to be statistically significant (Borsari et al. 152).

In the Comment (i.e., Discussion) section, the researchers claim that drinking game participation of incoming college students "warrants concern because games may place students on a trajectory for developing increasingly problematic alcohol use" (Borsari et al. 152). The researchers linked future behavior explicitly to the findings of their study, saying that "In the present study, we found that the most commonly endorsed motive to play drinking games was to get drunk. Therefore, precollege drinking-game participation and the heavy drinking that usually accompanies it may serve as a marker of those students who will develop problems with alcohol" (Borsari et al. 152). This link is supported, claim the researchers, by data that demonstrate that students who attended the summer orientation sessions "were twice as likely to be referred for violations of campus regulations as were students who did not attend" (Borsari et al. 153), apparently because the results of the survey showed that students who came for the orientation were a "high-risk sample" as compared with high school seniors nationally (Borsari et al. 153).

The authors then propose an educational program for incoming college students, to be conducted during the summer orientation sessions or during the first few weeks of the fall semester, that would address the risks of drinking games (Borsari et al. 153). Three topics, Borsari et al. contend, should be given attention:

1. Drinking games can result in high levels of intoxication over a relatively short time.
2. Making students aware of other socialization opportunities may reduce the need to play drinking games to meet others.
3. Women are at heightened risks for adverse consequences, especially sexual assault, following participation in drinking games. (Borsari et al. 153)

Borsari et al. conclude their article by noting some of the limitations of the study. "It is possible," they say, "that the students in our survey underreported their alcohol use" (Borsari et al. 153). Additionally, they contend that additional statistical tests (e.g., reliability coefficients) could potentially strengthen the results. Finally, the researchers discuss some of the potential biases of the data. One such bias is that the students who participated in the orientation sessions seemed to be a high-risk group as compared with a typical incoming college student; thus, the generalizability of the results is limited (Borsari et al. 153).

While students may be eager to discuss the article because it focuses on them in particular, they may simultaneously be quite reluctant to speak about their personal experiences or about experiences that they have heard about because of fear of being reported to campus or community authorities for underage drinking. Before beginning a discussion of the article with the class, the instructor may want to point out that he or she is not seeking to provide names to such authorities; the instructor may also encourage students to speak of hypothetical situations.

In their discussion of the article by Borsari et al., students may address a number of issues. One of the first questions that an instructor could ask is if the students are surprised that scientists study *them* in particular and if that awareness colors the way that they think about science. For some students at least, the discovery that *they* are under the microscope may be unsettling and quickly help to make science a much less abstract phenomenon consisting of principles such as photosynthesis, stoichiometry, and momentum;[1] instead, science becomes a process and institution that hits much closer to home. Because of this proximity, students may become more interested in and motivated to look at science in a critical way.

In terms of the article itself, some students, especially those who have some experience with the behaviors that the study investigates, may question the point of conducting the study at all. They may claim that the results that many students play drinking games to socialize are not at all surprising and are so commonplace as to hardly warrant a scientific study to confirm them. Additionally, they may assert that no amount of analysis will change the fact that many incoming college students choose to participate in drinking games and have done so for a long time. Indeed, the first sentence of the study states that drinking games have "reemerged as a substantial influence on undergraduate drinking" (Borsari et al. 149); a student may ask if such a reemergence is a case of rediscovering the wheel. All of these comments may lead to a broader discussion on the goals, scope, and costs and benefits of science in general and social science in particular.

Methodologically, students may question the validity of results that are gained via self-selection and self-reporting. Self-selection occurred in the study on two levels. First, attendance at the summer orientation program was voluntary, and second, although attendance at the assembly at which the survey was introduced was mandatory, participation in the survey was voluntary. Such self-selection, especially the second case, can skew the data. For example, students who have not participated in drinking games may have chosen not to participate or left responses blank because they felt that the research did not apply to them. This trend could have made the problem look worse than it actually is. Self-reporting is also not without its disadvantages. It is difficult to assess the accuracy and reliability of self-reported data. In an age of endless focus groups, telephone polls, and marketing surveys, some students who indeed volunteered to participate in the study may have taken sardonic pleasure in fictionalizing their answers.

In specific terms of the construction of an identity of incoming college students, the study makes assumptions about the ability of students to control their actions when drinking, and students may question the extent to which they do not possess free will as implied by this lack of control. For example, Borsari et al. state that one of the motives for drinking game participation is getting drunk quickly, and the authors say that slamming drinks—a rule in many drinking games—"may be especially attractive to individuals who do not enjoy the taste of alcohol" (Borsari et al. 149). Some students may contend that if someone doesn't like the taste of alcohol, she or he will simply choose not to drink. Elsewhere in the study, when discussing the topics to be discussed in a proposed educational program for students attending orientation sessions, Borsari et al. state "Players are not likely to be in control of their personal alcohol consumption during drinking games, which affect [*sic*] subsequent performance. Intoxicated players become more impaired, make more mistakes, and are required to drink more alcohol" (153). Some students may be offended by the implication that they are not "in control" of their actions and are "required" to drink more and may question the extent to which such characterizations are accurate. These questions could lead to an excellent discussion on the magnitude of power that peer pressure possesses.

The students characterized by the study by Borsari et al. enforce the rules of drinking games strictly, as implied by the authors' above-mentioned contention that students are "required" to drink and, in another part of the study, that students are "forced to drink quickly" (Borsari et al. 149). Students may question the perception that drinking games are so rigidly played. Indeed, the authors' own comments on the loss of control associated with drinking games mentioned above perhaps belie the notion that the rules of drinking games would be adhered to so closely. Instead, students may say, a more freewheeling atmosphere prevails.

Some students may be dismayed by the characterization of some incoming college students discussed in the study as predatory. In their discussion of motives for playing drinking games, Borsari et al. maintain that "Getting other players intoxicated is . . . [an] appealing aspect of drinking games" (149); indeed, their results indicate that 21 percent of students identified "to control others or get someone else drunk" as one of the reasons for participation. This desire to control others, say the authors, applies especially to newcomers to the game (Borsari et al. 149) and to women to whom a male player is sexually attracted (Borsari et al. 153).[2] Students may argue that, instead of trying to control their peers, they play drinking games to have fun, alleviate boredom, and (more innocently) socialize; indeed, the last of these motives was found to be statistically significant in the study.

The study's assumption that incoming college students would limit or stop playing drinking games altogether because of educational programs at summer orientation may prove amusing to some students. Some students will likely point out that no matter how much information they hear about the perceived risks of drinking game participation, they will begin or continue to play. Students may add that despite widespread knowledge of the risks of other activities such as smoking, many of their peers choose to smoke; other risky activities can be discussed as well. Such a discussion can be broadened to include deliberation on why, although science often provides useful, detailed data about risky behavior, human beings do not always react in what would be considered a rational manner.

Finally, the students may question the longer-term characterization of them as young adults who have alcohol problems that could be predicted specifically by drinking game participation in college. This risk exists, say the authors, because the "most commonly endorsed motive to play drinking games was to get drunk" (Borsari et al. 152); presumably, then, this motivation remains as students grow older and is associated with at least some level of addiction to alcohol. Indeed, in their literature review, Borsari et al. cite a study that demonstrated that "drinking game participation appeared to contribute uniquely to students' increased risk for alcohol-related problems, especially if the participants drank heavily during the games" (150). Borsari et al. then expend considerable effort on this possibility. Students may question how such an assertion can be made without studying an older cohort of students or young adults with alcohol problems and determining the extent to which these people participated in drinking games while attending college.

Some sharp-eyed students may notice some minor problems that crop up occasionally in the study. For instance, "binge" drinking is never defined in the study, although an accepted definition in the field of college health may very well exist and is simply not mentioned. It appears—although it is not made explicit—that binge drinking refers to "consumption of 5 or more drinks of alcohol on one occasion" (Borsari et al. 150). Additionally, when explaining their method, the authors list the least frequent category of drinking game participation as less than or equal to once per year, but in the Results section, this category becomes less than once per year.

Cultural Context of Drinking Games

Colleges and universities have waged a long campaign against student drinking, with questionable success. Drinking games, an integral part of the student drinking culture, may be as popular as ever, what with the availability of a multitude of websites on drinking games as well as books such as *The Complete Book of Beer Drinking Games* and *101 Drinking Games* available at Amazon.com, the same source that many students use to purchase textbooks. What may be of interest to students and instructors is not so much the virtually incontrovertible facts that drinking games are well entrenched at many colleges and universities throughout the country and that these institutions attempt to discourage students from participating in them, as the ways these games have become institutionalized and technologized in the past few years. These changes have allowed drinking games to transform from a local event to a connected, organized national community. Questions for students to consider are how these changes influence their decision to participate or not participate in drinking games and how the changes impact college and university efforts to deter them.

One of the most popular drinking games for the past several decades has been Beirut, or beerpong, and its evolution from an occasional party event to an Internet-based institutionalized "sport," complete with rules, equipment, a logo, bar leagues, and tournaments has been remarkable. Essentially, Beirut involves putting multiple cups of beer at the edges of a roughly four- by eight-foot table (a ping-pong table is often used for the purpose), and players attempt to throw ping-pong balls into the cups at the opposite end of the table. Players are required to drink beer if they miss; they designate a person on the opposite team to drink if they make the shot. For many years, many variations of the game existed; now, however, official rules govern the game. For example, Rule 1.1.2, Knocking Over Cups, states that "A cup that is knocked over by the force of the ball, or by contact with a player shall be deemed a missed shot unless it is ruled that the ball came into contact with the bottom of the cup prior to the cup being knocked over. If the shot is ruled a missed shot, then the cup shall be replaced approximately to it's [sic] former position" (Beirut-guide.com). This rule and others are used in "PlayBeirut-sanctioned tournaments" (PlayBeirut.com), including a national championship that includes cash awards. Beirut devotees do not have to rely on a ping pong table: an official Beirut table complete with cupholders and insets for ping pong balls is available for $300 from the sponsors of a website devoted to the game. Clothing and accessories can be purchased as well. Beirut has received coverage in mainstream media outlets such as the *New York Times* and National Public Radio.[3]

Websites such as Beirut-guide.com and playbeirut.net are some of the main reasons that Beirut has become institutionalized and, as a result, standardized. Complete with advertisements from major corporate sponsors, these sites enable Beirut enthusiasts from colleges and universities throughout the country to debate rules, keep statistics, plan tournaments (which are also advertised on the websites), and even play online. Online discussion forums contain thousands of postings.

Students may want to discuss the culture of drinking on campus more generally. Although a seemingly intractable problem with unceasing sermons from college administrators and law enforcement and a never-ending, devil-may-care attitude toward alcohol from students, one development has been potentially noteworthy: a small number of colleges and universities (e.g., Colby College) now allow of-age students to consume alcohol with their meals on campus. The hope is that students will learn to associate alcohol with occasions that do not valorize drunkenness.

Writing Science about College Students' Drinking Games

Writing science with respect to the study by Borsari et al. would involve students being asked to propose and perhaps conduct a study that would follow up the analysis and attempt to confirm, call into question, and/or extend its findings. A key difference from the study by Borsari et al. would be that students—peers—would be conducting the proposed research, thus allowing for some methodological possibilities that may not be as feasible with older, pseudo-authority figures such as the university psychologists and student affairs staff who performed the research in Borsari et al. The possibilities for such research are many; four are discussed here.

Participant Observers at Social Gatherings

To determine motivations for and predictors of drinking game participation, students might propose that they attend social gatherings where such games are played—something professors and administrators would have a much more difficult time doing—and act as participant observers. Students who would be conducting the research would only be those who are comfortable in such settings. They would not consume alcohol but a non-alcoholic beverage instead and would participate in the drinking games as well as collect data by talking to participants between games or to those students who are attending the party but not playing.[4] All of the students at the party would need to be informed of the research being conducted so that they could opt out if they so desired. Students interested in proposing this kind of research may devise a number of ways to accomplish this notification; one method would be to have a colleague inform party-goers as they arrive. Additionally, students at the party might be more cooperative and honest if they are assured of anonymity; the same student who asks for consent at the door could also pass along this information. It is likely that the act of conducting research at a social gathering could change the dynamic of the event; students may want to speculate on what such changes might occur and on if and how they can compensate for such change.

In terms of data collection, participant-observer students might first, when playing drinking games (but not consuming alcohol), watch the other players carefully and take notes in an effort to determine motives. It may become clear to the researcher that one player is playing to get drunk quickly, while another is attempting to meet people, while yet another is trying to control others. Combinations of motives are possible. Other motivations not mentioned in Borsari et al., where the motives were assumed *a priori*, may also become apparent. Second, students conducting the research could talk informally, again taking notes, to students at the party in an effort to determine why or why not they are playing drinking games. These encounters could also be used to gauge predictors. Students conducting the research could ask about other factors such as those assessed by Borsari et al.: gender, age at first alcohol use, frequency and quantity of alcohol consumption, use of marijuana. Other predictors—e.g., family attitudes toward alcohol or lack of participation in high school or college extracurricular activities because of penalties for alcohol use—could be discovered.

Looking at a Big(ger) Picture

To determine the numbers of incoming college students who participate in drinking games, students may propose to study a larger sample from a regional or nationwide cross-section of colleges and universities. The results of Borsari et al.'s study could be somewhat constrained because the institution at which they work may attract students who in general have a core set of cultural assumptions in common; thus, by limiting their data collection to one "large northeastern university" (150), Borsari et al. may not be getting as accurate a picture as possible about the broader population of incoming college students. Students may propose that they contact peers at a variety of other types of institutions—from large universities to small colleges, from conservative Bible colleges to liberal enclaves—and conduct an informal, e-mail-based survey of incoming college students similar to that used by Borsari et al. The peers at other colleges and universities could be, for example, students who are employed to help run summer orientation sessions; these students would be in a good position to collect data from incoming students at their institution. Students conducting the research or helping to gather data could also work with the admissions office at their school to perhaps mail a survey to incoming students. This research could not only generate more accurate numbers of students who participate in drinking games but also uncover motivations and predictors that may not be prevalent at a single campus.

Future Alcohol-Related Problems

Students may propose to follow up on Borsari et al.'s tenuous link between participating in drinking games while in college and future alcohol problems. One way to confirm or disprove this link would be to informally survey (again via e-mail to reduce costs) or interview alumni of the students' institution as well as students who transferred or dropped out. The logistical and, if a mailing is involved, financial help of the institution's alumni office (for alumni) or registrar's office (for transfers or drop-outs) could be enlisted to search for people to contact. These offices often conduct exit interviews of students who are graduating or leaving, and this research could be a part of that effort. Each of the groups contacted would be queried about drinking game participation while a student at the college or university and about whether they have experienced alcohol-related problems since the time that they attended the institution. Asking about alcohol problems would undoubtedly be a delicate process, but perhaps those who are or have been dependent on alcohol would appreciate knowing that their alma mater cares about their well-being. Another way that students may propose to conduct this kind of research is to attend meetings of alcohol problem support groups such as Alcoholics Anonymous. Students could ask meeting attendees if they attended college, where, and whether they participated in drinking games while a student. All former college or university students who are contacted in this manner could be asked if they think a link exists between their participation in drinking games in college and subsequent difficulties with alcohol.

Effectiveness of Educational Programs

Students could propose to evaluate the effectiveness of an educational program implemented to teach incoming students about the risks of playing drinking games if such a program is offered at their institution. Borsari et al. imply that these programs could reduce the number of students who participate in drinking games and recommend that programs focus on the speed with which playing drinking games can lead to serious intoxication, alternative social events at which drinking games are not played, and risks to women. At the conclusion of such a program—perhaps a week or two later, after those who took part in the program have had a chance to dwell on it and reach a decision on how much the program will actually influence their behavior—students who are conducting research could ask students if they worry about how quickly or the degree to which they become intoxicated, if they would attend alternative social events, and, for women, if they are concerned about the association between drinking game participation and sexual assault. Specifically, students conducting the research would seek evidence (or a lack thereof) that incoming students who participated in an educational program changed their behavior as it relates to drinking-game participation.

Students who conduct this type of research could also be asked to assume an additional responsibility of revising an educational program for their incoming peers, or even developing an initial program if none exists. In all likelihood, interested students would produce creative, innovative, and effective solutions to be considered.

Epilogue

S
ome 2,500 years ago, an anonymous Sophist wisely observed that "It belongs to the same man to be politician, speaker, scientist" (Freeman 162). I didn't know that until I was in my mid twenties. Earlier, when I was an undergraduate chemistry major, I took English classes for fun—a break, I thought, from the rigors of physical chemistry, instrumental analysis, and biochemistry. From the time I became literate, I had always been a writer and a reader, and I enjoyed the way in which those activities were privileged in English courses. Nevertheless, I would always make my way back to the science building so that I could get back to work on what I considered *true* knowledge—not that relativistic, fuzzy, gray-area material that passed for knowledge in the humanities.

Or so I thought. Now that I am (definitely) older and (arguably) wiser, I more readily recognize that I was (and still am) in many important ways a product of the culture in which I live(d). In this culture, science rules. The world is *represented* by science. The world cannot be changed without a firm grasp of that institution's discourse.

Foucault asks, "What is this Reason that we use? What are its historical effects? What are its limits, and what are its dangers? One should remain as close to this question as possible, keeping in mind that it is both central and extremely difficult to resolve" ("Space, Knowledge, and Power" 249). For most of the last three hundred years, once science won the culture wars of the seventeenth and eighteenth centuries, the "Reason that we use" has been science, and there is no reason to doubt that it will retain its privileged position. But such dominance should not lead to complacency or blind faith. Such a lack of awareness promotes a potentially dangerous isolation and intellectual atrophy. However, because science, like all cultural institutions, is manifested discursively, the ideas contained in this book will, I hope, begin a process by which students and instructors in rhetoric and composition will actively participate in discussing the questions that Foucault poses.

The goal of the study of scientific discourse by our students is not, of course, to produce a society ruled by scientists and engineers such as the one described in Vonnegut's sarcastically dystopic *Player Piano*. The goal is, instead, to establish a dynamic theory–practice equilibrium with respect to scientific discourse that gives students (and instructors) the confidence and expertise they need to engage the dominant institution of science. As philosopher of science Brown notes at the conclusion of *Who Rules in Science?* "Science is the most important institution in our lives. That claim ought to make us sit up and take notice—but it doesn't. We've become complacent" (212). As a society, we cannot afford such complacency, and rhetoric and composition should ensure that our discipline does not contribute to it. We cannot hope to effect change in society without effecting change in science.

Cultural change is much more likely to occur and is much more likely to be positive change if the ways in which the world is represented are understood by a broad spectrum of society. This representation takes the form of scientific discourse. The ideas presented in this book promote a more balanced, accurate perception of epistemological and ontological operations in science. Additionally, because of the exchange of ideas that will take place between and among scientists and nonscientists, the healthy skepticism toward neutrality and universality claims in science would, if artfully articulated, simultaneously promote the idea that scientific discourse is inherently rhetorical and validate other methods of producing knowledge and describing reality. Scientific discourse, which alone occupies the table of knowledge and reality in contemporary Western society, would then be joined by narrative and other forms of discourse on an equally privileged footing. Scientific discourse would thus take its rightful place among all the other messy, complex rhetorics of human existence.

Notes

Introduction

1. Some seventy-five reviews of *The Bell Curve* were published between October 1994, when the book was published, and the late summer of 1995 (McInerney 83).

2. By *rhetorician*, I mean one who studies rhetoric, as opposed to *rhetor*, who is anyone who writes or speaks.

3. Gregory and Miller make a similar point when they say that "much of the science that the public needs to know about is either hotly contested or is still on the assembly line" ("Caught in the Crossfire?" 62). This controversy or incompleteness is typically not presented in textbooks or media accounts of science, yet it is this cutting-edge work that requires an informed, scientifically literate populace most of all.

4. As discussed in more detail in chapter 2, a balance needs to be struck here. While I strive to teach material that I hope my students will find relevant, I don't think we can rely entirely on our students to tell us what captures their interest; part of our job as instructors is to challenge students with texts that will arouse their interest. Although I present pedagogical scenarios in chapters 6, 7, and 8 that involve health and the environment, topics that I think most students will enjoy, I also chose these topics because they involve the sciences with which I am the most familiar (i.e., chemistry and biology). Instructors should not, however, hesitate to employ texts that they believe will broaden their students' horizons.

5. As a consequence of a discussion of the genre, students may want to tinker with it or dismiss it entirely and try something new. I am certainly intrigued by the notion that students be asked to write science in their own way; undoubtedly, some fascinating ideas on the nature of scientific discourse would surface from such writing. However, for the moment, I consider such an activity to be counterproductive to this book's goal of achieving scientific literacy according to the terms of its most common usage—the scientific research article. See Martin for a discussion on how allowing Australian K-12 students to write science in their own words in elementary and middle school left them ill prepared for the rigor of secondary school physics and environmental science. "Without a clear understanding of the fundamental role of scientific language in doing science," states Martin, "this problem cannot be properly redressed" (167).

6. As this manuscript went to press, an excellent article entitled "Primary Science Communication in the First-Year Writing Course" by Moskovitz and

Kellogg was published in *CCC*. These authors argue, as I do, that "primary science communication" (their term) should be treated no differently than other kinds of complex texts that we ask our students to read (313–14).

7. I am not arguing that all research in the rhetoric of science should pursue a pedagogical angle. However, attempts to make the work of rhetoricians of science visible and useful to compositionists and others concerned with widespread literacy need to be made.

8. It is prudent to note, however, the experience of physicist N. David Mermin. In a book review on the science wars that he published in *Nature* in 1999, Mermin wrote that he would be satisfied "if one outcome of the science wars were to make physicists less uncomfortable with their professional deployment of rhetoric." A *Nature* editor changed Mermin's wording to "less uncomfortable with using rhetoric when describing their work," and this latter version is the text that was published in the journal. Mermin objected to the rewording on the basis that the change in fact separated rhetoric from scientists' work, i.e., producing scientific discourse. Mermin sought to restore his original wording in page proofs and asked for an erratum after publication, but to no avail.

9. Chris Mooney's *The Republican War on Science* and Esther Kaplan's *With God on Their Side* are two recent books that discuss the current (and future) political implications of a fundamentalist Christian, anti-science perspective.

1. The Dominance of Scientific Discourse: Theoretical Contexts

1. Occasionally, original research will appear in books or other venues without being peer reviewed, as *The Bell Curve* did, but this practice is strongly discouraged in the scientific community. One need look no further than the controversy sparked by Pons and Fleischmann's infamous 1989 press conference—which occurred well before peer review and duplication of their work on cold fusion were attempted—to understand the dismay engendered in other scientists when rhetorical protocol is breached.

2. Sullivan defines forum control as "the process of authorizing or de-authorizing speakers, writers, texts, or speeches" (128).

3. At issue is the idea that, as a result of the Big Bang, on a galactic scale, matter should be expanding in all directions and not coalescing around a certain point or plane, such as an axis. Mainstream physicists would most likely question the interpretation that such an axis exists, or if indeed it does, that it is sufficient to disprove the Big Bang Theory.

4. Indeed, disciplines are, says Foucault, "techniques for assuring the ordering of human multiplicities" ("Panopticism" 207).

5. It can certainly be argued that science is in fact a repressive state apparatus, or perhaps a "border" apparatus, in the Althusserian sense in cases where the products of science are military in nature or have potential military applications.

2. The State of Scientific Discourse in Rhetoric and Composition

1. In practice, topics for students' declamations could vary widely. They included "pirates, seducers, wronged heirs, poison cups, cruel husbands, contradictory laws, cures for the blind, shipwrecks, and a host of other calamities and dilemmas calculated to present the student orator with difficulty" (Murphy 66). Nonetheless, the fundamental goal of the declamation was to prepare students for forensic and deliberative rhetorical situations, both of which center on law, and even some of the more fantastic topics typically involved legal implications. See, for example, the example on pirates from Seneca's collection of declamations (Murphy 66).

2. This notion holds true most convincingly during the periods of genuine democracy in ancient Greece and Rome. During periods of more autocratic rule, the purpose of focusing on legal discourse was, perhaps, presented in a more circumspect manner. Indeed, a compelling argument could be made that Quintilian's students most likely did not put their rhetoric lessons on the law to use after they finished their education because of the autocratic political climate in Rome (Delli Carpini 22–23). However, the spirit of Quintilian's intent remains: that, given a more democratic environment, students would be able to engage skillfully in substantive debates about the law, which was the discourse that had the most powerful effect on them.

3. Compositionists may be starting to re-establish a connection with legal discourse. At the 2005 Conference on College Composition and Communication, a panel of three scholars presented a session entitled "Breaking Down the Law: Bringing Legal Writing into the Composition Class."

4. Celeste Condit is a notable exception. Condit submitted a letter to the prestigious journal *Science* that she wrote in response to a scientific research article on brain sex research. In the letter, Condit posited alternative hypotheses relating to morphological diversity that the scientists who conducted the work she was commenting upon did not consider (104–5). Though the letter was peer reviewed and the authors of the brain sex study responded to Condit, the letter itself was not published (91–97), thus ending a potentially highly fruitful exchange between humanists and scientists before it had even really begun.

More generally, I do not mean to say that scientists are not rhetors: they most certainly are. But they generally do not study classical rhetoric, audience, or any body of knowledge that illuminates their communicative practices. For both an acknowledgment of and an exception to this position, see Hass and Kleine's "The Rhetoric of Junk Science," written by a scientist (Hass) and a rhetorician (Kleine). In part of the article, Kleine recounts his experiences taking technical writing courses while thinking about a second career as a writer. He states that the most difficult part of being a scientist is writing papers, and he claims that many of his colleagues would agree with him (267). He adds, "A writer by necessity, but a rhetorician I certainly am not. . . . As I took the first introductory graduate courses [in Rhetoric and Writing at the University of Arkansas at Little Rock], I learned about the classical approach to the structure and theory of rhetoric. I discovered that the most basic of concepts was audience. I had never considered the concept of audience when writing scientific papers" (267). It is perplexing and ironic that one of the most powerful discourses in Western culture warrants such little rhetorical attention from its practitioners.

5. This generalization does not hold as true for medical rhetoric and technical communication as it does for the rhetoric of science; these areas are discussed in more detail later in the chapter.

6. Bazerman is careful to point out that he does not entirely discount the use of classical rhetoric to make sense of scientific discourse. See, for example, his work on nuclear information in *Written Communication*.

7. The lack of representation of empirical research in rhetoric and composition has not gone unnoticed, nor is it viewed favorably by everyone in the field. See, for example, Haswell's "NCTE/CCCC's Recent War on Scholarship" in *Written Communication*.

8. Indeed, many instructors of graduate research methods courses in rhetoric and composition make use of books such as Lauer and Asher's *Composition Research: Empirical Designs*, fully half of which deals with quantitative research methods. Even so, most graduate students and dissertation directors in rhetoric and composition specifically and in the humanities generally shy away from quantitative research.

9. There is no compelling reason for scientific discourse to be stylistically barren. Another benefit of a closer connection between rhetoric and composition and science would be a greater appreciation of prose style by scientists.

10. Indeed, a community of scholars within science studies examines this very question. The movement is often referred to as Public Understanding of Science and Technology, or PUST. Many rhetoricians and compositionists would probably view this issue more broadly and familiarly as a matter of literacy.

11. According to the National Science Foundation, "Nearly everyone is interested in new medical discoveries. Year after year, more people express interest in this subject than in any other. In 2001, about two-thirds of the NSF survey respondents reported they were *very interested* in new medical discoveries. None of the other survey items, except local school issues, received such a high percentage of *very interested* responses" ("Info Brief" 7–5).

12. In addition to editorials, featured articles are often accompanied by more journalistic "news" articles in journals that publish such sections. Such journals include *Science, Nature,* and the *Journal of the National Cancer Institute*.

13. For a fascinating look at the history of the institutionalization of *p* values—the gold standard when deciding the value of scientific research—see Little's "Understanding Statistical Significance: A Conceptual History." Little asks, "What, then, is so special about 0.05? What theoretical or mathematical

rationale warrants its privileged status over other *p* values, such as 0.045 or 0.078? Remarkably, the answer is: nothing" (364).

14. Other composition texts, such as Hawisher and Selfe's *Literacy, Technology, and Society* and Holeton's *Composing Cyberspace*, focus on technology only. In this book, I distinguish between science and technology: the process of scientific inquiry (i.e., the scientific method) and its impact on culture is more prominent in the study of science than it is in technology studies. Also, several readers have sections on science in them (e.g., "Science and the Environment" in *The Conscious Reader*, edited by Shrodes, Finestone, and Shugrue, which I use). While encouraging, these sections basically operate in the same way, on a smaller scale, as the readers that devote themselves entirely to science and suffer from the same shortcomings.

15. The rhetorical function described by McLeod is now more commonly associated with Writing in the Disciplines (WID) (Bazerman and Russell xv, Peritz 431). However, for the purposes of this book, I believe that enough overlap still exists to use "WAC" to discuss both functions.

16. The *Journal of Chemical Education* is a widely read journal, and its influence cannot be underestimated. Interestingly, however, although one of the authors, Labianca, is listed as a chemistry professor, Reeves is an English professor. Resistance to WAC is thus not limited to disciplines outside of English.

17. As this book went to press in early 2006, a deep revision of Gross's book, newly titled as *Starring the Text: The Place of Rhetoric in Science Studies* was released by Southern Illinois University Press.

18. For an exception, see Schryer's "Genre Time/Space: Chronotopic Strategies in the Experimental Article." Schryer proposes that, in associating genre with time and space, IMRAD-based scientific discourse represents an "attempt to control the time not only of past events but also the reader's future actions" (86), thus initiating a focus on specific material effects that correspond to specific scientific texts. Schryer presents the idea only, and it needs to be tested by attempting to determine how actions of individuals are influenced by a scientific research article.

19. I do not know of any studies of the "Drug Facts Panel" or other information that is a part of the packaging of over-the-counter medications and prescription medications, and I am somewhat surprised that this genre, like that of the nutrition information that is a part of food packaging, has not been examined closely.

20. In many technical communication textbooks, the scientific research article is in fact mentioned—as one of the many forms a report can take. Typically, for example, the scientific research article is listed as an empirical research report along with other types of reports such as a progress report or a recommendation report. However, no technical communication class that I know of has ever paid much attention to an empirical research report; instead, technical communication

courses usually focus on the other types of reports. Technical communication courses that focus on science writing specifically may spend more time and effort on scientific research articles. Hutto, for one, advocates reading and writing summaries of and responses to scientific research articles in his courses (220). He says that "Scientists must regularly interact with what other people have said and are saying in print, and participation in this dialogue is important for science students to learn. The most effective science writers are the most thoroughly engaged in that dialogue, altering and reinterpreting their own ideas in a social interactive invention that depends heavily on critical reading" (220).

3. Scientific Discourse as a Cultural Studies Issue

1. Lessl's description of a scientist's *ethos* as a "priestly voice," mentioned in chapter 2, reinforces this comparison.

2. This book is the first overview of science studies to include a chapter devoted to the "rhetoric and discourse" of science (chapter 14).

3. For another take on this debate, see Ian Hacking's *The Social Construction of What?*

4. For a more general description of the transformation of the university into a site of "capital accumulation" (Noble 433), see Noble's "Digital Diploma Mills" in *Science Bought and Sold: Essays in the Economics of Science.*

5. The National Science Foundation defines the "R&D [research and development] plant" as "facilities and fixed equipment, such as reactors, wind tunnels, and particle accelerators . . . [and which] includes acquisition of, construction of, major repairs to, or alterations in structures, works, equipment, facilities, or land for use in R&D activities at Federal or non-Federal installations. Excluded from the R&D plant category are expendable or movable equipment (e.g., spectrometers, microscopes) and office furniture and equipment. Also excluded are the costs of redesign studies (e.g., those undertaken before commitment to a specific facility). These excluded costs are reported under 'total conduct of research and development.' Obligations for foreign R&D plants are limited to Federal funds for facilities that are located abroad and used in support of foreign research and development" ("Info Brief").

6. In 2003, *The Scientist* published an article on how and why English has become the standard in science. See "No Pardon for Poor English in Science," by Sam Jaffe, in the March 10, 2003, issue.

4. Scientific Discourse as a Literacy Issue

1. By "emic," Halloran draws on Black and defines the term as "criticism that begins with the particular instance and aims toward the development of theories comprehending more general principles that operate across larger bodies of discourse" (81).

2. A 2004 study by Miller puts the figure at 17 percent by the end of the 1990s. While this figure is certainly more encouraging than Shamos's 5 percent,

Miller laments that "the current level is still problematic for a democratic society that values citizen understanding of major national policies and participation in the resolution of important policy disputes" (273), most of which incorporate scientific data.

5. Popularizations of Science

1. It is interesting to note, in light of Lawrence Summers's controversial comments in early 2005 on the possibility of gender-specific differences in science and math aptitude, that a significant portion of the most important work in nuclear physics during the twentieth century was performed by women. Marie Curie, her daughter Irena Curie, and Lise Meitner were at the center of exciting breakthroughs in the field. Indeed, Meitner and Frisch cite the work of Irena Curie in their letter.

2. Indeed, Gould required students to read Vonnegut's *Galápagos* in science courses for which he covered the idea of contingency.

3. For a detailed study of the development of a visual scientific icon that became a part of popular culture, see Myers's "The Double Helix as Icon."

4. The association of science with theater does have a precedent. Among the better known plays about science are Frayn's *Copenhagen*, Capek's *R.U.R.*, Brecht's *Galileo*, and Durenmatt's *The Physicists*. There are stage versions of Shelley's *Frankenstein* as well. Gould was something of a playwright himself: he was commissioned by the Piccolo Theater in Milan to write a play about Darwin. Among contemporary playwrights, perhaps Stoppard is best known for incorporating science into his work in, for example, *Hapgood* and *Arcadia*.

5. Given this argument, one may consider the extent to which Gould may have thought that Darwin is the person most responsible for the existence and methodologies of historical science in the same way that Bacon is for experimental science.

6. This situation is strikingly similar to the one Mendel found himself in during the nineteenth century, as described by Foucault (see chapter 1). Whittington, as Mendel did, possessed compelling data, but it was not "in the true" of the propositions of the time.

6. Scientific Discourse of Another Culture

1. Weight loss via surgery has grown in popularity in recent years. However, questions about its safety and long-term effects remain. Because of these questions and because of its cost (it is almost always a cosmetic procedure in the eyes of medical insurance companies), surgery is thus relatively uncommon compared with the four strategies discussed here.

2. Unlike acupuncture, Chi Kung has never been studied by Western scientists, to my knowledge.

3. The FDA, as a result of the 1994 Dietary Supplements Health and Education Act, is unable to monitor herbal supplements and other over-the-counter

diet drugs closely. Before this legislation took effect, says Fraser, "if the FDA had a health or safety question about a food product, the burden of proof was on the manufacturers to show that it was safe. Now it's up to the FDA to prove, in a lengthy and expensive investigation, that a product is dangerous before it can be pulled from the shelves. And despite its increased burden, the FDA has received no additional resources to conduct investigations of potentially harmful products" (83).

4. This issue is addressed in the book. In chapter 5, the author reports that he hosted fourteen Japanese guests who had no background in Chi Kung. While the guests stayed with the author, they tried Chi Kung. After four days, the average weight loss for this group was 2.43 kg (5.35 pounds).

5. If language barriers can be surmounted, the student may want to investigate the possibility of collaboration with students and faculty at a Chinese university to help assemble the traditional Chinese lifestyle group.

7. Classics

1. Again, Odum proved to be prophetic, as many dams have been dismantled in the United States in recent years.

2. Odum may have been especially careful with his tone because Rachel Carson, in *Silent Spring*, was accused repeatedly of using a panicked tone to gain attention for her arguments. These accusations were, of course, made because Carson was a woman; some critics even accused her of being hysterical. Carson was proven right in the long run. Additionally, Odum's discourse is "harder" science than Carson's. This fact is not surprising given Odum's audience of scientists both in the speech and in the journal *Science*, but it may also represent an attempt on his part to convince scientists of the validity of Carson's arguments, which instead of being directed to scientists, were written for a more general audience.

3. I suspect that this mention of "urban sprawl" has to be one of the earliest uses—if not the earliest—of this term. If it was in the speech version of the text, it would have been introduced in 1966.

8. You Are What Science Says You Are

1. Of course all of these processes directly affect human beings in critical ways. Photosynthesis produces oxygen, stoichiometry governs proportions and conservation of matter and energy in all types of chemical reactions, including those that take place in our bodies, and momentum is the product of mass and velocity. But sometimes the connection to human beings is lost, given that physical manifestations outside of the human body are the object of study. Research such as that conducted by Borsari et al. can remind students that a great deal of science studies human beings and that *all* science impacts the human race in one way or another.

2. The authors base the gender-related conclusion—undoubtedly valid—on other research. Their own data, however, do not support such a conclusion: "We found no gender differences in students' motives for playing drinking games," say the authors (Borsari et al. 151). Even so, the researchers list danger to women as one of three areas on which the proposed education program should focus.

3. Beirut was mentioned in the *Times* as part of a larger story on the future of sororities and fraternities. See the *New York Times* Educational Supplement from November 7, 1999. The National Public Radio report was part of NPR's Next Generation Radio project; this report discussed college students knowing the game of Beirut but not the city of Beirut as part of the context for a story about student reaction to the Iraq war. See http://www.npr.org/about/nextgen/ stitch/beirut.html for the text of the report, which was available as of December 31, 2005.

4. Talking to students who are at a social gathering but who are not playing drinking games may help shed some light on just how much peer pressure is exerted for participation.

Works Cited

aaas.org. 2003. American Association for the Advancement of Science. June 20, 2003. <http://www.aaas.org/>.

Alford, Elisabeth M. "Thucydides and the Plague of Athens: The Roots of Scientific Writing." *Written Communication* 5 (1988): 131–53.

Althusser, Louis. *Lenin and Philosophy and Other Essays*. New York: Monthly Review Press, 1971.

Anderson, Richard C., et al. "Use of Partial Information in Learning to Read Chinese Characters." *Journal of Educational Psychology* 95 (2003): 52–57.

Aronowitz, Stanley. *Science as Power: Discourse and Ideology in Modern Society*. Minneapolis: University of Minnesota Press, 1988.

Aronowitz, Stanley, Barbara Martinsons, Michael Menser, and Jennifer Rich, eds. *Technoscience and Cyberculture*. New York: Routledge, 1996.

Atkinson, Dwight. *Scientific Discourse in Sociohistoric Context: The Philosophical Transactions of the Royal Society of London, 1675–1975*. Unpublished manuscript. 1996.

Barton, Ellen. "Literacy in (Inter)Action." *College English* 59 (1997): 408–37.

Bazerman, Charles. "What Written Knowledge Does: Three Examples of Academic Discourse." *Landmark Essays on Writing Across the Curriculum*. Eds. Charles Bazerman and David R. Russell. Davis, CA: Hermagoras Press, 1994. 159–88.

———. H-Rhetor (listserv). February 18, 2003.

———. "Nuclear Information: One Rhetorical Moment in the Construction of the Information Age." *Written Communication* 18 (2001): 259–95.

———. *Shaping Written Knowledge: The Genre and Activity of the Experimental Article in Science*. Madison: University of Wisconsin Press, 1988.

Bazerman, Charles, and David Russell. "Writing Across the Curriculum as a Challenge to Rhetoric and Composition." *Landmark Essays on Writing Across the Curriculum*. Eds. Charles Bazerman and David R. Russell. Davis: Hermagoras Press, 1994. xi–xvi.

Bell, Heather D., Kathleen A. Walch, and Steven B. Katz. "'Aristotle's Pharmacy': The Medical Rhetoric of a Clinical Protocol in the Drug Development Process." *Technical Communication Quarterly* 9 (2000): 249–69.

Beirut-guide.com, December 31, 2003. <http://beirut-guide.com/>.

Berkenkotter, Carol, and Thomas Huckin. "You Are What You Cite: Novelty and Intertextuality in a Biologist's Experimental Article." *Professional Communication: The Social Perspective*. Eds. Nancy Roundy Blyler and Charlotte Thralls. Newbury Park, CA: Sage Publications, 1993. 109–27.

Bernhardt, Stephen A. "The Writer, the Reader, and the Scientific Text." *Journal of Technical Writing and Communication* 15 (1985): 163–74.

Body Positive.com. July 10, 2003. <http://www.bodypositive.com/>.

Borsari, Brian, Dessa Bergen-Cico, and Kate B. Carey. "Self-Reported Drinking-game Participation of Incoming College Students." *Journal of American College Health* 51 (2003): 149–54.

Brandt, Deborah. "Literacy and Knowledge." *The Right to Literacy.* Eds. Andrea A. Lunsford, Helene Moglen, and James Slevin. New York: MLA, 1990. 189–96.

Brennan, Richard P. *Dictionary of Scientific Literacy.* Hoboken: John Wiley & Sons, 1991.

Brown, James Robert. *Who Rules in Science?: An Opinionated Guide to the Wars.* Cambridge: Harvard University Press, 2001.

Brown, Lester R. "Rescuing a Planet Under Stress." In Easton 216–23.

Bruce, Bertram. "The Discourses of Inquiry: Pedagogical Challenges." In Keller-Cohen 289–316.

Bucchi, Massimiano. "The Uses of Scientific Fact: Pasteur's Public Experiment on Anthrax in the Popular Press of the Time." *Appropriating Technology: Vernacular Science and Social Power.* Eds. Ron Eglash, Jennifer L. Croissant, Giovanna Di Chiro, and Rayvon Fouché. Minneapolis: University of Minnesota Press, 2004. 5–32.

Burroughs-Boenisch, Joy. "International Reading Strategies for IMRD Articles." *Written Communication* 16 (1999): 296–316.

Bushnell, Jack. "Writing through Science." *Technical Communication Quarterly* 12 (2003): 251–66.

Calfee, Robert. "Critical Literacy: Reading and Writing for a New Millennium." *Literacy: A Redefinition.* Eds. Nancy J. Ellsworth, Carolyn N. Hedley, and Anthony N. Baratta. Hillsdale, NJ: Lawrence Erlbaum Associates, 1994. 19–38.

Carpenter, Harrison. "Scientific Research and Writing in the Composition Classroom." Paper presented at the Conference on College Composition and Communication, San Antonio, Texas, March 2004.

———. "Why Should Science Matter? Composition and its Consideration of Scientific Writing." Paper presented at the Conference on College Composition and Communication, San Francisco, California, March 2005.

Ceccarelli, Leah. *Shaping Science with Rhetoric: The Cases of Dobzhansky, Schrödinger, and Wilson.* Chicago: University of Chicago Press, 2001.

———. "Neither Confusing Cacophony Nor Culinary Complements: A Case Study of Mixed Metaphors for Genomic Science." *Written Communication* 21 (2004): 92–105.

Charney, Davida. "Lone Geniuses in Popular Science: The Devaluation of Scientific Consensus." *Written Communication* 20 (2003): 215–41.

———. "Introduction: The Rhetoric of Popular Science." *Written Communication* 21 (2004): 3–5.

cnn.com. 2003. "U.N. Official: World can't afford rich China." July 16, 2003. <http://www.cnn.com/2003/TECH/science/07/16/China.un.reut.index.html>.

Coletta, W. John. "The Ideologically Biased Use of Language in Scientific and Technical Writing." *Technical Communication Quarterly* 1 (1992): 59–70.

Condit, Celeste. "How Bad Science Stays That Way: Brain Sex, Demarcation, and the Status of Truth in the Rhetoric of Science." *Rhetoric Society Quarterly* 26 (1996): 83–109.

Conference-board.org. May 22, 2003. <http://www.conference-board.org/>.

Council of Biology Editors Style Manual. 5th ed. Bethesda, MD: Council of Biology Editors, 1983.

Davis, Abiola C. "Expenditures on S&E Research Facilities at Historically Black Colleges and Universities Continue to Decline." 1997. <http://www.nsf.gov/>.

Delli Carpini, Dominic F. "The End(s) of Civic Education: Banning the Poet from the Republic of Composition, from Plato to Pragmatism." *Composition and/or Literature: The End(s) of Education.* Eds. Linda S. Bergmann and Edith M. Baker. Urbana: NCTE, 2006. 17–35.

Dickson, Barbara, and Ellen Barton. "Leaving Science and Technology for Business and Management: Quality Control as a Discourse on the Move." *Rhetoric Society Quarterly* 26 (1996): 41–63.

Dodd, Janet S., ed. *The ACS Style Guide: A Manual for Authors and Editors.* Washington, DC: American Chemical Society, 1986.

Dombrowski, Paul M. "Plastic Language for Plastic Science: The Rhetoric of Comrade Lysenko." *Journal of Technical Writing and Communication* 31 (2001): 293–333.

Dorr, Aimeé. "What Constitutes Literacy in a Culture with Diverse and Changing Means of Communication?" In Keller-Cohen 129–53.

Downing, David B., Patricia Harkin, and James J. Sosnoski. "Configurations of Lore: The Changing Relations of Theory, Research, and Pedagogy." *Changing Classroom Practices.* Ed. David B. Downing. Urbana: NCTE, 1994. 3–34.

Doyle, J. "Introduction to Acoustics." July 17, 2003. <www.btinternet.com/~j.doyle/Mus-Tech/Units/Unit4/Unit4-OHs/Unit4-OH1-Introduction-to-Acoustics.htm>.

Easton, Thomas A., ed. *Taking Sides: Clashing Views on Controversial Environmental Issues.* 11th ed. New York: McGraw Hill/Dushkin, 2005. 214–15, 231.

Etzkowitz, Henry, and Andrew Webster. "Science as Intellectual Property." *The Handbook of Science and Technology Studies.* Eds. Sheila Jasanoff, Gerald E. Markle, James C. Petersen, and Trevor Pinch. Thousand Oaks, CA: Sage Publications, 1995. 480–505.

Fahnestock, Jeanne. "Series Reasoning in Scientific Argument: *Incrementum* and *Gradatio* and the Case of Darwin." *Rhetoric Society Quarterly* 26 (1996): 13–40.

———. "Accommodating Science: The Rhetorical Life of Scientific Facts." *Written Communication* 3 (1986): 275–96.

———. *Rhetorical Figures in Science*. New York: Oxford University Press, 1999.

Faigley, Lester. "After the Revolution." *College Composition and Communication* 48 (1997): 30–43.

Federal Trade Commission. "Weight-Loss Advertising: An Analysis of Current Trends," 2002.

Flower, Linda, et al. *Reading-to-Write: Exploring a Cognitive and Social Process.* New York: Oxford University Press, 1990.

Foster, Gary D., et al. "A Randomized Trial of a Low-Carbohydrate Diet for Obesity." *New England Journal of Medicine* 348 (2003): 2082–90.

Foucault, Michel. "The Means of Correct Training." *The Foucault Reader*. Ed. Paul Rabinow. New York: Pantheon Books, 1984. 188–205.

———. "Truth and Power." *The Foucault Reader*. Ed. Paul Rabinow. New York: Pantheon Books, 1984. 51–75.

———. "Panopticism." *The Foucault Reader*. Ed. Paul Rabinow. New York: Pantheon Books, 1984. 206–13.

———. "Space, Knowledge, and Power." *The Foucault Reader*. Ed. Paul Rabinow. New York: Pantheon Books, 1984. 239–56.

———. "The Order of Discourse." *Untying the Text: A Post-Structuralist Reader.* Ed. Robert Young. Boston: Routledge and Kegan Paul, 1981. 48–78.

Fraser, Laura. *Losing It: False Hopes and Fat Profits in the Diet Industry*. New York: Plume, 1998.

Freeman, Kathleen. *Ancilla to the Pre-Socratic Philosophers*. Cambridge: Harvard University Press, 1948.

Fuller, Gillian. "Cultivating Science: Negotiating Discourse in the Popular Texts of Stephen Jay Gould." *Reading Science: Critical and Functional Perspectives on Discourses of Science*. Eds. J. R. Martin and Robert Veel. London: Routledge, 1998. 35–62.

Garwin, Laura, and Tim Lincoln, eds. *A Century of* Nature: *Twenty-One Discoveries That Changed Science and the World*. Chicago: University of Chicago Press, 2003.

Geisler, Cheryl. *Academic Literacy and the Nature of Expertise: Reading, Writing, and Knowing in Academic Philosophy*. Hillsdale, NJ: Lawrence Erlbaum Associates, 1994.

Göçek, Fatma Müge. "Shifting the Boundaries of Literacy: Introduction of Western-Style Education to the Ottoman Empire." In Keller-Cohen. 267–88.

Goldberger, Arthur S., and Charles F. Manski. "The Bell Curve." *Journal of Economic Literature* 33 (1995): 762–76.

Gopen, George. "A Short History of the Scientific Article: The Evolution of a Genre." Paper presented at the Conference on College Composition and Communication, Washington, DC, 1995.

Gopen, George, and Judith A. Swan. "The Science of Scientific Writing." *American Scientist* 78 (1990): 550–58.

Gould, Stephen Jay. "Curveball." *The Bell Curve Wars: Race, Intelligence, and the Future of America.* Ed. Steven Fraser. New York: Basic Books, 1995. 11–22.

———. "Women's Brains." *The Panda's Thumb.* New York: W. W. Norton & Company, 1980. 152–59.

———. *Wonderful Life: The Burgess Shale and the Nature of History.* New York: W. W. Norton & Company, 1989.

Graff, Harvey J. *The Labyrinths of Literacy.* London: Falmer Press, 1987.

Graves, Heather Brodie. "Marbles, Dimples, Rubber Sheets, and Quantum Wells: The Role of Analogy in the Rhetoric of Science." *Rhetoric Society Quarterly* 28 (1998): 25–48.

———. *Rhetoric in(to) Science.* Cresskill, NJ: Hampton Press, 2005.

Gregory, Jane, and Steve Miller. "Caught in the Crossfire?" *The One Culture? A Conversation about Science.* Eds. Jay A. Labinger and Harry Collins. Chicago: University of Chicago Press, 2001. 61–72.

———. *Science in Public: Communication, Culture, and Credibility.* New York: Plenum Press, 1998.

Gross, Alan G. *The Rhetoric of Science.* Cambridge: Harvard University Press, 1996.

Gross, Paul R., and Norman Levitt. *Higher Superstitions: The Academic Left and its Quarrels with Science.* Baltimore: Johns Hopkins University Press, 1994.

Haas, Christina. "Learning to Read Biology: One Student's Rhetorical Development in College." *Written Communication* 11 (1994): 43–84.

Hacking, Ian. *The Social Construction of What?* Cambridge: Harvard University Press, 1999.

Halliday, M. A. K., and J. R. Martin. *Writing Science: Literacy and Discursive Power.* Pittsburgh: University of Pittsburgh Press, 1993.

Halloran, S. Michael. "The Birth of Molecular Biology: An Essay in the Rhetorical Criticism of Scientific Discourse." *Rhetoric Review* 3 (1984): 70–83.

Halloran, S. Michael, and Annette N. Bradford. "Figures of Speech in the Rhetoric of Science and Technology." *Essays on Classical Rhetoric and Modern Discourse.* Eds. Robert J. Connors, Lisa S. Ede, and Andrea A. Lunsford. Carbondale: Southern Illinois University Press, 1984. 179–92.

Halloran, S. Michael, and Merrill D. Whitburn. "Ciceronian Rhetoric and the Rise of Science: The Plain Style Reconsidered." *The Rhetorical Tradition and Modern Writing.* Ed. James J. Murphy. New York: Modern Language Association of America, 1982. 58–72.

Haraway, Donna. "The Virtual Speculum in the New World Order." *Feminist Review* 55 (1997): 22–72.

Harding, Sandra. *Is Science Multicultural? Postcolonialisms, Feminisms, and Epistemologies.* Bloomington: Indiana University Press, 1998.

————. *Whose Science? Whose Knowledge? Thinking from Women's Lives.* Ithaca: Cornell University Press, 1991.

————, ed. *The "Racial" Economy of Science: Toward a Democratic Future.* Bloomington: Indiana University Press, 1993.

Harris, Randy Allen. "Rhetoric of Science." *College English* 53 (1991): 282–307.

Hartley, James. "From Structured Abstracts to Structured Articles: A Modest Proposal." *Journal of Technical Writing and Communication* 29 (1999): 255–70.

Hass, Bruce, and Michael Kleine. "The Rhetoric of Junk Science." *Technical Communication Quarterly* 12 (2003): 267–84.

Haswell, Richard H. "NCTE/CCCC's Recent War on Scholarship." *Written Communication* 22 (2005): 198–223.

Hatton, John, and Paul B. Plouffe, eds. *The Culture of Science.* New York: Macmillan, 1993.

Hawisher, Gail E., and Cynthia L. Selfe. *Literacy, Technology, and Society: Confronting the Issues.* Prentice Hall, 1996. .

Hazen, Robert M., and James Trefil. *Science Matters: Achieving Scientific Literacy.* New York: Doubleday, 1991.

Henze, Brent. *Scientific Rhetorics in the Emergence of British Ethnology, 1808–1848: Discourses, Disciplines, and Institutions.* Unpublished dissertation. Pennsylvania State University, 2002.

Herndl, Carl G. "Cultural Studies and Critical Science." *Understanding Scientific Prose.* Ed. Jack Selzer. Madison: University of Wisconsin Press, 1993. 61–81.

Herndl, Carl G., Barbara A. Fennell, and Carolyn R. Miller. "Understanding Failures in Organizational Discourse: The Accident at Three Mile Island and the Shuttle *Challenger* Disaster." *Textual Dynamics of the Professions: Historical and Contemporary Studies of Writing in Professional Communities.* Eds. Charles Bazerman and James Paradis. Madison: University of Wisconsin Press, 1991. 279–305.

Hess, David J. *Science Studies: An Advanced Introduction.* New York: New York University Press, 1997.

Holeton, Richard. *Composing Cyberspace: Identity, Community, and Knowledge in the Electronic Age.* Boston: McGraw Hill, 1998.

Holmes, Frederic L. "Scientific Writing and Scientific Discovery." *Isis* 78: (1987): 220–35.

Humphreys, Russell. "Light from Creation Illuminates Cosmic Axis." May 22, 2003. <http://www.icr.org/headlines/cmbaxis.html>.

Hutto, David. "When Professional Biologists Write: An Ethnographic Study with Pedagogical Implications." *Technical Communication Quarterly* 12 (2003): 207–23.

Irwin, Alan. "Constructing the scientific citizen: science and democracy in the biosciences." *Public Understanding of Science* 10 (2001): 1–18.

Jennycraig.com. Fact_sheet. July 10, 2003. <http://jennycraig.com/corporate/news/industry>.

Johnson, Gordon. "Using Science, Technology, and Society Issues to Achieve Scientific Literacy." *HortScience* 28 (1993): 93–95.

Kamin, Leon J. "Lies, Damned Lies, and Statistics." *The Bell Curve Debate: History, Documents, Opinions.* Eds. Russell Jacoby and Naomi Glauberman. New York: Times Books, 1995. 81–105.

Kaufer, David, and Richard Young. "Writing the Content Areas: Some Theoretical Complexities." *Theory and Practice in the Teaching of Writing: Rethinking the Discipline.* Ed. Lee Odell. Carbondale: Southern Illinois University Press, 1993. 71–104.

Keller-Cohen, Deborah, ed. *Literacy: Interdisciplinary Conversations.* Cresskill, NJ: Hampton Press, 1994.

———. "Introduction." In Keller-Cohen 1–29.

Kennedy, Donald. "The State of the Profession." *Science* 294 (2001): 265.

Kevles, Daniel J., and Leroy Hood. "Reflections." *The Code of Codes.* Eds. Daniel J. Kevles and Leroy Hood. Cambridge: Harvard University Press, 1992. 300–328.

Kinneavy, James. *A Theory of Discourse.* New York: W. W. Norton & Co., 1971.

Kinsella, William J. "A 'Fusion' of Interests: Big Science, Government, and Rhetorical Practice in Nuclear Fusion Research." *Rhetoric Society Quarterly* 26 (1996): 65–81.

Kirscht, Judy, Rhonda Levine, and John Reiff. "Evolving Paradigms: WAC and the Rhetoric of Inquiry." *College Composition and Communication* 45 (1994): 369–80.

Knoblauch, C. H., and Lil Brannon. *Critical Teaching and the Idea of Literacy.* Portsmouth, NH: Boynton/Cook, 1993.

Knorr-Cetina, Karin. *Science Observed: Perspectives on the Social Study of Science.* London: Sage Publications, 1983.

Koszinowski, Konrad, Detlef Schröder, and Helmut Schwarz. "Reactivity of Small Cationic Platinum Clusters." *Journal of Physical Chemistry A* 107 (2003): 4999–5006.

Krieger, Barbara Jo, Paul G. Saint-Amand, and Robert W. Emery. *Dialogue and Discovery.* New York: St. Martin's Press, 1996.

Kuhn, Thomas S. *The Structure of Scientific Revolutions.* 2nd ed. International Encyclopedia of Unified Science, Vol. 2. No. 2. Chicago: University of Chicago Press, 1970.

Labianca, Dominick A., and William J. Reeves. "Writing Across the Curriculum: The Science Segment. A Heretical Perspective." *Journal of Chemical Education* 20 (1985): 400–402.

Latour, Bruno. *Pandora's Hope: Essays on the Reality of Science Studies.* Cambridge: Harvard University Press, 1999.

———. *Science in Action.* Cambridge: Harvard University Press, 1987.

Latour, Bruno, and Steve Woolgar. *Laboratory Life: The Social Construction of Scientific Facts.* Beverly Hills, CA: Sage Publications, 1979.

Lauer, Janice M. "Rhetoric and Composition Studies: A Multimodal Discipline." *Defining the New Rhetorics.* Eds. Theresa Enos and Stuart Brown. Newbury Park: Sage Publications, 1993. 44–54.

Lauer, Janice M., and J. William Asher. *Composition Research: Empirical Designs.* New York: Oxford University Press, 1988.

LeCourt, Donna. "WAC as Critical Pedagogy: The Third Stage?" *Journal of Advanced Composition* 16 (1996): 389–405.

Lee, Stuart, and Wolff-Michael Roth. "Science and the 'Good Citizen': Community-Based Scientific Literacy." *Science, Technology, and Human Values* 28 (2003): 403–24.

Lenoir, Timothy. *Instituting Science: The Cultural Production of Scientific Disciplines.* Stanford: Stanford University Press, 1997.

Lessl, Thomas M. "The Priestly Voice." *Quarterly Journal of Speech* 75 (1989): 183–97.

Lewontin, Richard C. *Biology as Ideology: The Doctrine of DNA.* New York: HarperCollins, 1991.

Little, Joseph. "Analogy in Science: Where Do We Go From Here?" *Rhetoric Society Quarterly* 30 (2000): 69–92.

———. "Understanding Statistical Significance: A Conceptual History." *Journal of Technical Writing and Communication* 31 (2001): 363–72.

Longo, Bernadette. "An Approach for Applying Cultural Study Theory to Technical Writing Research." *Technical Communication Quarterly* 7 (1998): 53–73.

Lunsford, Andrea A., Helene Moglen, and James Slevin. "Introduction." *The Right to Literacy.* Eds. Andrea A. Lunsford, Helene Moglen, and James Slevin. New York: MLA, 1990. 1–6.

Lyotard, Jean-François. *The Postmodern Condition: A Report on Knowledge.* Trans. Geoff Bennington and Brian Massumi. Minneapolis: University of Minnesota Press, 1979.

MacDonald, Susan Peck. "Syntax and Verb Choice in Journalistic Treatments of Scientific Research." Paper presented at the Conference on College Composition and Communication, New York, 2003.

Macedo, Donald. *Literacies of Power: What Americans Are Not Allowed to Know.* Boulder: Westview Press, 1994.

MacKenzie, Nancy R. *Science and Technology Today.* New York: St. Martin's Press, 1995.

Magnotto, Joyce Neff, and Barbara R. Stout. "Faculty Workshops." *Writing Across the Curriculum: A Guide to Developing Programs.* Eds. Susan H. McLeod and Margot Soven. Newbury Park: Sage Publications, 1992. 32–46.

Marketdata Enterprises. "The U.S. Weight Loss and Diet Control Market." 7th ed. July 10, 2003. <http:// www.mkt-data-ent.com>.

Martin, J. R. "Chapter 9. Literacy in Science: Learning to Handle Text as Technology." *Writing Science: Literacy and Discursive Power*. M. A. K. Halliday and J. R. Martin. Pittsburgh: University of Pittsburgh Press, 1993. 166–202.

McComiskey, Bruce. *Gorgias and the New Sophistic Rhetoric*. Carbondale: Southern Illinois University Press, 2002.

McInerney, Joseph D. "Why Biological Literacy Matters: A Review of Commentaries Related to *The Bell Curve: Intelligence and Class Structure in American Life*." *Quarterly Review of Biology* 71 (1996): 81–96.

McLaughlin-Jenkins, Erin. "Walking the low road: the pursuit of scientific knowledge in late Victorian working-class communities." *Public Understanding of Science* 12 (2003): 147–66.

McLeod, Susan H. "Writing Across the Curriculum: An Introduction." *Writing Across the Curriculum: A Guide to Developing Programs*. Eds. Susan H. McLeod and Margot Soven. Newbury Park: Sage Publications, 1992. 1–11.

Meitner, Lise, and Otto Frisch. "Disintegration of uranium by neutrons: A new type of nuclear reaction." In Garwin and Lincoln 70–72.

Menser, Michael, and Stanley Aronowitz. "On Cultural Studies, Science, and Technology." In Aronowitz et al. 7–29.

Mermin, N. David. "Readings and Misreadings." *The One Culture? A Conversation about Science*. Eds. Jay A. Labinger and Harry Collins. Chicago: University of Chicago Press, 2001. 275–79.

Milbrath, Lester W. "Environmental Education for the 21st Century." *Literacy: A Redefinition*. Eds. Nancy J. Ellsworth, Carolyn N. Hedley, and Anthony N. Baratta. Hillsdale: Lawrence Erlbaum Associates, 1994. 271–79.

Miller, Carolyn R. "*Kairos* in the Rhetoric of Science." *A Rhetoric of Doing: Essays on Written Discourse in Honor of James L. Kinneavy*. Eds. Stephen P. Witte, Neil Nakadate, and Roger D. Cherry. Carbondale: Southern Illinois University Press, 1992. 310–27.

Miller, Carolyn R., and Jack Selzer. "Special Topics of Argument in Engineering Reports." *Writing in Nonacademic Settings*. Eds. Lee Odell and Dixie Goswami. New York: Guilford Press, 1985. 309–41.

Miller, Jon D. "Public understanding of, and attitudes toward, scientific research: what we know and what we need to know." *Public Understanding of Science* 13 (2004): 273–94.

Minter, Deborah Williams, Anne Ruggles-Gere, and Deborah Keller-Cohen. "Learning Literacies." *College English* 57 (1995): 669–87.

Moore, Randy. "Writing as a Tool for Learning Biology." *BioScience* 44 (1994): 613–17.

Moore, Stephen. "Body Count." In Easton 224–30.

Morris, Paul J. II, and Stephen Tchudi. *The New Literacy: Moving Beyond the 3Rs*. San Francisco: Josey-Bass Publishers, 1996.

Moskovitz, Cary, and David Kellogg. "Primary Science Communication in the First-Year Writing Course." *CCC* 57 (2005): 307–34.

Moss, Jean Dietz. *Novelties in the Heavens: Rhetoric and Science in the Copernican Controversy.* Chicago: University of Chicago Press, 1993.

———. "The Interplay of Science and Rhetoric in Seventeenth-Century Italy." *Rhetorica* 7 (1989): 23–43.

Murphy, James J. "Roman Writing Instruction as Described by Quintilian." *A Short History of Writing Instruction from Ancient Greece to Twentieth-Century America.* Ed. James J. Murphy. Davis: Hermagoras Press, 1990. 19–76.

Myers, Greg. "Out of the Laboratory and Down to the Bay: Writing in Science and Technology Studies." *Written Communication* 13 (1996): 5–43.

———. "The Double Helix as Icon." *Science as Culture* (9) 1990: 49–72.

———. "The Social Construction of Two Biologists' Proposals." *Written Communication* 2 (1985): 219–45.

Nagelhout, Edwin R. "Writing and Professional Apprenticeship: Case Studies of Biology Graduate Students' Entry into the Scientific Community." Dissertation. Purdue University, 1996.

National Science Foundation. "Info Brief." Washington, DC: Division of Science Resources Statistics, National Science Foundation, 2003.

———. "Science and Engineering Indicators—2002." Washington, DC: National Science Foundation, 2002.

nea.gov. June 20, 2003. < http://www.nea.gov/>.

neh.gov. June 20, 2003. <http://www.nea.gov/>.

Nelkin, Dorothy. "Perspectives on the Evolution of Science Studies." In Aronowitz et al. 31–36.

———. *Selling Science: How the Press Covers Science and Technology.* 2nd ed. New York: W. H. Freeman, 1995.

Noble, David F. "Digital Diploma Mills." *Science Bought and Sold: Essays in the Economies of Science.* Eds. Philip Mirowski and Esther-Mirjam Sent. Chicago: University of Chicago Press, 2002. 431–43.

Norgaard, Rolf. WAC-L (Writing Across the Curriculum Listserv). March 6, 1998.

Norris, Stephen P., Linda M. Phillips, and Connie A. Korpan. "University students' interpretation of media reports of science and its relationship to background knowledge, interest, and reading difficulty." *Public Understanding of Science* 12 (2003): 123–45.

Odum, Eugene P. "The Strategy of Ecosystem Development." *Science* 164 (1969): 262–70.

Ohmann, Richard. *Politics of Letters.* Middletown, CT: Wesleyan University Press, 1987.

Orr, David W. *Ecological Literacy: Education and the Transition to a Postmodern World.* Albany: SUNY Press, 1992.

Patterson, Orlando. "For Whom the Bell Curves." *The Bell Curve Wars: Race, Intelligence, and the Future of America.* Ed. Steven Fraser. New York: Basic Books, 1995. 187–213.

Paul, Danette. "Spreading Chaos: The Role of Popularizations in the Diffusion of Scientific Ideas." *Written Communication* 21 (2004): 32–68.

Peeples, Tim. *Professional Writing and Rhetoric: Readings from the Field.* New York: Longman, 2003.

Peritz, Janice. "When Learning is Not Enough: Writing Across the Curriculum and the (Re)turn to Rhetoric." *Journal of Advanced Composition* 14 (1994): 431–54.

Petryna, Adriana. *Life Exposed: Biological Citizens after Chernobyl.* Princeton: Princeton University Press, 2002.

PlayBeirut.com. December 31, 2003. < http://beirut-guide.com/>.

Prelli, Lawrence J. *A Rhetoric of Science: Inventing Scientific Discourse.* Columbia: University of South Carolina Press, 1989.

Quintilian. *Institutio Oratorio.* Trans. H. E. Butler. Cambridge: Harvard University Press, 1920.

Rorty, Richard. "Solidarity or Objectivity?" *Objectivity, Relativism, and Truth: Philosophical Papers, vol.1.* Cambridge: Cambridge University Press, 1991.

Rose, Mike. *Lives on the Boundary: The Struggles and Achievements of America's Underprepared.* New York: Free Press, 1989.

Ross, Andrew. "Cultural Studies and the Challenge of Science." *Disciplinarity and Dissent in Cultural Studies.* Eds. Cary Nelson and Dilip Parameshwar Gaonkar. New York: Routledge, 1996. 171–84.

Rotblat, Joseph. "From nuclear physics to nuclear weapons." In Garwin and Lincoln 63–69.

Roth, Wolff-Michael, and Stuart Lee. "Scientific literacy as collective praxis." *Public Understanding of Science* 11 (2002): 33–56.

Rowntree, Derek. *Statistics Without Tears: A Primer for Non-Mathematicians.* New York: Charles Scribner's Sons, 1981.

Russell, David. *Writing in the Academic Disciplines, 1870–1990: A Curricular History.* Carbondale: Southern Illinois University Press, 1991.

Samaha, Frederick F., et al. "A Low-Carbohydrate as Compared with a Low-Fat Diet in Severe Obesity." *New England Journal of Medicine* 348 (2003): 2074–81.

Santa-monica.org. 2003. July 17, 2003. <http://santa-monica.org/home/index.asp>.

Schryer, Catherine F. "Genre Time/Space: Chronotopic Strategies in the Experimental Article." *Journal of Advanced Composition* 19 (1999): 81–89.

Science and Society. New York: HarperCollins, 1992.

"Science Wars and the need for respect and rigour." *Nature* 385 (1997): 373.

Secor, Marie, and Lynda Walsh. "A Rhetorical Perspective on the Sokal Hoax: Genre, Style, and Context." *Written Communication* 21 (2004): 69–91.

Selzer, Jack, ed. *Understanding Scientific Prose.* Madison: University of Wisconsin Press, 1993.

Shamos, Morris H. *The Myth of Scientific Literacy.* New Brunswick: Rutgers University Press, 1995.

Shapin, Steven. "The House of Experiment in Seventeenth-Century England." *The Science Studies Reader*. Ed. Mario Biagioli. New York: Routledge, 1999. 479–504.

Shrodes, Caroline, Harry Finestone, and Michael Shugrue. *The Conscious Reader*. 9th ed. New York: Pearson Longman, 2004.

Sismondo, Sergio. *An Introduction to Science and Technology Studies*. Malden, MA: Blackwell Publishing, 2004.

Snow, C. P. *The Two Cultures and the Scientific Revolution*. New York: Cambridge University Press, 1962.

Soven, Margot. "The Advanced Writing Across the Curriculum Workshop: The Perils of Reintroducing Rhetoric." *Journal of Teaching Writing* 12 (1994): 277–86.

Sprat, Thomas. *History of the Royal Society*. Eds. Jackson I. Cope and Harold Whitmore Jones. St. Louis: Washington University Press, 1958.

Staessen, Jan A., et al. "Hypertension Prevalence and Stroke Mortality Across Populations." *JAMA* 289 (2003): 2420–22.

Street, Brian V. *Literacy in Theory and Practice*. Cambridge: Cambridge University Press, 1984.

Strickling, Chris. "E309K Syllabus." Austin: University of Texas, 1999.

Sullivan, Dale. "Keeping the Rhetoric Orthodox: Forum Control in Science." *Technical Communication Quarterly* 9 (2000): 125–45.

Swales, John, and Hazem Najjar. "The Writing of Research Article Introductions." *Written Communication* 4 (1987): 175–91.

Swan, Judith A. "Reflections Across the Divide: Written Discourse as a Structural Mirror in Teaching Science to Nonscience Students." *Writing on the Edge* 6 (1995): 55–73.

Thacker, Brad, and James F. Stratman. "Transmuting Common Substances: The Cold Fusion Controversy and the Rhetoric of Science." *Journal of Business and Technical Communication* 9 (1995): 389–424.

Thompson, Dorthea K. "Arguing for Experimental 'Facts' in Science: A Study of Research Article Results Sections in Biochemistry." *Written Communication* 10 (1993): 106–28.

Traweek, Sharon. "When Eliza Doolittle Studies 'enry 'iggins." In Aronowitz et al. 37–56.

Tuana, Nancy. *The Less Noble Sex: Scientific, Religious, and Philosophical Conceptions of Woman's Nature*. Bloomington: Indiana University Press, 1993.

Uno, Gordon E., and Rodger W. Bybee. "Understanding the Dimensions of Biological Literacy." *BioScience* 44 (1994): 553–57.

Usher, Robin, and Richard Edwards. *Postmodernism and Education*. New York: Routledge, 1994.

Vande Kopple, William J. "Noun Phrases and the Style of Scientific Discourse." *A Rhetoric of Doing: Essays on Written Discourse in Honor of James L.*

Kinneavy. Eds. Stephen P. Witte, Neil Nakadate, and Roger D. Cherry. Carbondale: Southern Illinois University Press, 1992. 328–48.

Varghese, Susheela Abraham, and Sunita Anne Abraham. "Book-Length Scholarly Essays as a Hybrid Genre in Science." *Written Communication* 21 (2004): 201–31.

"Vindication for the Atkins diet?" *CNN.com*. Cable News Network. May 21, 2003. <http://www.cnn.com/2003/HEALTH/diet.fitness/05/21/diet.studies.ap/index.html>

Waddell, Craig. "The Role of *Pathos* in the Decision-Making Process: A Study in the Rhetoric of Science Policy." *Quarterly Journal of Speech* 76 (1990): 381–400.

Walvoord, Barbara. "Getting Started." *Writing Across the Curriculum: A Guide to Developing Programs*. Eds. Susan H. McLeod and Margot Soven. Newbury Park: Sage Publications. 12–31.

Watson, J. D., and F. H. C. Crick. "A Structure for Deoxyribose Nucleic Acid." *Nature* 171 (1953): 737–38.

WebMd.com. June 30, 2003. <http://www.webmd.com/>.

Wertheim, Margaret. *Pythagoras' Trousers: God, Physics, and the Gender Wars*. New York: W. W. Norton & Company, 1995.

Winsor, Dorothy A. "Constructing Science and Knowledge in Gould and Lewontin's 'The Spandrels of San Marcos.'" *Understanding Scientific Prose*. Ed. Jack Selzer. Madison: University of Wisconsin Press, 1993. 127–43.

Winterowd, W. Ross. *The Culture and Politics of Literacy*. New York: Oxford University Press, 1989.

Wolf-Maier, Katharina et al. "Hypertension Prevalence and Blood Pressure Levels in 6 European Countries, Canada, and the United States." *JAMA* 289 (2003): 2363–69.

Yutopian Enterprises. *Oriental Secrets to Weight Loss, Beautiful Skin and High Energy*. Santa Monica: Yutopian Enterprises, [1990?].

Zappen, James P. "Historical Studies in the Rhetoric of Science and Technology." *The Technical Writing Teacher* 14 (1987): 285–98.

———. "Historical Perspectives on the Philosophy and the Rhetoric of Science: Sources for a Pluralistic Rhetoric." *PRE/TEXT* 6 (1985): 9–29.

Zerbe, Michael J. "What's Up, Doc? Approaching Medicine as a Cultural Institution in the Technical Communication Classroom by Studying the Discourses of Standard and Alternative Cancer Treatments." *Innovative Approaches to Technical Communication: Teaching, Administration, and Curriculum*. Eds. Tracy Bridgeford, Karla Saari Kitalong, and Dickie Selfe Logan: Utah State University Press, 2004. 183–96.

Zerbe, Michael J., Amanda J. Young, and Edwin R. Nagelhout. "The Rhetoric of Fraud in Breast Cancer Trials: Manifestations in Medical Journals and the Mass Media—And Missed Opportunities." *Journal of Technical Writing and Communication* 28 (1998): 39–61.

Zimmerman, Michael. *Science, Nonscience, and Nonsense: Approaching Environmental Literacy*. Baltimore: Johns Hopkins University Press, 1995.

Žižek, Slavoj. *Looking Awry: An Introduction to Jacques Lacan through Popular Culture*. Cambridge: MIT Press, 1991.

Index

Michael J. Zerbe teaches rhetoric, composition, and professional writing and editing courses at York College of Pennsylvania, where he is an assistant professor of English and humanities. He is the recipient of a Health Communications Fellowship from the National Cancer Institute in Bethesda, Maryland, and his work has appeared in the *Journal of Technical and Scientific Communication*, *Innovative Approaches to Teaching Technical Communication*, and *The Rhetoric of Health (or Healthcare): Toward a New Disciplinary Inquiry*.